Social Collaboration

FOR DUMMIES®

A Wiley Brand

by David F. Carr

FOR DUMMIES®
A Wiley Brand

Social Collaboration For Dummies®

Published by: **John Wiley & Sons, Inc.,** 111 River Street, Hoboken, NJ 07030-5774, www.wiley.com

Copyright © 2014 by John Wiley & Sons, Inc., Hoboken, New Jersey

Published simultaneously in Canada

For general information on our other products and services, please contact our Customer Care Department within the U.S. at 877-762-2974, outside the U.S. at 317-572-3993, or fax 317-572-4002. For technical support, please visit www.wiley.com/techsupport.

Wiley publishes in a variety of print and electronic formats and by print-on-demand. Some material included with standard print versions of this book may not be included in e-books or in print-on-demand. If this book refers to media such as a CD or DVD that is not included in the version you purchased, you may download this material at http://booksupport.wiley.com. For more information about Wiley products, visit www.wiley.com.

Library of Congress Control Number: 2013948026

ISBN 978-1-118-65854-3 (pbk); ISBN 978-1-118-65853-6 (ebk); ISBN 978-1-118-65855-0 (ebk); ISBN 978-1-118-65856-7 (ebk)

Manufactured in the United States of America

10 9 8 7 6 5 4 3 2 1

Contents at a Glance

Table of Contents

Introduction

This book is about getting work done with social media and social networking technologies. This is what's often described as the use of "an internal Facebook" or "Facebook inside the enterprise" — even though many of those who work with the technology have grown to hate the comparison as trivializing what they do.

What is true is that social collaboration products humanize the online workplace by putting a friendlier face on it. We get to know our online collaborators better in something like the way we get to know our Facebook friends and friends of friends. Public social networks are great for the joy of discovering a long-lost high school friend or making a connection with a favorite author. The business equivalent would be connecting with others around the company whom you may never have met in person but who share a professional interest or are willing to share tips and make helpful introductions.

The more expansive enterprise social networking platforms go far beyond cloning Facebook, also including tools for maintaining internal blogs, wikis, document repositories, and project workspaces.

Because this is a book about a category of software products and cloud services, rather than any single social collaboration platform, I can't promise detailed instructions on how to perform every task or configure every feature, although I do provide examples.

Consider this your guidebook to what is possible with social collaboration and how to get the most out of it.

About This Book

This book is for social business strategists, community managers, and company leaders seeking to put social collaboration to work. I also want you to consider this a resource to share with others in your organization whom you'd like to give a basic understanding of the principles of social collaboration.

If you're using the software, rather than driving the strategy for its use, I hope I can help orient you to use it more effectively.

There are many business uses of social networking, but *Social Collaboration For Dummies* specifically focuses on software and cloud services that make it easier for employees to connect with each other in productive ways. It's about busting communications out of the e-mail inbox and turning them into corporate knowledge that makes the organization smarter. In a well-run, social collaboration network, everyone from the CEO to the new hire gets a better picture of activities from throughout the organization, plus the ability to network with others in specific professional disciplines.

I won't tell you how to market your business on Facebook or respond to customer complaints posted to Twitter. Behind the scenes, social collaboration can be a tool for helping you do those things better. Internal and external uses of social media are complementary as part of a complete social business strategy.

Like every book in the *For Dummies* series, this one is designed to deliver information in easily digestible chunks, translating jargon and breaking procedures into simple steps wherever possible. As you read, you will notice a few standard typographical conventions:

- ✔ Web addresses appear in monofont. This information is also used for Twitter handles like `@davidfcarr`. If you're reading a digital version of this book on a device connected to the Internet, note that you can click the web address to visit that website, like this: `www.dummies.com`.
- ✔ New terms are highlighted with *italics* the first time they are used.

Foolish Assumptions

This book assumes some basic familiarity with consumer social media although I also explain some of its conventions (such as the use of hashtags) and how they apply to social collaboration for business.

I try not to make many assumptions about your familiarity with social collaboration software. I assume some readers will just be getting started with or planning for a social collaboration initiative. Others may have some social software in use, or even several such products, in which case I hope this book can be useful for developing a better strategy for using it effectively.

Although I tried to make the material in this book relevant to small businesses, some of the concerns I raise will be more relevant to large, complicated enterprises. Social collaboration can be useful for small businesses, particularly those that operate across multiple locations, or employ home-based workers, or forge virtual teams with contractors or business partners.

Multinational corporations may get even more value out of some key enterprise social networking applications, such as the ability to locate experts from throughout the organization and connect them with each other. At the same time, big companies must manage more complexities in terms of technical integration and regulatory compliance.

If I'm spending too many words on a topic that's not relevant to your organization, you have my permission to skip ahead.

Icons Used in This Book

The Tip icon marks tips (duh!) and shortcuts that you can use to make social collaboration easier or more effective.

Remember icons mark the information that's especially important to know. To siphon off the most important information in each chapter, just skim through these icons.

The Technical Stuff icon marks information of a highly technical nature that nontechnical readers can skip.

The Warning icon tells you to watch out! It marks important information about pitfalls and headaches to avoid.

Beyond the Book

This book is not the last word on social collaboration. It's not even my last word. Here are the additional resources you can find online:

- ✔ The Cheat Sheet for this book is at

  www.dummies.com/cheatsheet/socialcollaboration

  Here you'll find a summary of the essential elements for social collaboration success.

- ✔ Online articles covering extra topics are available at

  www.dummies.com/extras/socialcollaboration

- ✔ You can find significant updates from the world of social collaboration at

  www.dummies.com/go/socialcollaborationupdates

  Social software is a very fast-moving market, so there may be surprises like acquisitions of major players between the completion of the manuscript and its publication. If readers point out errors that the editors and I didn't catch, this is also where corrections and clarifications will be posted.

Where to Go from Here

This book is addressed to those planning a social collaboration initiative, as well as those who are farther along in their journeys and striving to get more value out of social software. Depending on who you are and what you're trying to accomplish, you may want to skip or skim certain chapters and jump ahead to others. Like all *For Dummies* books, this one is structured so you don't have to read it in a linear fashion — you can start anywhere.

If you're just getting started with social collaboration, start at the beginning so you understand the basics of what social collaboration, how it relates to public social media, and how the private business applications of social software are different.

For more specifics about how to communicate, build a productive network, and manage projects on a social platform, read Part II.

If you're in the process of selecting a social collaboration software product or cloud service, you may want to jump ahead to Part III.

In Part IV, the focus shifts to ongoing community management, which is something that you should plan for from the beginning but which requires even more attention as an online community matures.

I included Part V because I expect this book to be read by CEOs, CIOs, sales leaders, and human resources directors, all of whom will have different ideas of what would make social collaboration useful to their organizations and all of whom have a different role to play in making it successful. If you are in one of those roles, that may be the chapter you want to read first. I'd recommend you read the other chapters in this section, too, so you will understand what the other constituencies in your organization are likely to want from a social platform.

The Part of Tens chapters and the case studies in the Appendix round out the book with tips and examples of social collaboration success. Honestly, I want you to read all of it, but I'll understand if you don't.

If you have a complement, a criticism, or a suggestion for further research, you can reach me at david@carrcommunications.com or @davidfcarr on Twitter. Use #SocialCollaborationForDummies in tweets or the subject line of e-mail to make sure you get my attention.

Part I
Getting Started with Social Collaboration

In this part . . .

✔ Understand social networking and how it complements business collaboration.

✔ Find out what collaboration networks borrow from consumer social networks and how they are different.

✔ Discover how to put social collaboration to work.

Chapter 1

Connecting Business Collaboration with Social Networking

In This Chapter

▶ Understanding what social collaboration means

▶ Moving beyond the "Facebook inside your company" slogan

▶ Accessing new resources in social collaboration systems

▶ Competing and coexisting with e-mail

▶ Finding practical applications for social collaboration

*W*e often talk about having a social life, separate from our work lives, recognizing that mingling the two can be hazardous. *Social Collaboration For Dummies* isn't a book about being social at work, in the sense of flirting or sharing jokes. By *social collaboration,* I mean recognizing that business is inherently social, even when social interaction is constrained within the bounds of professionalism.

In this chapter, I help you understand what social collaboration is (and what it isn't), outline some of the benefits of implementing a social collaboration system in your business, and suggest some ways that you can help colleagues shift from e-mail to social collaboration tools (and know when to use one over the other). I also give you some real-world examples of how social collaboration can help employees solve specific problems and complete tasks more efficiently.

Defining Social Collaboration

Social collaboration comprises social networking and social media for the purpose of getting work done in an enterprise setting. The collaboration part is just as important as the social part. In this context, collaboration is about getting work done with teams of people, working together toward a common goal — which is essential to any business.

Used properly, social collaboration widens exposure to corporate knowledge, streamlines the flow of ideas, and gets everyone thinking about how to improve processes, products, and services.

Social collaboration is also known as *enterprise social networking,* and the products to support it are often branded enterprise social networks (ESNs). However, you don't have to be running a huge enterprise to benefit from social collaboration because the same sorts of tools can be used by small businesses and nonprofit groups. That's one reason I'll stick to social collaboration as my preferred term — beyond the fact that it's in the title of this book. I also use the term "collaboration networks," used as shorthand for private social networks (as opposed to public ones).

You've probably heard the maxim "people do business with people they know, like, and trust." My local Chamber of Commerce parrots this endlessly as a reason why salespeople and small business owners should attend its networking breakfasts and other events. And it's true: Successful salespeople tend to be talented networkers. In the same way, people within organizations who have all the right connections often can accomplish tasks that others cannot — or at least not as quickly. When a company's standard formal processes break down, the employee with a strong network knows who's who and what's what and how to get the job done anyway.

Social collaboration is nothing new, in that sense. What is new is the digitization of the social network and the transformation of what used to be dry, impersonal corporate collaboration tools into friendly places filled with smiling faces. Online social networking has become famous for reconnecting long-lost lovers and sparking friendships between people who never would have met in the offline world. In a business or enterprise setting, social networking can be just as effective at connecting employees with other employees who share a common interest, or skill, or have the answers to each other's questions, even though they might be in offices in different states or on opposite sides of the world.

So, this is what I mean by "social collaboration." The collaboration element comes into play when employees use a social network to share their progress on a common project and work together on digital artifacts of that project, such as a sales proposal or a presentation to management.

Social collaboration initiatives have many fathers and mothers. Often, though, the impetus doesn't come from the IT department but from a particular project team that experiments with the technology and finds it worthwhile. Other drivers could be

- A CEO wanting a way to unite business units that have come in through acquisition

- The head of HR wanting to promote a more collaborative workplace

- A sales leader wanting to speed sharing leads, production of proposals, and closing of deals

- An early adopter of new technologies anywhere within the company

  At the energy company Apache Corporation, social collaboration champion Randy Wagner's official title is "drilling advisor," and the success stories he tells revolve around the science and engineering of drilling for oil.

The specific interests of these different constituencies in social collaboration are discussed in Part V.

In this section, I explain social collaboration and the benefits it offers for doing business. I also clarify how social media tools like Facebook are different from social collaboration tools, which connect colleagues so that they can work together to solve problems and complete tasks.

Seeing how social collaboration can help your business

By definition, an enterprise social network has different aims than a public social network or any consumer website. Some reasons why organizations invest in social collaboration include:

- **Embrace social everywhere.** Mirror the increasingly important role of social media interaction in customer communications, enabling internal collaboration that delivers results for external customers.

- **Improve sales efficiency.** Speed the production of proposals and improve the sharing of tips and leads within sales teams.

- **Share information.** Capture more of the tacit knowledge of the organization — that is, the knowledge not recorded in any formal document — by encouraging communications that are shared broadly rather than trapped in e-mail or discussed only offline.

✔ **Promote agility.** Allow employees to make the connections they need to create workarounds when formal processes break down or to react quickly to unanticipated events or opportunities.

✔ **Improve the workplace atmosphere.** Humanize the workplace and improve morale by encouraging employees to make more varied connections and recognize each other publicly for good work. In Figure 1-1, you see co-workers thanking Celeste, the creator of a helpful sales document. This example is from Jive Software's social collaboration platform, and the comment I added includes a *badge,* a graphical symbol of recognition, created using Jive's Props app.

✔ **Coordinate activities.** Improve coordination of routine work activities, such as gathering information for a proposal or resolving a customer complaint.

✔ **Help colleagues connect.** Bridge organizational divisions by department, work function, or geography, enabling productive collaboration between employees who otherwise never would have met, even online.

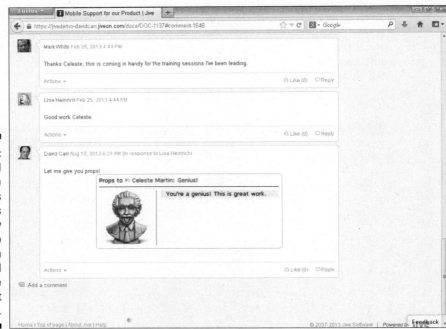

Figure 1-1:
Social collaboration gives co-workers many ways to thank each other and recognize excellent work.

A social collaboration environment like Yammer (see Figure 1-2) looks a whole lot like Facebook. Scratch beneath the surface, though, to find tools that promise secure business collaboration. Here, you can see that Yammer is built around a central *news feed,* a listing of recent messages, links, and documents shared by co-workers that is similar to the listing of updates shared by friends on Facebook, except that here the context is work rather than play. This user interface format for presenting a stream of messages is also known as an *activity stream* and can be used to represent all sorts of social and application events.

Yammer makes a distinction between the news feed, which is limited to updates posted by people, and the activity feed, which includes automated updates. Other environments mix the two, and the terms are often used interchangeably.

One of the most important elements of social collaboration is that you can view a customized and personalized activity stream of all the things that are most important to you. You see the updates posted by your closest collaborators, answers to questions you have posed, and feedback on documents or links you have shared. You pick the people and groups you want to follow, rather than having their messages broadcast to you whether you find them relevant or not. That also means you can share information with the people and groups most likely to care about it, rather than trying to e-mail everyone you can think of who may care, which often means spamming co-workers who don't care and missing some who do.

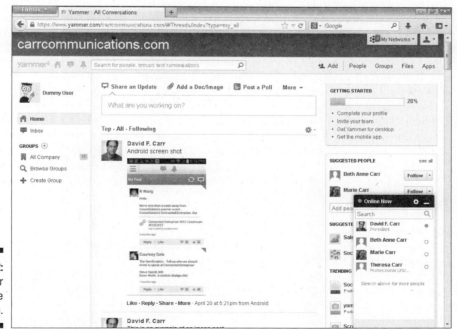

Figure 1-2:
The Yammer home screen.

The language of social business

You may be hearing a lot of talk about "social business," which is a broad term that encompasses both social collaboration and techniques for using public social networks for marketing, market research, and customer service. A variation that turns up in vendor marketing, as well as press and analyst reports, is "social enterprise."

One source of confusion: Both terms are also used in other contexts to refer to the business of running charities and social service organizations.

To my mind, a social business is a business with a coherent approach to applying the power of social networking internally and externally, in complementary ways. For example, when a customer service organization picks up on complaints being aired on Twitter or Facebook about your company's products (or even in a public forum on your company's website), internal social collaboration can help the service organization connect with the employees who have the right expertise or authority to answer questions or resolve a problem on behalf of those customers. Social business is about more than collaboration, but social collaboration is an important element of success for social business.

Social collaboration: not about cloning Facebook

Many social collaboration advocates are wary of the easy and obvious comparison to Facebook, which has positive but also some negative connotations. To describe a corporate collaborative application "as engaging and easy to use as Facebook" is a good thing in terms of getting people to use it. On the other hand, do companies really want employees posting the same sort of things on a corporate system that they would post on Facebook? No way.

By definition, an enterprise social network has different aims than a public social network or any consumer website. For example, Facebook says its mission is "to make the world more open and connected" (even though critics often charge that its mission is to get people to share even more than they realize they're sharing). In contrast, corporate network managers may be very concerned about making sure that sharing is carefully controlled and that proprietary information won't leak outside the company. And although I'm using the big company, self-important word "enterprise," these confidentiality concerns also apply to smaller businesses.

Of course, social collaboration tools have indeed been heavily influenced by the design and functionality of public social networks like Facebook, Twitter, LinkedIn, and Google+, often with elements of Wikipedia, YouTube, and other popular consumer websites mixed in. Many basic social collaboration functions for posting, sharing, tagging, Liking, and commenting on content are judged at least partly on how well they mirror those functions on the consumer sites. (I discuss this idea in greater detail in Chapter 2.)

If you're the person trying to sell social collaboration to the boss, arguing that it will be "just like Facebook inside our company" could be counter-productive, given that Facebook is associated with frivolity. So, if you find comparisons to Facebook troublesome, you might work LinkedIn into the conversation, given its reputation as the site for professional social networking. (You won't see a lot of beer bash photos or tasteless jokes posted on LinkedIn.)

The social collaboration system inside your business should have a similar professional focus. People use LinkedIn to burnish their professional reputations and find their next jobs. Employees use social collaboration to build professional connections at work and do their current jobs better.

Socializing software

This isn't the place to explain all your social collaboration software options — that's what Part III of this book is for — but let me pause for a quick rundown of the major products and types of products I will be using frequently as examples.

I've already mentioned Jive and Yammer. Jive was the first independent social software maker to become a public company and has many large enterprise customers. Yammer has to be counted a major social collaboration platform if for no other reason because it is part of Microsoft, which bought the cloud software startup in 2012.

Some definitions: By *cloud* software, I mean software sold on a subscription basis, where the subscription gives you access to software running on a remote server (or in a pool of remote servers). That's in contrast to traditional packaged software that an organization buys and installs on its own servers (or remotely hosted servers that it controls directly). You will also see references to *the cloud,* which essentially means the same as saying the Internet or the web — think of the cloud as the web of software and storage resources as opposed to publishing and marketing content. The rise of social collaboration is intertwined with cloud computing. I address the relationship in Chapter 10.

By *platform,* I mean a software or cloud product is more than an isolated software application but a foundation that multiple applications build on. Most social collaboration vendors would call their products platforms. I'm usually pretty generous about using the term where others might argue whether a particular product deserves it.

Here are a few of those platforms:

- ✔ **Jive Software Platform:** The enterprise social networking and collaboration product from the leading independent software vendor focused entirely on social software for businesses.

- ✔ **IBM Connections:** Like Jive's platform, IBM's platform provides a broad array of tools that include blogs, wikis, task management, and document management, in addition to social networking.

- ✔ **Yammer:** The one that looks most like a Facebook clone. You know you are on an enterprise social network because your co-workers are sharing spreadsheets instead of cat photos. Originally a spunky independent startup, Yammer was acquired by Microsoft in 2012.

- ✔ **Chatter:** The social collaboration companion to Salesforce.com's software for sales and customer service.

- ✔ **Tibbr:** Social software from Tibco, a company better known for its application and data integration products.

- ✔ **SharePoint:** Widely deployed for document sharing and other collaboration applications, Microsoft SharePoint has been adding social features, most notably with its SharePoint 2013 release. However, Microsoft is signaling that its future social software plans revolve more around Yammer.

- ✔ **NewsGator Social Sites:** Adds more sophisticated and extensive social collaboration features to Microsoft SharePoint.

Those are the ones I have the most case studies on, although there are many others.

All of the products mentioned here are available on a cloud subscription basis. Yammer and Chatter are exclusively cloud-based. Jive, IBM Connections, and NewsGator are relative newcomers to the cloud, whereas Tibbr was created in the cloud era but offers an on-premises installation option.

Within an online collaboration tool, the activity stream is an important concept (and I tell you more about that in Chapter 2). A photo is just as important as information that you find in the activity stream because a profile photo puts a face on a collaborator or potential collaborator.

Within a social collaboration tool, you can click the face and go straight to that colleague's profile page where you can learn more about that person — not just that person's position on an org chart but the projects and interest groups the colleague is associated with and the ideas she's been sharing. Even if you never make it to the profile page, ambient exposure to faces seen on the company activity stream can help you recognize those people if you run into them in the hall or build long-distance relationships that feel a little more real than an interaction with a faceless collaborator.

Figure 1-3 shows how profile photos are displayed on a NewsGator home screen that has been configured to show multiple streams of information. NewsGator calls this multistream feature Lookout, and it's one of several home screen layouts a user can choose. By hovering my mouse over any user's photo or name, I can see what's commonly called a *contact card,* a compact representation of that person's profile with essential information such as title, e-mail, and phone number.

I have seen all sorts of new software products on the market that include the user interface elements of social networks, including activity streams with profile photos. However, often these products require the user to create a social profile just for that one application. There may or may not be a convenient way of synchronizing those profiles or sharing those feeds on a company-wide collaboration network. The danger of these products is that while they look "social," they can create silos of social activity disconnected from the rest of the network.

Figure 1-3:
A social collaboration activity stream lets you see the faces of your co-workers and easily get more information about them.

On the other hand, with proper integration, this boom in social applications can result in many more ways of getting work done through the network. Such integration will be simpler, as a matter of IT architecture, if you settle on one central social collaboration platform all others should feed into.

One argument in favor of using social collaboration is that most employees are familiar with social networking. In fact, organizations that fail to implement some form of social collaboration are likely to find employees grumbling about basic computing tasks that they can perform easily at home, but not at work. For example, consumer social networks boast slick apps that work well on a smartphone, which isn't true of most enterprise systems but is a major focus of social collaboration software makers.

Familiarity carries you only so far, however. Even though a social collaboration system may mimic modes of interaction found on public social networking sites, it's not the same. Certainly, the type of information users are expected to share is different. Social collaboration platforms typically include whole suites of tools for document collaboration, file management, and project management — and there is no equivalent to those on Facebook.

I talk more about the virtues and limitations of familiar social networking conventions in Chapter 2.

Making social networking serve business purposes

Using social collaboration isn't socializing for the sake of socializing. If employees become friends through the network and then go out and socialize after work hours, that's wonderful and may even have soft benefits for the business in terms of team cohesion — but that's really beside the point.

The purpose of social collaboration is to get work done better or faster. That means aligning the types of connections people make, the content that is shared, and the functions that are available for goals like accelerating projects, solving business problems, and generating ideas for new products.

Probably the biggest distinction between enterprise and public social networking is that business conversations require privacy and security. Business collaboration is often restricted to employees only, maybe with a few trusted contractors treated as "honorary employees." And even within a company, departments and project groups likely want to carve out private collaboration areas off-limits to other employees. Certainly, sometimes businesses find that it makes sense to extend access to a specific collaboration group to a

Figure 1-5 shows how you post a question in NewsGator, one of several social platforms that treats questions as a distinct content type. Here, the question is targeted at one person, but others could also jump in and answer it. If I specifically classify a post as a question, I can go back and mark it answered when I get a satisfactory response. Other users and forum moderators can also filter to see just the unanswered questions requiring follow-up. IBM Connections and Jive provide similar functionality in their discussion forums.

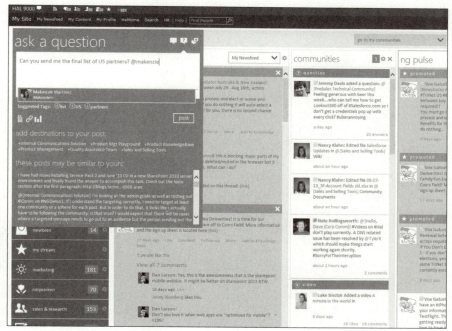

Figure 1-5: Classifying a post as a question in NewsGator.

Distinguishing between Collaboration and Social Networking

 Whenever a buzzword runs hot in the information technology world, vendor marketing folks rush to apply that term to their products, whether it fits or not. "Social" is a hot buzzword these days, giving way to a whole lot of "social software" even though many of these products do very different things. Here are the important distinctions in "social" terminology:

- ✔ **Social media:** Websites used primarily for socializing with friends and family. Facebook is the most successful example of this.

- ✔ **Social networking:** Socializing for a personal or professional purpose or benefit. LinkedIn is an example of professional social networking.

- ✔ **Social collaboration:** Socializing to achieve a common goal. Websites such as Yammer are considered social collaboration sites because they offer colleagues the tools to collaborate in an online social environment.

Tony Byrne, founder of The Real Story Group advisory service, tries to use more precise language in discussions with customers seeking help with product selection. One of the main distinctions he makes is between collaboration and social networking, which are two different things even though many organizations are finding they are complementary.

"When we collaborate, we work jointly on an activity, toward a common goal," Byrne says. "When we network, it's really about connecting with others for its own sake — it's about the relationship. Also, this is about humanizing the digital experience. Much of our software, to date, has assumed we were autonomous robots working in a cube."

To create, manage, or improve a social collaboration system, it helps to understand how social networking and social collaboration are different as well as how they come together.

Accelerating teamwork with collaboration

Collaboration tends to be more focused than social networking, meaning that it's associated with a specific project and involves a smaller number of people. To achieve their goals, team members share digital assets, such as documents and project schedules.

For instance, if the goal of the project is to create a document — say, a proposal — the online collaborative experience may revolve around exchanging drafts of the document or working on it in an environment that allows synchronous editing. Or, the digital assets may be planning tools used to coordinate work that occurs offline.

Figure 1-6 shows a series of revisions collaborators have made to a PowerPoint presentation shared in Jive. Any of these collaborators can download the document, edit it, and upload a new version. Revisions are tracked, making it possible to go back to an older version if necessary.

*ACR
Bulletin

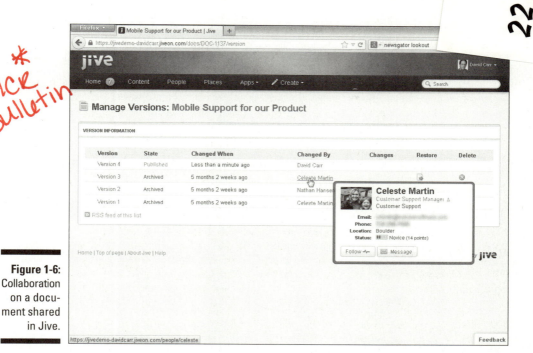

Figure 1-6:
Collaboration
on a docu-
ment shared
in Jive.

Either way, the point of collaboration is to get work done efficiently, whereas social networking focuses on making connections, not necessarily in the context of an immediate project.

In the offline world, two employees sitting together at the same desk, working together intensively on a common problem, are collaborating. Two people who run into each other in the hall and learn and casually exchange information about their respective projects are networking. You might interact with the same person in both modes on the same day, collaborating in the morning and networking in the evening.

Reaching across the organization with social networking

Offline social networks within business consist of the connections between people who work together, as well as the more extended connections between employees who run into each other in the hallway or tell jokes at the water cooler.

The evolution of social collaboration tools

Digital collaboration tools have been around for a long time. Lotus Notes, one of the first popular online collaboration systems for businesses, had its first release in 1989 and still enjoys a following. IBM bought Lotus in 1995 and continues to rely on that business unit for many of its collaboration software innovations.

However, until recently, corporate collaboration tools weren't very social. They might let you participate in discussion forums, but you didn't see the faces of the other participants, just names and subject lines. Perhaps the company provided an online directory, but the entry for each person provided little insight into expertise or interests, let alone personality.

The idea of using exciting new modes of web-based interaction in business actually predates the rise of Facebook and Twitter. Harvard Business School Professor Andrew McAfee coined the term "Enterprise 2.0" in 2006 to describe the business applications of Web 2.0 technologies, which at the time meant things like blogs and wikis — ways of using the web for community interaction, as opposed to one-way publishing.

McAfee saw great potential for these tools to be used effectively in business, and his Enterprise 2.0 concept generated some buzz. Software and software as a service companies like Socialtext and Jive Software began to promote wiki and blogging tools designed for business.

That first wave of Enterprise 2.0 technologies was social, but not as social as what we see today. Blogging is social in the sense that it allows the blogger to express his personality, and other people can comment back, but it's still the blogger on his soap box and the audience down below. Networks of blogs with a shared account structure start to get more interesting, allowing bloggers to comment on each other's articles and have their comments accompanied by a profile photo or avatar image and a link back to their own blogs.

From this pattern evolved current social networks, which resemble networked blogs with a central feed of all posts, organized for easy browsing. The term that came to be associated with Twitter is "microblogging," reflecting a design that encourages brief status posts rather than long diatribes. Social activity streams make it possible for the feed to also include summaries linked to other resources as they are added, such as documents, discussion posts, or notifications from other applications that are linked to the social network.

Online social networking is a digital representation of the networks that exist between people and an aid to expanding those networks. In addition to connecting you with people you know, they allow you to discover people you would like to get to know. In a business context, this means keeping tabs on people who have expertise or authority relevant to your work. Adding them to your database of contacts makes it easier to keep track of them. Meanwhile, the social nature of the environment makes it easier to connect names with faces, navigate to a person's profile with a click, and monitor posts or other activity updates from our contacts.

Figure 1-7 shows the NewsGator social profile for Jenay Sellers, an online marketing manager for the software vendor. Her profile makes it easy to see the topics she posts about most frequently (based on tags used in those posts), which is a clue to interests or expertise. We can also see who else follows her posts, and other tabs on her profile would allow us to see colleagues in her network and content she has posted.

Part of the theory of why social networking is so powerful lies in the strength of weak ties: that is, more casual connections, as opposed to strong ties with close friends or co-workers you know better. For example, if you lose your job, having a large network of connections on LinkedIn (and in your offline social networks) significantly boosts your chances of coming up with a lead on a new opportunity, even if those connections might be weak ties. Better yet, if you can persuade your connections to share the news of your availability with their own networks, you're getting exposure to people with whom you previously had no tie at all. Of course, after you land an interview and are trying to seal the deal, your tighter connections are the ones you will turn to for a recommendation.

In the same way, when you have a problem to solve at work or a question you need answered, the answer may come from a weak tie connection or even a connection a few degrees removed. Social networking can naturally lead to social collaboration. Over time, these new connections may become strong ties, or at least stronger ones, if you find they consistently have the answers you need for your work. Someone who starts out as a social connection may also become a collaborator. If someone has been consistently helpful, maybe you can return the favor by recommending that colleague for a choice project.

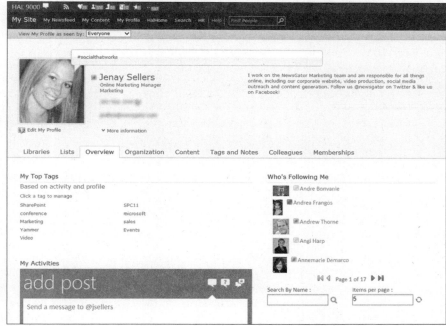

Figure 1-7:
A NewsGator social profile lets you see a colleague's connections, as well as the subjects she posts about frequently.

Bringing Collaboration and Social Networking Together

When evaluating enterprise social collaboration products and platforms, you might opt for a robust collaboration environment with a little social functionality sprinkled on top, or perhaps a slick social tool with only lightweight collaboration tools.

Although understanding the distinction between social networking and collaboration is important, social collaboration brings them together in an effective way. For example, a project workspace may be used primarily for small group collaboration, but if it includes a social network-style feed, then you can also get to know your collaborators better, maybe even staying in touch with them as contacts after the project is over.

Keep reading to discover more ways social networking makes collaboration work better.

Sharing expertise within the organization

Sharing expertise within the organization is paramount. After all, I don't have all the answers, and neither do you, but if we work together, we ought to have more answers between us. When a group of collaborators come together to accomplish a big, important goal, ideally they will know what they're doing — but that doesn't mean the team members will have all the answers or expertise or skills to get it done. Occasionally, they may not even know whom to ask. Or, maybe they just want a second opinion from someone who has the right expertise but hasn't been directly involved in the project.

And that's where the social network comes in. One of the main purposes of an employee social network is to act as a medium for discovering and sharing expertise.

Employees reveal their expertise in several ways, both explicitly and implicitly:

- **Profiles:** Colleagues can spell out areas of expertise on their profiles, which can also be seeded with details about academic and professional credentials imported from human resources databases.

- **Status updates:** Posting status updates about what colleagues are working on or links to documents, blogs, or activities relevant to their work can reveal a colleague's areas of expertise.

✓ **Group discussions:** Colleagues can display their knowledge by participating in topical or functional discussion groups, such as a community of interest for auditors or a project group in a division on the other side of the world tackling problems similar to those you and your collaborators are addressing. Figure 1-8 shows a discussion in Jive. If one of the participants in the discussion is making good points or displaying expertise on a topic you care about, you can easily get more information about that person or start following his posts.

As you learn the value of the social network to make connections and discover information, that should motivate you to refine your profile and share useful posts. By advertising your expertise, you not only make yourself easier to find, but you also boost your professional reputation within the organization.

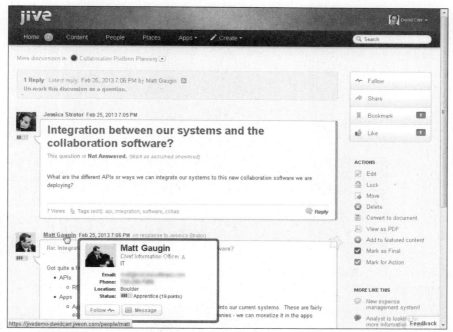

Figure 1-8: Participation in discussions is one way to show expertise.

Introducing new collaborations

Ideally, employees who connect through the social network, with common professional interests, will spark ideas that lead to new projects, allowing them to progress from social connections to active collaborators. If lightning strikes, this could be where your organization's next million-dollar (or multi-million-dollar) idea comes from.

Such spontaneous generation of ideas for collaborations can be particularly fruitful for research and development specialists or ideas that come from cross-disciplinary collaboration.

On a more routine basis, project managers may learn to think twice before they round up the usual suspects for a new project, instead prospecting for new blood on the social network.

Finding new connections through existing connections

The digitization of the social network has the advantage of making the connections between people visible. Users can navigate from one good connection to another, finding other people with related expertise and competencies.

A good place to start would be looking at the lists of connections shown on the profiles of our close collaborators. In Jive, you can browse to the Connections tab on any user's profile to see related profiles, as shown in Figure 1-9.

Figure 1-9: Browsing the connections of another member of a Jive social collaboration network.

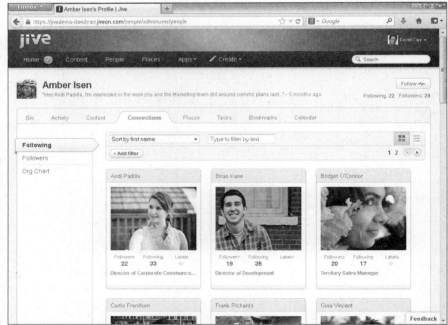

By mapping the connections between people, you can also see any common connections who can help introduce you to some senior executive you might be uncomfortable approaching directly. Other times, established connections might proactively introduce you to new connections who can help get things done.

In life and business, it helps to be connected, and the social network can help you be better connected.

Linking knowledge, documents, and projects to people

Social collaboration stands on the shoulders of several previous generations of knowledge management, document management, content management, and collaboration technologies. The need to organize documents and knowledge hasn't gone away, but now when folks find an internal business document, for instance, they also expect to be able to find our way to the profile of its author.

So exactly why is that so valuable? Suppose the document you found is a competitive intelligence report on a key market segment that was compiled two years ago. Since then, new competitors have entered the market, and others have merged or gone out of business. The report hasn't been updated. Hmm. If you can easily locate the author's profile, maybe you'll find that she posted informal updates as a blog or a series of posts to the social network. No? Then contact her and ask about any unpublished insights she can share. Maybe you can enlist her to produce a new edition of the report or provide tips on other ways to research the topic.

The social dimension moves online collaboration away from merely being an exchange of documents and data, adding people to the mix. When you can look at any document or report and see the people behind it, you boost your ability to find information because not all the needed information is already written down or neatly organized in a database. Often, people are the best resource.

One of the mantras of social collaboration is the capability of finding people through documents, and documents through people. The same goes for connecting people and customer records, people and sales reports, people and projects, and so on.

Data is important, but people make an organization work.

Competing and Coexisting with E-Mail

Social collaboration addresses some of the weaknesses of e-mail, particularly the use of mailing lists, broadcast messages, and inappropriate use of the Reply to All function.

Social collaboration does not necessarily replace e-mail. Anyone who attempts to frame a social collaboration initiative that way is likely to be disappointed, given how ingrained the use of e-mail is in business. When setting metrics of success, reducing the total volume of e-mail is likely to be a false or frustrating goal. On the other hand, tracking the number of mailing lists converted to more productive social collaboration groups would be a productive goal.

Social collaboration can replace many types of discussion or collaboration-oriented internal communications for which e-mail is an awkward match.

Consider the weaknesses of e-mail compared with social collaboration:

- **E-mail discussions can be confusing.** In any extended discussion, context is easily lost in a mess of quoted text from prior messages. It can be difficult to sort out the original question or problem posed. Social collaboration tools typically do a better job of organizing message threads and making it easier to scan a list of messages to see who has been participating in the discussion.

- **Private replies restrict the flow of information.** The easiest way to start an ad hoc group discussion via e-mail is to include the e-mail addresses of several people in the Cc field and have the discussion continue by having everyone click Reply to All rather than Reply. However, if anyone included in the distribution list unintentionally clicks Reply, a message intended for the whole group will be transmitted to only one person (the author of the currently selected message).

- **Reply to All can cause trouble.** Most organizations have a story about the person who clicked Reply to All by mistake and wound up sending a rude or disrespectful comment to the whole company, when it was intended for only one person. When employees participate in a discussion on a social collaboration system, the group discussion context is explicit; private messaging in these environments is the exception to the rule.

- **Sharing information is sometimes too easy.** Proprietary information easily can be shared outside the organization, either unintentionally (an employee failed to understand that some of the participants on an e-mail discussion thread were outsiders) or maliciously (an employee forwards the message to an outsider).

✔ **Version control can be difficult through e-mail.** When collaborators exchange documents through e-mail, there is room for confusion about who has the latest version. Documents shared in a social collaboration workspace are less subject to this confusion, particularly if the collaborators make their edits within the web-based system rather than downloading them for offline editing. Or, a document management system can be used to enforce checking in and checking out documents in an orderly way.

✔ **E-mail strains IT resources.** E-mail distribution of documents consumes more bandwidth and storage than necessary because a complete copy of the document is transmitted to every recipient (including people who may never read it). Sharing a link to that same document in a centralized repository, whether through e-mail or a message on the social collaboration system, makes more frugal use of network resources.

✔ **E-mail is private by default.** Information that ought to be shared more widely can end up trapped in the inbox of one person or a small number of people. That same information shared on a social collaboration system would be broadly available (either to the whole company or members of an interest or project group) and searchable.

Social collaboration doesn't hold all the advantages, however. Here are some of the strengths of e-mail:

✔ **E-mail is an Internet standard.** You can send business e-mail to any e-mail addresses inside or outside your company (if you have the e-mail addresses, obviously).

✔ **E-mail programs work together.** You can use the same e-mail software for both internal and external communication, and you can send an e-mail to someone using a different program than he will use to receive it. In contrast, every social collaboration system is isolated. This may be an advantage in terms of organizational control, but it does mean you can't invite an outsider into a discussion without specifically creating an account for him on your social collaboration system.

✔ **E-mail support is widely available.** E-mail is an established technology for use in corporate settings, which means that supporting tools for administration, archiving, and compliance are also well established.

✔ **E-mail works well for private messages.** Social collaboration systems may provide their own private messaging systems, but most employees still find sending an e-mail faster, easier, and more familiar. Conservative organizations may also be more willing to trust e-mail with private messages on sensitive topics or the transmission of documents, such as drafts of contracts.

Your social collaboration strategy must account for e-mail's strengths as well as its weaknesses. The goal should be to use each medium according to its strengths. In the following sections, I discuss some of the appropriate uses of social collaboration in more detail.

Providing social discussions as an alternative to Reply to All

Red Robin CIO Chris Laping told me that his company's implementation of Yammer could be justified with the elimination of Reply to All e-mail alone, given that it's so annoying and nonproductive. He tells employees to not expect him to reply to their e-mails unless they have a very good reason for communicating via e-mail rather than the social network. Of course, he still has to use e-mail to communicate with people outside the company; e-mail remains the standard for intercompany communication.

Here are the two types of email-based messaging that fall into this Reply to All category:

- ✔ **The common ad hoc, Reply to All discussion thread:** Replies go to all the recipients of the original message. Users may also add or delete addresses from the distribution list for the message at will.

- ✔ **The mailing list, configured at the network level:** A mailing list allows employees to write to a single address and have their messages distributed to a list of people. Messages relayed through the list can be set to have the Reply To field in the e-mail header set to the list e-mail address. In that case, replies are effectively Reply to All by default.

Mailing lists are the easiest targets to replace with social collaboration. All it takes is a message to the group saying that the list has been deactivated and that future discussions will take place in a shiny new social workspace. Or at least, that should be about all that's required at the system administration level. The politics of taking away a familiar resource and replacing it with something new can definitely be tricky. The list owner and other key stakeholders in the discussion group will need to be convinced that the social collaboration environment is an improvement. You might consider running the two in parallel for a test period, but ultimately the benefits of replacing the e-mail list will be realized only when you shut it off.

Eliminating ad hoc Reply to All e-mail is a tougher problem — and perhaps not even a worthwhile goal. Brief, focused Reply to All exchanges among a small group of collaborators may be perfectly productive. After all, if employees are getting their work done, don't get in their way. On the other hand, if employees are frustrated with long, confusing e-mail discussions, they may be looking for a better way.

Dictating that Reply to All conversations must stop is unlikely to work. There's no quick technical fix. I have heard social collaboration boosters talk about wanting to deactivate the Reply to All button on Microsoft Outlook, but as far as I can tell, that's just talk.

There may also be cases where social collaboration isn't a perfect replacement for information sharing via e-mail. For example, one tech firm I spoke with couldn't deactivate some e-mail lists used by programmers — at least not immediately — because the social collaboration system that the company had implemented didn't do as good of a job of preserving the formatting of code snippets. So while the system administrators sought a workaround, it was better to leave those mailing lists turned on.

The best way to sell social collaboration to employees is demonstrating the productive uses of social collaboration on a routine basis. I've seen this as an employee of UBM (the publisher of *InformationWeek* and organizer of trade shows, including the E2 Conference on social business). I got training on using UBM's Jive software implementation (The Hub), when I first joined the company. Whenever the CEO or one of the other top executives puts out a message to the whole company, it's published on The Hub rather than sent by e-mail. (For an important announcement, employees get an e-mail including a link pointing to the executive's blog post on the Hub, just so no one misses it.) Comments and feedback can then be managed through The Hub, as are comments on the blog post, rather than as exchanges of e-mail messages.

Besides de-cluttering inboxes, this promotes greater participation and more productive conversations. Employees would be foolish to do Reply to All on a company-wide e-mail. They might also be too shy to send a personal e-mail back to the CEO. On the other hand, the comments field on an internal blog post is a clear invitation to feedback. Other employees can choose to follow the conversation closely, or not at all.

Linking to documents rather than attaching them

Another habit that is difficult to break is e-mailing file attachments. The argument against this practice is not new. Generations of document management and file sharing tools have come and gone, and yet the use of file attachments remains common.

Once again, e-mail is the lowest common denominator, working for both internal and external sharing of files. Once again, that is both a strength and a weakness. Every business works with sensitive documents that should not be shared with anyone other than employees and, perhaps, a small number of trusted external collaborators. That provides organizational motivation for dictating that those should be shared and accessed through a centralized and controlled system. To get better compliance with such dictates, it helps to also provide individual motivation.

If a social collaboration environment can make it as easy (or ideally, easier) to share documents on a network, rather than through e-mail, employees will be more likely to change their habits. If that's one of your goals for social collaboration, you want to take a close look at how well your software vendor or cloud service provider is delivering on that ease of use promise.

Another increasingly popular way of improving e-mail and document file sharing (outside of social collaboration) is using cloud-based file sharing tools. The cloud file sharing service Box, for example, has positioned itself as an alternative to established enterprise tools for document management such as SharePoint. Box also provides a little bit of social collaboration functionality, in the form of comments on files, but does not try to deliver a full-blown enterprise social network. However, it has recently promoted a partnership with Jive Software to make Box available as an embedded application within Jive's social collaboration platform, while also synchronizing files and discussions about files between the two systems.

Encouraging sharing beyond the personal inbox

The executive sponsors of social collaboration projects frequently seek to encourage innovation and broaden knowledge sharing within their organizations. When an employee details an undocumented procedure in a private e-mail conversation, that's *knowledge creation* — except that the knowledge is now buried in another employee's inbox. Maybe only one person asked for the information, but perhaps many others would also find it valuable.

Social collaboration makes sharing of knowledge the default, so information is kept private only when there is a good reason for it to be private.

One of the implicit assumptions of e-mail communication is knowing who needs to receive your message or is likely to have the answer to your question. You have to know the right e-mail addresses to plug into the To and Cc lines in your e-mail client. On the other hand, when knowledge is shared through social collaboration, it might be delivered, so to speak, to colleagues who the sender doesn't even know.

When you make an announcement to the stream on a social collaboration network, you have the option of tagging or mentioning users or groups of users whom you want to be notified of your message. (I give you more details about tagging and mentioning in Chapter 4.) However, by posting a widely distributed message on a social collaboration network (without tagging or mentioning a specific person), you also open up the possibility of getting a response from someone in another part of the company, maybe on the other side of the world, whom you never would have known to reach out to. There is more chance involved, which means there is also the possibility that your message won't be seen by just the right person with the answer to your question. But when these chance encounters happen, they can be magic.

Skilled social collaborators also learn to boost the odds by including topical tags on their messages (I tell you more about topical tags in Chapter 4) or targeting them to communities where they are more likely to find the right audience.

Bridging the gap between social collaboration and e-mail habits

E-mail isn't going away any time soon. The most productive approach to users who are wedded to e-mail may be this: If you can't beat 'em, join 'em — or more specifically, integrate 'em.

- ✔ **E-mail notification messages:** Most social collaboration systems provide an option for e-mail notifications, allowing users to get e-mails alerting them to things they have to pay attention to in the social collaboration system even if they don't participate actively. For example, you might want to get an e-mail notification whenever someone edits or comments on a document you originally posted. Figure 1-10 shows the configuration of e-mail notifications in Yammer, most of which are turned on by default.

- ✔ **Plug-ins:** Another approach is to use a plug-in to Microsoft Outlook (assuming it's your standard corporate e-mail client) that displays social conversations side by side with e-mail threads. For example, Jive for Outlook allows Outlook users to participate in social community discussions. You can also take a discussion that started out as an e-mail thread and convert it into a social discussion hosted in Jive. Figure 1-11 shows an e-mail exchange with one of my co-workers at the media and events company UBM, showing the social context I can get from integration with our Jive-based social network, the Hub.

For those employees who "live in e-mail," Outlook integration can be a good bridge to social collaboration.

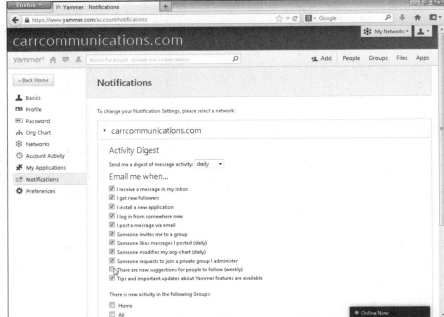

Figure 1-10:
E-mail notifications in Yammer can be configured by checking or clearing check boxes.

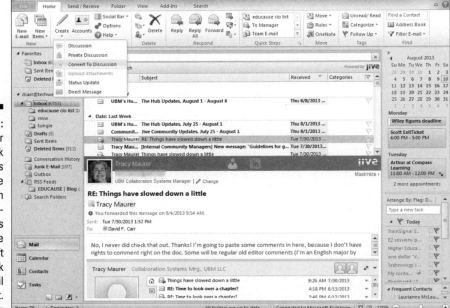

Figure 1-11:
Jive for Outlook displays Jive profile information and integration options within the Microsoft Outlook e-mail client.

> ✓ **E-mail as part of the social collaboration platform:** Another approach, seen in products such as IBM Connections, is to provide integrated web-based e-mail, making e-mail access just another tab within the social collaboration system. The IBM Notes e-mail client (also known as Lotus Notes) has also been adding social features to be a better companion to Connections.

The more that users can move smoothly between e-mail and social modes of communication, the better.

Exploring Practical Applications of Social Collaboration

Successful social collaboration is ultimately judged by business results, not theoretical advantages of one mode of collaboration over another. Part of what distinguishes a successful implementation from an unsuccessful one is a strategy for achieving some initial results quickly, giving the network time to deliver more substantial results over time. This analysis of potential payoffs will be different for every business, but here are some of the usual suspects.

Helping sales teams close more deals with social collaboration

Organizations increasingly market their products through social media, seeking to spark viral sharing and bring in tons of sales leads. It's a beautiful thing when it works. Individual salespeople also use social networks a number of ways: as a medium for prospecting and researching opportunities, as well as a way of promoting themselves and forging connections with potential customers.

The potential of internal collaboration to drive sales may be less obvious, mostly a matter of making connections behind the scenes that make a difference. Particularly in business-to-business (B2B) sales, a complex internal process is often involved in formulating a proposal and putting a price on it. Cutting the time required to produce a proposal is one way how social collaboration can pay off. The proposal may also be more likely to succeed if the salesperson can tap the knowledge of the right people, including product experts and people who have worked with the prospect in the past.

The synergy of social collaboration and sales tools was sufficiently obvious to Salesforce.com (the leading vendor of cloud-based Customer Relationship Management (CRM) software used for sales, marketing, and support) that it created its own social collaboration tool: Chatter. When Salesforce.com and Chatter are used together, the activity surrounding a sales opportunity can be represented in the Chatter feed. Employees can choose to follow Customer and Opportunity records in Salesforce.com, just as they might follow an individual. Viewing one of these records in Salesforce.com CRM also brings up a listing of Chatter commentary about it, as shown in Figure 1-12. This can provide context that goes beyond the neatly organized fields of the record. Having the social profiles of collaborators on the record displayed within it also makes it easy to reach out to one of those people with a question in a couple of clicks.

Microsoft has created a similar integration between Yammer (a cloud-based social platform it acquired in 2012) and Microsoft Dynamics CRM.

A social collaboration environment need not be joined at the hip with a CRM tool to be useful to sales teams. Social collaboration software vendors such as Jive also say that sales collaboration is one of the main uses of their platforms.

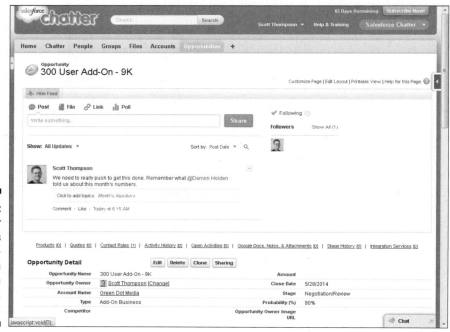

Figure 1-12:
Chatter
provides
social com-
menting on
records in
Salesforce.
com CRM.

For example, Unisys sales teams use Chatter with their Salesforce.com implementation, but the company-wide enterprise social network is based on a combination of NewsGator Social Sites and Microsoft SharePoint. Chatter is perfect for discussions between salespeople comparing notes on an account. At the same time, there are many cases when salespeople need to tap the knowledge of the broader organization. For example, a salesperson visiting a customer site might need to quickly locate the right subject matter expert in the Unisys consulting organization to answer an obscure customer question. NewsGator is the better tool for the job, then, particularly in combination with mobile device access that allows the salesperson to post the question immediately and perhaps get an answer before leaving the customer location.

That's the sort of thing that keeps a customer happy, makes the salesperson look like a hero, and leads to more business down the road.

Finding answers to questions

If you've got questions, the social network has answers. Even if you have no idea who to ask, you can post your question to a general feed and see who answers.

If your question has been asked before, you may be able to search to find your answer without having to pose it again. When the same questions come up again and again, it makes sense to organize them into some sort of knowledge base or frequently asked questions document. That doesn't always happen, however, making the ability to search the social stream an important capability.

 Even if you don't find the answer to your specific question, you may find people who have posted on related topics. (I tell you how to do that in Chapter 2.) Remember that social collaboration is about people, not just data. Find the people with the right expertise and ask them your question.

Very likely, your search will also turn up social collaboration groups associated with professional interests, projects, or departments, all of which can be avenues to finding either the information you seek or the right people to ask.

The payoff here is in the form of less time wasted, less guesswork, better knowledge sharing, and smarter business decisions.

Coordinating projects from the social activity stream

Every organization runs at least partly on projects: groups of people working together to accomplish some common goal. That's essentially the definition of collaboration I use earlier. One simple way how the social component of social collaboration can contribute to better project management is with the routine sharing of project status updates from all participants. The traditional way is to hold a status report meeting, where participants talk about their piece of the project and their progress. By most accounts, this can be really tedious. When project participants share their statuses online, though, the need for the status meeting goes away. To the extent that participants can be persuaded to share their project statuses regularly, project managers may also be alerted to problems sooner and have an opportunity to make course corrections.

The need for meetings in general may be reduced to the extent that decisions can be driven through social collaboration. And when meetings are truly necessary, folks can focus on decision-making rather than status reports.

Some social collaboration environments also provide features specific to project and task management. Often, this is positioned as lightweight project management that doesn't attempt to replicate all the capabilities of the tools used by professional project managers. In other words, you might not want to use a social collaboration tool like the Activities function in IBM Connections to build a bridge or an airplane (a complex technical project with dependencies between tasks requiring precise tracking), but using it to plan a conference would be perfectly appropriate. In fact, that's one of the things IBM uses the software for internally.

Social project collaboration puts the emphasis on integration with the social environment, providing a smooth transition from a social post *(Hey, somebody ought to do this!)* to creating a task *(Good idea; you do it, and your deadline is Friday at 5 p.m.)*. Assigning a task becomes as simple as tagging someone in a post.

Social networking and project management have been converging in another way, as project management tools vendors add social feeds to their products. I have more to say about this in Chapter 6 where I talk about managing projects and tasks.

Generating ideas for products and business improvements

No company can afford to rest secure that the products that sustain its business today will continue to support it in the future. In fact, many companies are under considerable pressure to find their next hit, or even to turn around a struggling company.

Ideally, some of these ideas will arrive spontaneously through ongoing discussions in the social collaboration system. A great idea is proposed, refined, and recognized by someone with the power to make it happen. That's great when it happens, but sometimes innovation needs a little nudge.

One way to seek ideas for new products and services, as well as money-saving ideas for current operations, is to leverage the power of the crowd. This can be done informally (through questions or challenges posted to social collaboration streams) or in a more structured way (using an application geared to gathering and organizing ideas). Often, this includes a voting mechanism for identifying the best ideas.

Some crowdsourcing initiatives are public, such as appeals to customers, consumers, and freelance inventors to come up with new product ideas. There may be a prize and certainly will be public recognition for the best ideas, providing motivation for members of the public to contribute.

This kind of online brainstorming also can work internally, with employees encouraged to contribute their best ideas. Employees have the advantage of knowing the company and its capabilities (as well as its shortcomings) and probably will be happy to be asked for their opinion.

Applied to internal brainstorming, this process is also known as "ideation." The best known ideation software specialist is Spigit, which offers its Spigit Engage product as a standalone cloud service with its own built-in social features and also supports integrations with Jive, Yammer, and SharePoint. IBM Connections has its own ideation module, as does NewsGator.

As with any social application, the virtue of integration with a core enterprise social network is to provide a unified social experience, rather than a bunch of social applications each of which has its own system for managing user profiles and connections. I tell you more about choosing the right software in Part III.

Chapter 2

Getting Familiar with Social Collaboration Tools

*S*ocial collaboration takes advantage of many of the user interface conventions and styles of interaction that many of your employees will have encountered in their personal use of the web. This includes the basic elements of social networks for making connections, sharing links and status posts, and clicking Like or Favorite on content to recommend to others. Other familiar features will likely include elements of web software: search engines, web-based calendar and event invitation apps, or even e-commerce sites, such as automated recommendations of connections or content (à la Amazon.com personalized product recommendations).

These familiar elements give social collaboration a head start toward employee adoption. At the same time, they set high expectations for the functionality a social collaboration system should deliver.

Adoption of social collaboration systems also requires that business leaders who implement them explain to colleagues how social collaboration in the workplace is different from participation in social media. I tell you how to approach that issue in this chapter. I also introduce the social graph and ways that you can collaborate on projects.

Introducing Social Collaboration Tools

The status post is one of the most recognizable elements of social media that flows into social collaboration. Collaborative platforms provide many more focused tools, but the ability to post a message for everyone to see can be very powerful for the employee who has an observation or question of general interest. The main company feed is also a natural place to post short messages from company leaders or links to longer blog posts.

Figure 2-1 shows the kind of information a traveling executive might post to let workers in a particular office or region know she is coming to town.

Figure 2-1:
A basic
social post
in Jive.

The mechanics of the posting and browsing updates to the social network are intentionally familiar to public social media users. The content is what's different.

Even to the extent that Facebook familiarity is an asset, you can't start with the assumption that every employee is a Facebook user. As big as Facebook's audience has grown, some people have never tried it — or have tried it but don't like it. Too, some of your most experienced employees may think of social networking as something "kids are doing these days," which they don't have time for, or necessarily want to learn.

In this section, I tell you what a social collaboration system typically looks like and introduce you to some of the tools available to users.

Taking a look at corporate activity streams

What Facebook calls its News Feed and Twitter calls its Timeline is known generically as an *activity stream*. Every member of the social network generates a stream of posts and other records, which you can see by navigating to that user's profile. In addition to showing a person's latest status posts, the system might show groups joined, connections made, and documents created or uploaded. Each user can also view a merged activity stream that provides an overview of everything going on in the organization that has been recorded on the collaboration network. If the entire feed is too overwhelming, you can filter it down to show just items related to people you follow and groups you have joined.

Applications connected to the social network can also generate activity stream posts, such as notifications of deals recorded as closed in a Customer Relationship Management (CRM) system.

Evolution of the activity stream

Early versions of Facebook called the view of a user's activity stream "the Wall," and a typical mode of interaction was to navigate to the Wall of other users to see what they posted and perhaps "write on their Wall" (a message directed at them) or a comment on a post. In 2006, Facebook introduced its News Feed, which is a merged view of posts from all your Facebook Friends. This shift was controversial because people felt that what they'd posted was a lot more "public" — one of many instances when Facebook users have been shocked to realize how much they are sharing. When that controversy blew over, the News Feed emerged as one of Facebook's most popular features, and today users can't imagine the service working any other way.

Twitter had the notion of a merged feed of posts from the beginning, with its short messages functioning like a headline service about the lives and thoughts of all the people you have chosen to follow. Over time, it has become more populated with companies and media organizations sharing links to their content. Twitter also introduced several key techniques for making even simple text-based posts richer, such as "@mentioning" another user (referencing them with their username preceded by the @ sign) and informally categorizing posts with hash tags (labels preceded by the # sign).

Social collaboration systems borrow from these conventions.

The notion of a social-style feed or stream has also become a run-away success in the world of enterprise applications. Even outside enterprise social networking platforms, many software products mimic the format of a social feed to represent important events in the form of a social feed. Ideally, these feeds and the user profiles associated with them should be synchronized with other social applications in use across the company.

Having separate feeds for specific functions and applications isn't necessarily bad, but one of the goals of social collaboration is to be able to get a bird's-eye view of everything going on in the organization.

A user on Jive Software's social collaboration platform who navigates to the Activities tab will find more listed there than just status posts. Oh, you can filter the feed to show just status posts, if you like. Normally, however, you would see all sorts of updates, revolving around documents, projects, tasks, and messages from executives posted as blog entries. Jive provides a much broader set of options for creating or sharing content than Facebook or even some of the other products for business, such as Yammer. That means there is more going on here that you may want to be notified about.

Notions of what a corporate activity stream ought to look like vary between social collaboration platform providers, but here are some of the common elements:

- ✔ **Status updates:** Short posts employees use to share what they're working on, where they're traveling, or pithy thoughts about life and business.

- ✔ **Photo and profile:** Every post includes a photo or an avatar of the author, linked back to that person's profile.

- ✔ **Activity stream organization:** Posts and other items in the stream are listed in reverse chronological order, at least by default. Comments posted as replies are often indented under the original post to keep the entire discussion together.

  - *Ranking:* The most important content tends to rise to the top. For example, posts that may be older but are the subject of active discussion will tend to rank higher than newer posts that have attracted no attention. Every social collaboration platform has its own algorithms for determining importance.

  - *Filtering:* The stream can be viewed through a variety of filters. For example, users should be able to filter the stream to display posts from only those people they chose to follow (as opposed to all employees) and in either strict chronological order or through an algorithm that promises to display the most significant content. To illustrate the possibilities, I captured images of several different filters on the same user's activity stream in Jive. The same basic concept is present in all the major social collaboration platforms, although the specific options will be different.

The Activity tab in Jive 6 displays all activity from all employees, but in Figure 2-2 I've filtered it to just the status posts.

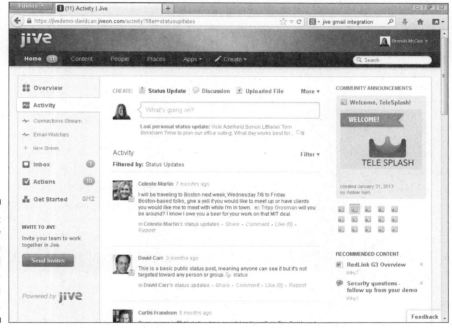

Figure 2-2:
The Activity tab in Jive shows all recent messages and updates.

Figure 2-3 shows what Jive calls the Connections Stream, which is limited to whoever you follow on the network.

Figure 2-4 shows the Jive Inbox, which is where you can see all the messages specifically addressed to you.

Figure 2-3:
The Jive
Connections
Stream
narrows
the activity
stream to
activities
from the
people,
groups, and
documents
you follow.

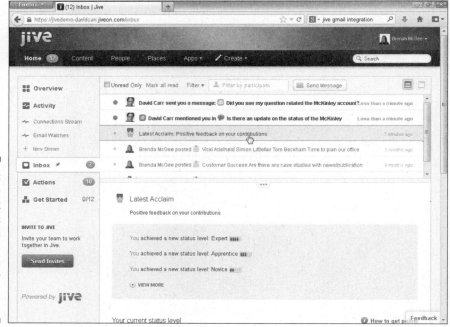

Figure 2-4:
The Jive
Inbox
displays
messages
and noti-
fications
specifically
addressed
to you.

Finally, Figure 2-5 shows how you can create your own custom filter, for example to track employees who report to you separately from the rest of your connections. You do this by clicking the New Stream link and selecting specific co-workers to include.

✔ **Links and documents:** In an activity stream, you can post links to other web pages and upload documents to share with colleagues. I tell you more about that in the next section and in Chapter 4 (on social posts) and Chapter 7 (on document collaboration).

✔ **Embedded applications:** Increasingly, social collaboration systems embed application objects in the stream, allowing users to interact with them in the social context. This is similar to the way Facebook will let you view a YouTube video using a player embedded in the stream, rather than clicking away to the YouTube site. The business equivalent may be a requisition approval form embedded in the stream.

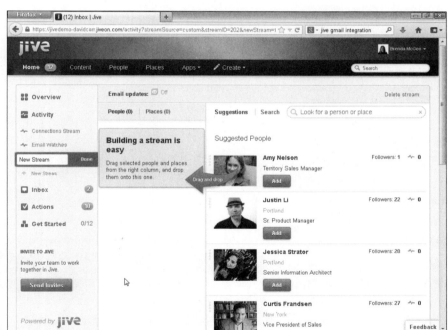

Figure 2-5: Creating a Jive custom stream.

Sharing links, media, and documents

One of the things that makes the web so powerful is the ability to link to and embed other resources. In addition to sharing simple text-based status messages, social collaboration includes the ability to share links, media, and other documents.

One of the most basic forms this takes is, "You really should read this article on teamwork if you want to understand how organizations are changing," followed by the link. Figure 2-6 shows link sharing on a Yammer social collaboration network. Note that when the user adds the web address for an article as part of the body of a post, Yammer automatically retrieves a preview of the article, in this case from the Harvard Business Review Blog Network.

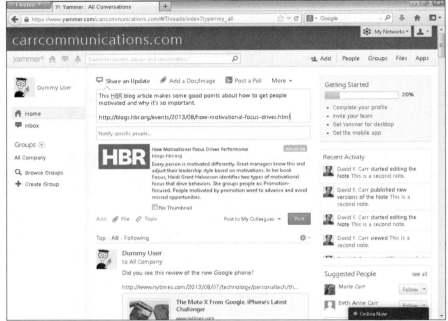

Figure 2-6:
Posting links to a Yammer social collaboration network.

Social collaboration tools are also good for basic document sharing. Some provide more sophisticated features for document management and collaborative editing. Whether simple or sophisticated, the point of sharing documents in a social context is to be able to comment on them as well as share them across the internal social network.

Determining what to post to an activity stream

For social collaboration to be useful, status posts cannot focus as much on entertainment and idle chatter as they do on Facebook or Twitter. An occasional, tasteful joke that brightens someone's day can be fine, but most posts ought to be about getting work done or brainstorming ideas for making the company and its products better.

Regardless of the social collaboration platform, in the status update text box, you simply type your message and then click the appropriate button (Update in Yammer; Post in Jive). Your status then appears in the activity stream of everyone in that network. Useful post types include

- ✔ **Basic:** *Here is what I'm working on.* Broadcasting this information opens the possibility of connecting with others working on something complementary, or perhaps preventing duplication of effort.

- ✔ **Progress:** *I just finished the preliminary sketches and will be sharing with the team at Friday's meeting.* Keep other project team members informed of your progress and allow managers to monitor it from a distance.

- ✔ **Question:** *Has anyone in marketing worked with Xenon? Any advice on how to approach the company for a partnership deal?* Asking questions is not only a great way of encouraging engagement in social collaboration, but often it produces answers not gotten any other way — along with introductions to people who can answer further questions you may have on related topics.

- ✔ **Company news:** *The Xenon partnership deal was signed on Friday. Great work everyone!* Celebrate achievement in a way that allows everyone to comment back with reactions.

- ✔ **Announcement:** *The Newark office will be closed Friday as well as Monday for the Labor Day weekend.* Share basic information and reminders.

Before you make a post to the company-wide stream, consider carefully whether it really should be made to a more focused audience, such as a group associated with a project, department, or professional specialty. Strategies for posting to the activity stream are discussed in more detail in Chapter 4.

Monitoring an activity stream

Most social collaboration systems allow you to view a company-wide activity stream, with all the most recent public updates from every employee, everywhere. There is no real parallel to that in public social media. Even if you could tune in to all the posts from all Facebook users, the messages would scroll by too fast to read. There are automated systems, primarily for marketing analytics, that try to digest the full "fire hose" of all the posts coming in to Twitter, but that would be no fun for a mere human.

Instead, in ordinary social media, you choose who to follow or make online "friends" with, and the websites show you items associated with those people. At most, you may get a peek at content from friends of friends (and from advertisers). Even that can get overwhelming if you add connections too liberally.

The scale of social collaboration within a company isn't quite as extreme as the broader social web. Still, a company-wide feed is most useful for small organizations that find it a good way to keep everyone on the same page. On the other hand, the company-wide feed from a large global corporation wouldn't be very useful as your default view of the stream.

Fortunately, you can make the feed more manageable by narrowing it to only activity from your connections on the social network or by applying other filters. For example, Jive provides a standard filter that looks at your profile, your connections with other employees, and the projects you are involved in to identify items that are likely to be interesting or useful to you.

You can also make the feed more useful for everyone by giving feedback and sharing good content from other participants with your own networks or with specific people for whom it is relevant.

Connecting external applications to an activity stream

Activity streams can include feeds from automated systems as well as activity from individuals. Application feed items from automated systems can then include links back to a related form or report, or embedded functionality (like the ability for a user with the right authority to approve an invoice).

Application feeds can be useful as long as the information in them doesn't drown out human activity, defeating the goal of making social collaboration personal and welcoming rather than impersonal and robotic. For example, you wouldn't want an activity stream notification about every updated field in a customer record. On the other hand, a status change from prospect to signed customer could be a significant event worthy of sharing.

Depending on which social collaboration platform you choose, you can manage activity stream clutter with the following:

- **Limiting an activity stream for only application updates:** One way of keeping activity streams from becoming cluttered with application activity is to provide a stream just for application updates.

- **Post ranking within the platform:** Alternatively, the platform may weight automated posts lower in the rankings of the posts that should be displayed first, elevating them only if users comment on them or mark them important. The platform designers make many of these choices, at least in terms of deciding the default behaviors.

If you're the system administrator or community manager, your job is to decide which application feeds make sense and how to configure them to be productive rather than distracting.

Automated feeds aren't the only way applications can be integrated with the feed. Another approach is to embed a social comment feed within the application and have comments posted there mirrored in the main feed. An example would be commenting on a Salesforce.com CRM customer account record, rather than entering data into the record itself, leveraging Salesforce.com's Chatter social collaboration tool, as shown in Figure 2-7. This can be a good way for employees to document their work, allowing others to see the history of a customer relationship.

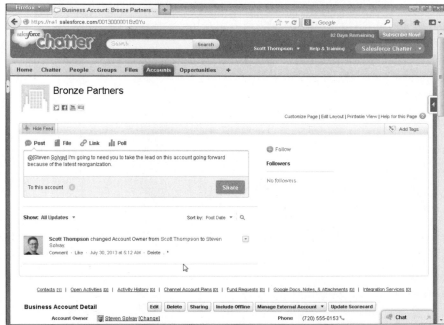

Figure 2-7: Adding Chatter comments to a Salesforce. com customer account record.

Even in the absence of such tight integration, it may be possible to link to content in web-based applications that provide a distinct web address for each record and share comments on the collaboration network. Jive, for instance, provides the Jive Anywhere browser extension that makes that sort of loose application integration easier.

Jive Anywhere also provides a convenient way of referencing external websites and resources. When the plug-in is installed and activated, your browser displays a Discuss button on the right margin of every web page. Clicking that button reveals the commenting user interface shown in Figure 2-8. In this example, I show how to link to a publicly accessible demo of Good Data's web-based business intelligence tool and add comments about it. The comment or question I post in this sidebar will also be displayed in my Jive collaboration network. A collaborator who follows the link and also has Jive Anywhere installed can continue the discussion using the same social sidebar user interface.

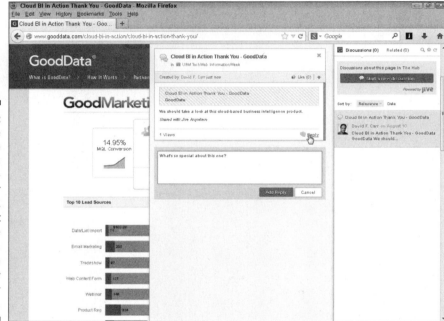

Figure 2-8:
Jive Anywhere adds a social sidebar to your browser, making it possible to start a discussion from any web page or application.

Addressing your post to a specific person or group

Tagging or mentioning other users in your posts is an important technique for making sure your messages will reach the right audience.

In social networking communication, this can be accomplished with an @mention or a similar method of referencing one or more users or user groups. Individuals mentioned in this way will get a notification — in the social stream and possibly also by e-mail — that they have been mentioned in a post.

Figure 2-9 shows a post in Jive that mentions both a group (Marketing) and a user (Tom Beckham). The text of each mention appears in a different font color (blue) and links, respectively, to the group and user profile. As a result of this tagging, the post shows up in the marketing group feed, as well as the public activity feed. Tom Beckham gets a notification that he has been mentioned and responds. The message has achieved both the broadest distribution and delivery to a more focused audience.

Group   User

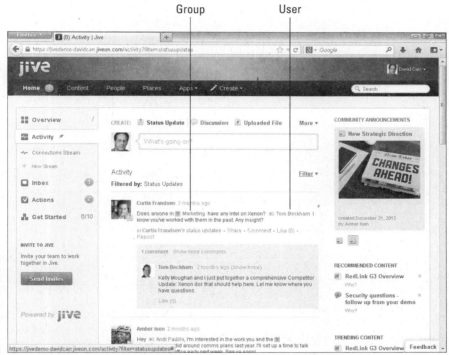

Figure 2-9:
User and group mentions show up in Jive.

When you post to the company-wide activity stream, your potential audience is the entire company, but that does *not* mean the entire company will see your post. And in many ways, that's a good thing. You can post something to the company-wide stream that you would never want to send to a company-wide e-mail alias — as in, items with the potential to be of interest in many parts of the company but not necessarily to every individual within the company. And that's okay because the activity stream doesn't demand an employee's attention the same way that an e-mail inbox does.

Employees may be reasonably expected to read all internal company e-mail, but a large organization with a busy activity stream can't reasonably expect the same of the global stream. Instead, employees skim the social feed looking at the most recent items and the ones with the most comments or other activity. If some posts stream past unread, that's just the nature of the medium.

Harnessing the energy of consumerization and rapid innovation

The rise of social collaboration tools can be seen as a symptom of a broader trend — consumerization — that's having a sweeping impact on the world of enterprise technologies. Instead of the most advanced technology originating within businesses and slowly trickling out, the best technologies have begun flowing the other way, from the consumer world into the enterprise.

Consumer web applications and consumer devices are setting new expectations of ease of use and personal productivity. They may not meet corporate requirements like security and regulatory compliance. If your organization fails to provide an alternative that is at least roughly comparable, employees will be tempted to use the consumer version, anyway, though.

For example, the best smartphones today are developed as consumer devices first, with features for corporate environments added as an afterthought. Thus, the Apple iPhone has become one of the most popular corporate smartphones because so many executives were eager to switch from the longtime corporate mobile king, the BlackBerry. The iPhone came into many companies as an unsanctioned device, but then became popular enough that companies decided to make it an officially sanctioned and supported one.

The story of Yammer is similar: In many cases, employees initially sign up with the cloud collaboration service on their own initiative. In some cases, IT administrators who belatedly find out employees are doing business in the cloud react by trying to shut it down. On the other hand, if the Yammer experiment goes on long enough to show business results, the unofficial choice may be adopted as the official one. Or, even if administrators decide that Yammer use is unacceptable, the Yammer experience may lead to the adoption or increased use of another social collaboration environment.

Consumerization also means bringing some of the energy and innovation from consumer technology and consumer websites into corporate technology. As cloud services, products like Yammer are subject to continuous improvement, with updates released several times per year and immediately available to all subscribers. Like consumer websites, cloud applications tend to see frequent updates and improvements. Even if your organization elects to host social collaboration software independent of the cloud, the social collaboration experience is subject to the same expectation of continuous improvement.

Items you post to the stream will therefore be subject to all sorts of possibilities for serendipitous discovery. But what if you want to make sure someone sees your post, because your post is a public thank you to that person and you want to make sure they see it. Or, you think they're likely to have the answer to the question you are posing. You're posing it to the general feed in case someone else has the answer, but you also have a short list of people you suspect can answer it. By tagging those people with an @mention, you can ensure they will be notified that you particularly want to hear their thoughts.

Moving Beyond Social Media

Familiarity with the social networking concepts implemented by public social networks and consumer websites is a good thing, in general. Although the functions of a social collaboration platform may be slightly different, they are similar enough that many employees can draw parallels with websites and web apps they've used before.

In this section, I tell you how to emphasize the differences to colleagues who are familiar with social media platforms such as Facebook and Twitter. All colleagues will need some guidance on how to use the system in a way that's productive and appropriate, so I advise you on how to set acceptable use policies and choose a community manager.

Introducing Facebook and Twitter users to social collaboration

Employees who are active on a social network like Facebook or Twitter may come up to speed quickly using social collaboration, but they may not understand how it's different from the social networks they know and love or how to apply social networking to their work.

For those employees, you probably won't have to spend much time telling them how to post, but that doesn't mean they understand what to post.

Here's an example of how one company introduced social collaboration to its colleagues:

> ✔ **Provide guidelines.** When social collaboration was first introduced at Mercer (a management consulting firm that helps other companies design benefits plans and other employee programs), employees were presented with a series of "quick guide" documents on what was and wasn't appropriate.

✔ **Discuss appropriateness.** Marcia Robinson, leader of the Mercer Global Knowledge Management team, says Facebook and Twitter users took to the collaboration network more easily, but they still needed guidance on what was and was not appropriate. Her short version: "You should not be microblogging that you had Corn Flakes for breakfast, but you could post that you had Corn Flakes for breakfast with the CEO and here is what he said."

✔ **Explain who sees what.** At the same time, other employees were afraid to post, partly because they were not clear where their posts would show up or who would see them, says Barbara Fiorillo, the enterprise content management leader on Robinson's team. Posting to the main corporate feed ". . . can be scary for people, putting yourself out there like that — knowing your boss sees it." In Mercer's social collaboration setup, based on SharePoint and NewsGator social sites, every employee is automatically assigned followers including their supervisor and departmental co-workers. "I think we've been really good about creating a culture that says it's okay to post — and don't worry if there's a typo," she says.

✔ **Help colleagues choose the right audience for messages.** Still, employees needed guidance about what to post where — whether in the company-wide stream or a group for a particular professional interest — and who would see it. The Who Sees My Post infographic shown in Figure 2-10 is the result. In addition to calming fears about broadcasting too widely, this summary helped employees understand how to tag their posts to get them seen by the right people.

A Facebook user encountering a broad-based social collaboration platform like Jive or IBM Connections for the first time may also be overwhelmed by the number of options for creating content as an ordinary status post, a blog entry, or a wiki document. Should the post be directed to the main activity stream or to a feed associated with a project or a community relevant to the topic? The transition to Yammer may be smoother, given how closely that cloud-based collaboration service mirrors the major features and the layout of Facebook. Yammer adds more sophisticated, business-specific features, but the emphasis still tends to be on simplicity over sophistication. (Now that the product is owned by Microsoft, SharePoint is supposed to provide the sophistication.)

I would argue that the notion of software being "as easy as Facebook" starts from a false premise. The Facebook user interface can be quite confusing, particularly to the uninitiated. Facebook fans put up with it anyway because their friends are on the service. Then, just when they've learned their way around, Facebook changes everything. Or so it seems, sometimes.

WHO SEES MY POST?

The four examples below are viewable in your activity stream when **My Newsfeed**, the default view is selected. You can view more microblogs -- posts, questions, comments, and likes -- by changing the view to **All Public Microblogs**.

WHO SEES IT? 👁

ANY POST

I have a new client with workforce turnover issues. Excellent possibility of doing multi-LOB work for them.

Colleagues following you

POST TARGETING A COLLEAGUE

*@**jane-smith**, I heard you worked on mobility issues for financial services clients. Do you have insights to share?*

Colleagues following you + Targeted colleague

POST TARGETING A COMMUNITY

*@**Energy**, I'm working on a job leveling proposal for a US Northeast prospect. Anyone have proposals I can leverage?*

Colleagues following you + Targeted colleague

POST WITH A HASHTAG

*I'm helping my #**retail** client with a #**[pension buyout]**; anyone done similar work in that industry?*

Colleagues following you + Colleagues/communities following the hashtagged term

? Want to learn more? Go to the Mercer Link Help community for quick guides, FAQs and training videos

Figure 2-10: Create simple training examples for posting.

 My point is that the power of a social network comes at least as much from the people participating in it as from anything coded in software. Having the right people involved can overcome a few shortcomings in the underlying software. It may even motivate people to train themselves on the elements of the system that aren't immediately obvious. However, a social collaboration system only gains that momentum after you have people actively using it.

By all means, exploit the power of familiarity. Just don't expect it to eliminate the need for training and support.

Keeping social collaboration productive with policies and community management

The champions and managers of social collaboration must take the good that comes from the expectations and training provided by public social networks and filter out the bad. Then, they must set new expectations for productive uses of social collaboration. This means setting acceptable use policies, which typically includes basics like ruling out profanity, personal attacks, and other objectionable content, as well as detailing what information can and cannot be shared in the system. For example, the internal social network may be ruled an inappropriate system for sharing sensitive information like employee Social Security numbers that should not be shared any more widely than necessary.

Rules imply enforcement, meaning that system administrators and community managers must be empowered to moderate discussions by removing posts and comments as necessary. If employees are trained adequately and understand the company's professional culture, it should not be necessary very often.

Keeping the social network healthy and productive is the job of the community manager or team of community managers. (I tell you more about the community management responsibilities in Part IV.) In a large organization, someone is typically in charge of overall community management, plus employees with part-time community management responsibilities and authority for specific communities within the social collaboration system. Usually, they are much more concerned with promoting discussion and engagement than they are with playing the moderator on discussions.

If you take the role of community management, part of your job is to start conversations by posting questions, documents, and media, as well as jumping in to conversations and encouraging other employees to join in. You must model the behavior you want to see others exhibit and lavish praise on those who are using the system effectively.

Social collaboration is a tool for open discussion and transparency within the organization. That is precisely why some executives fear it: They envision an unending complaint session starting as soon as employees are given permission to voice their thoughts. I have yet to talk to anyone who has encountered this as a serious problem. Yes, there is also a possibility someone could post a really nasty note on the internal social network, just as an employee could send a Reply to All e-mail condemning the company and its management. If it happens at all, this would be the last act of an employee who has decided to burn all bridges on his way out the door (if he hasn't already been fired, it's likely he will be).

On the other hand, the company and its executives need to be prepared to shrug off most milder forms of criticism. I have heard stories of social collaboration initiatives that lasted about a day. After all the effort spent on setting up a productive online community, the CEO responds harshly to the first criticism he sees. Game over.

Remember, though, that one of the common aims of social collaboration is to get more employees thinking and contributing ideas about how to make the organization more innovative, productive, and effective. So, an organization that's serious about using social collaboration to perform better must accept that the road to better products and processes is sometimes paved with frank criticism of the current ones. Employees are understandably reluctant to speak their minds if they fear retribution. In fact, they may be skeptical of all reassurances about the company's policy of transparency until they see repeated examples of criticisms offered and accepted gracefully.

In a healthy community, you would expect comments like *That's the stupidest idea I've ever seen!* to be strongly discouraged (and rare, if you set some minimum standards of civility). A more constructive criticism may be something like *This plan strikes me as unnecessarily expensive. I recommend talking with our procurement folks, who may be able to get us significantly better pricing if you can explain exactly what you're looking for.* Polite, specific criticism combined with a suggested alternative is the ideal.

Navigating the Enterprise Social Graph

Because social collaboration is as much about people as it is about content, understanding how a collaboration platform represents the connections between people is important.

The "social graph" is a term popularized by Facebook for the network of connections between people in an online system, particularly the Friend connections between Facebook users. An *enterprise social graph* is the same sort of thing applied to organizations.

In addition to allowing users to make spontaneous connections, an enterprise social graph may apply some relationships taken from an org chart. In this section, I tell you what you need to know about the social graph.

Defining the social graph

The social graph is an algorithmic representation of the connections between people, direct and indirect. The name comes from the mathematical concept of a graph representing the links between pairs of objects.

People, or user accounts that represent people, can be represented as nodes linked directly to some other people yet indirectly to others — "friends of friends" as well as people who may be three or four connections removed in the social network. One way that you can expand your social network (your social graph) is by having intermediate connections introduce you to someone you want to meet.

People are also linked to content they view or comment on, social applications they activate, and other objects represented within the social network. Figure 2-11 shows a portion of a work-based social graph featuring reciprocal connection and follower relationships between employees, as well as "Like" and viewing relationships with a document and a video.

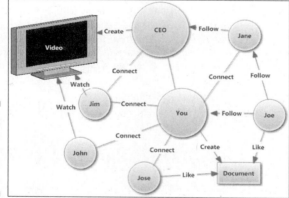

Figure 2-11:
A sample workplace social graph.

The social graph is roughly akin to the network of links between documents on the web, which Google and other search engines use for clues to relationships between concepts and ideas. A web page linked to as an authoritative reference from many other web pages is ranked higher in search results because it looks more important. Similarly, a social network user with a large number of connections is also treated as important, partly because other network users can easily navigate through that person's profile to reach other connections.

How all this works depends a great deal on the model the social network imposes for how connections are made, as I describe in the following sections.

Making friends with reciprocal links

Facebook was built around reciprocal connections, meaning that the connection exists only if both parties agree. Someone sends you a friend connection, and you approve it or not. Connection requests on LinkedIn work similarly, based on the assumption that we will make professional connections with people we have either worked with or whose work we know in some other professional context. I'm always happy to approve a connection with a current or former co-worker but will ignore the random LinkedIn requests from someone I don't know.

On Facebook, LinkedIn, and other social networks that use this model, users can share content that's accessible to their contacts only. This mode of private communication among friends used to be the default on Facebook although the service has moved to make more content public by default (so keeping it private takes more effort on behalf of the user).

The model of requiring reciprocal connections is not commonly used in social collaboration, though, because the entire network is supposed to be private to the company. Content may also need to be contained within a particular workgroup. Other than that, content shared on the social network is generally meant to be viewable and searchable by anyone within the organization.

Following people and subscribing to their feeds

Following people is the Twitter model. To *follow* another person on a social network is to subscribe to updates from that person. You generally don't need another user's permission to follow their feed. Although Twitter users can configure their profiles for greater privacy, individually approving follower requests, doing so still doesn't create a reciprocal relationship because it doesn't automatically mean the person agreeing to be followed will in turn follow the person who issued the request.

When reciprocal connections are formed — that is, people decide to follow each other — that's still a signal of a tighter affinity that the social software can use to grant additional privileges. On Twitter, only reciprocal connections can send each other *direct messages,* which are a form of private messaging.

The follower model is also implemented in other social networks, including Facebook, as a way of forming one-way connections that don't require individual approval. This became important originally as a way for celebrities and brands to participate in social networking by creating Facebook pages that users could subscribe to by becoming a Fan rather than a Friend. More recently, Facebook has added the option for individuals to add a Follow button to their personal profiles so people who aren't necessarily personal friends can still subscribe to their public posts.

Social collaboration systems generally employ the follow model for connections between people, although they can also analyze reciprocal connections to construct a better model of organizational dynamics and do a better job of recommending people and content.

Subscribing to feeds about documents, events, projects, or customer records

The follow model is a good match for social collaboration because it's easy to generalize. You can follow people and also groups, projects, documents, event listings, or records in an enterprise application: any object represented in the enterprise social graph. Following an object just means following the stream of updates about its status — say, when a document is updated or an order ships — as well as any comments attached to that object.

Searching for expertise

One classic application of collaboration networks is locating expertise on any work-related activity or topic, whether research and development findings, management strategies, or company history.

- ✔ **Connections:** When you view a profile in a social collaboration tool, you can also browse a listing of that person's connections. Again, in a social collaboration context, think Twitter (where the list of a member's connections is public) rather than Facebook or LinkedIn (where access to your list of friends or connections is limited to existing friends or connections).

  In other words, even if you can't get a response from one representative of a product team (maybe because that person is on vacation), you can probably click through to the profile of another team member and make your request. You simply look at the relationships represented on the contacts list and in the social stream and choose the most appropriate person to contact.

- ✔ **Tags:** Some of this comes from explicit tagging of profiles, based on extracts from human resources systems and other information entered manually by the user.

- ✔ **Posts:** The social component comes from relationships that can be derived about interests and knowledge based on content postings and participation in online discussions. For instance, if someone consistently posts and participates in discussions about the industrial design of the company's products, then that person looks like an expert — or at least, someone with strong opinions on the topic.

- ✔ **Content:** Because the social graph includes both people and content, you can navigate from one to the other, finding more resources than if you were exploring a directory of people or a repository of content alone.

Say you found a terrific document on a topic of intense, ongoing interest to you. Look up the author with a click on his name or profile photo. Maybe you and the author of the document work in research and development for different parts of the company but have been investigating related topics. Now, you can follow this person or send her a message, perhaps proposing that you two collaborate on future research. From her profile, you can also see some of the other content she has posted, including several other research papers and a blog post or two that are all relevant to your work.

Expertise location is important as a way of locating organizational knowledge that may not be explicitly documented anywhere.

It works the other way, too, where the personal connection comes first. Maybe you only looked at the other person's profile because you noticed she had started following you online. You see from her recent activity on the network that she is someone you should follow. Meanwhile, you find your way to the wiki she maintains with several other collaborators on her team. In addition to finding useful content in the wiki, you follow the profile links to the other wiki authors, each of whom is also someone you will want to follow.

Searching the social graph

As a side effect, social collaboration should improve search results in internal web networks: *intranets*. One reason why intranet search tends not to be as good as Internet search is the quantity of links between documents is far smaller, making them less reliable as an indicator of quality or authority.

One of the ways Google gained fame was by going beyond indexing all the words on a web page and counting links to that page as votes in favor of it. In a collaboration network, users generate additional links to content that they share. They may also vote on its importance explicitly by clicking a Like button or implicitly by commenting on it.

By including both people and content, social search results also provide avenues for answering questions that may not exist in the online system at all. Or maybe you find that the document you're looking for does turn up, connected to the profile of one of the people turned up by your search, even though the keywords you entered for your search query did not find it.

I should caution that here I'm giving the theoretical argument about why search *ought* to be better in a social collaboration system. The actual quality of search results may vary considerably from one platform to the next. For example, there is a lot to like about Podio, a cloud-based social collaboration product (purchased by Citrix in 2012), but at this writing the search provided within the tool is basic. For example, you can look up a user by name but not expertise, and a content search will cover text in the content of a post but not in the attached document.

Forming Groups

Most of the real work accomplished through collaboration networks happens through groups rather than the main company feed. I use the word "group" generically here because the terminology varies between social platforms, and some of the more sophisticated products provide multiple types of groups and communities.

For example, Jive has basic collaboration groups, project groups, and *spaces,* which are sort of super-groups that can include subspaces and projects, each of which has its own associated content and activity. Only an administrator or community manager can create Jive Spaces, which are often more formal reflections of the corporate hierarchy, such as a space for the human resources department used to post benefits plan descriptions and policy documents or host discussions about how policies are being interpreted. On the other hand, Jive Groups can be created and administered by ordinary users to discuss a common professional interest, which may cut across the hierarchy, such as sales presentation tactics. The approval of a community manager may or may not be required, depending on how Jive is configured.

In IBM Connections, a group is a Community, and a project is an Activity.

In any social collaboration platform, you can use a Groups tool to gather everyone into a virtual workspace to collaborate on a project and manage tasks free from the distractions of the main activity stream.

Making room for projects

Project workspaces focus collaboration around multiple people working toward a single goal or set of goals. Social networking within a project group can be good for eliminating status report meetings. After everyone can easily keep tabs on everyone else, there is little need to make everyone go around the table announcing their progress.

Social network communication can be good for loose project coordination, where it's helpful to know who is running behind or running into trouble but project outputs do not need to be precisely sequenced.

For instance, Yammer doesn't provide specific project or task management functionality, but many of its users say their projects run more smoothly anyway as the result of team members sharing their status on a regular basis and heading off problems more promptly.

Social software that defines a specific group type for projects typically provides additional tools for structuring and sequencing tasks, as well as visualizations like Gantt charts for measuring progress toward project completion. Social project management can also take advantage of the graph structure of social collaboration, making it possible to assign tasks with @mention references to a user profile from the status line or a drop-down list based on the user's connections.

One reason for segmenting collaborative activity using groups is to avoid distractions from the purpose of that group, whatever it may be. The group activity stream can be kept free of irrelevant posts by only admitting people with relevant interests and expertise.

Meanwhile, content of interest to only that group can be prevented from cluttering the main company feed.

Configuring levels of privacy in a group

Groups can be configured to be open to anyone who wants to join, or they can be *closed,* meaning that every member of the group must individually be granted admission by the group manager or administrator. Groups can also be secret and invitation only, with their existence and all the content associated with them invisible in search results.

The exact gradations vary between platforms, making it important to understand what configuration options such as open, closed, public, private, and secret mean in practice. For example, is activity within a group displayed in the company-wide feed as well? Is content created within a group displayed in global search results? Can you do a targeted search of just the content contained within the group?

Working Together on Content

When people work together to create a document — be it a sales proposal, project plan, or policy — the collaboration network can serve as the joint writing desk for collaborators and discussion forum for reviewers. Social collaboration on documents comes in a few flavors: web native and desktop document sharing.

Creating, editing, and linking documents wiki-style

The purest form of web-based document collaboration is the wiki (from the Hawaiian word for "fast" or "quick"), a mechanism for creating sets of linked documents collaboratively written and edited by multiple people. Early wiki tools had a user interface only a techie could love, and the concepts of collaborative editing and easy linking between documents remain less well understood than some other types of social media. The average consumer has browsed Wikipedia (a very large wiki) articles but not created or edited them.

As a result, social collaboration tool makers are tending to drop the wiki label but keep the underlying concepts.

Wiki concepts are also merging with ideas drawn from other web-based document editors, such as the Google Docs word processor (now part of Google Drive). Traditionally, collaborators on a wiki document would alternate posting edits. In Google Drive and other tools that implement a similar realtime collaborative editing capability, collaborators can edit a document simultaneously, watching changes made by the other person appear in the text as they work.

Web native documents are easy to share on the web and can make use of the web's capabilities for linking to or embedding other digital resources.

Incorporating file sharing

Sharing files and documents through the collaboration network is more appropriate when the output of the collaboration is a printed document or some other format (as opposed to a web document).

In that case, the collaboration network can provide a place to post drafts of a document produced with desktop software. Some systems may provide at least basic file management and version tracking capabilities. Otherwise, the file associated with the most recent activity stream item can be assumed to be the most current version. This is still an improvement on e-mailing files back and forth. Part of the collaboration may take place in the form of comments and discussion attached to the file posting in the activity stream. However, the actual editing will take place offline.

Integration between social collaboration products and cloud-based file sharing services, such as Box and Dropbox, is also common.

Forecasting the Future of Social Collaboration

Many of the visionaries trying to foresee the future of business, the future of work, and the future of enterprise systems see social collaboration as part of something larger.

Over the next few years, social collaboration will combine even more with other trends like the rapidly increasing business use of mobile devices, plus advanced analysis of all the clues in our social posts and GPS location data.

"By 2020, we will get to the point where all apps are social and support decisions," predicts Michael Fauscette, group VP of software business solutions at the market analysis firm IDC. (I'm quoting from a speech at the E2 Conference in 2012.) "We won't talk about social software. Every application is a system of relationships because we have to connect with people to get things done." In other words, social software will become so pervasive that we won't notice it's there anymore. Meanwhile, with all those rich contextual clues to work with, software products will start to tell us what we need to know before we know to ask for it, he says.

That vision is a bit over the horizon, but this book will show you the steps you can take toward it today.

Chapter 3

Putting Social Collaboration to Work

In This Chapter

▶ Harnessing the energy of social networks for business

▶ Gearing up for implementation

▶ Addressing enterprise requirements for social collaboration

▶ Viewing an alternate vision of workplace software

*I*n the first chapters of this book, I define social collaboration and cover its history as well as some of the megatrends driving changes in collaboration technology and its use. In this chapter, I talk about how to put social collaboration to work, pivoting from theory to practice. After all, where do you begin? Keep reading to find out about common requirements for the implementation and rollout of any social collaboration platform.

You can find more on product selection in Part III.

Harnessing the Energy of Social Networks for Business

Seeing the potential for social networks to streamline collaboration within your organization is a good start but only a start. How are you going to make it happen? Where are the biggest opportunities?

Developing specific business scenarios for how you think social collaboration can be used productively is an important way of focusing your efforts. Particularly at first, set a template for the use of social technologies at work. After you set the example, employees will be more likely to figure out their own inventive uses of the platform. If you present them with nothing but a blank Set Your Status field, you will fail.

You may have a short list of business uses in mind for the platform already. Better yet, there may be a department or project team within the company that has been actively clamoring for access to tools of this type. Take the time to brainstorm a longer list, and then whittle it down and prioritize it. This list will suggest the business units or business functions that would make the most sense to start with. In addition to meeting their specific needs, you want to have an idea of the payoff you're looking to achieve. They should be candidates to produce the early wins you will showcase when you later make your case for broader adoption across the enterprise.

Consider making one of those target audiences sales or another group with a direct connection to revenue or new product development. That will tend to make whatever success you can claim later more attention-getting.

Other good candidates may include employee teams who already actively use the latest collaboration technologies, regardless of whether they were officially authorized and endorsed by IT. Most large corporations have pockets of adoption of Yammer, or other team collaboration tools like Basecamp (a cloud-based project collaboration tool) or cloud file sharing tools like Box and Dropbox. Whether or not these ad hoc tools earn a place in your official company strategy, they provide clues to the kind of work environment employees have been stitching together in a do-it-yourself fashion. If you will be asking colleagues to give up their established collection of tools, be sure you can make a strong case for how the social collaboration platform you choose is an improvement — more integrated and capable, easy to work with, and productive.

In addition to deciding where to start, some of the questions you need to answer up front include

- ✔ **What's in it for me?** Employees being asked to change their established work habits will want to know how they will personally benefit. This is where you need to be ready with your case for how the social collaboration system will help salespeople sell, managers manage, and everyone save time.

- ✔ **When is it appropriate?** Clarify when social collaboration is the right way to share information and when e-mail is still preferred.

- ✔ **What are the ground rules?** If the etiquette on the social collaboration system is the same as for e-mail, that's easy to communicate to colleagues. However, if the new system requires tweaks to corporate policies for acceptable use of the network, make sure that you communicate those policies to all employees. Is there any sort of information employees are prohibited or strongly discouraged from sharing on the social platform? For example, some organizations may discourage discussion of sensitive personnel matters or sharing personal data, such as Social Security numbers, preferring to restrict those to systems with more tried-and-tested information security.

✔ **What are the pitfalls?** Rather than treating social collaboration as a magical cure-all, acknowledge the ways it can fail and have a strategy for avoiding those pitfalls. Do not let fear, uncertainty, and doubt fester.

✔ **How will we measure success?** Stake out at least a few metrics for the key business processes you are targeting for improvement.

Gearing Up for Implementation

Some of the project steps I outline in this section may seem like overkill if your organization is relatively small, or if you select a cloud-based solution that promises to dramatically simplify the implementation process. Of course, these are just guidelines. You should scale and adapt them to your needs. Still, think through how these requirements are being satisfied, even if one person on your team will be fulfilling multiple roles or some of the tasks will be outsourced.

Forming the team

Here are some constituencies that should be considered as part of the product team.

✔ **IT:** Regardless of whether a project is initiated by IT or a business-led group with IT playing a supporting role, someone needs to evaluate the social collaboration platform against the organization's minimum technical requirements to determine how it will be implemented and supported. In an on-premise implementation of a product like IBM Connections, the IT team will have many decisions to make about systems architecture, such as whether multiple servers and databases will be required to support a large or geographically distributed employee population. For more on this perspective, see Chapter 16.

✔ **Senior leadership:** The more you can get the CEO and other executive leaders involved, the better. Their presence in detailed planning sessions may be rare, but their endorsement of the concept will be invaluable.

✔ **Business unit leadership:** Your pilot or showcase business units should be actively involved in helping you field an environment that will meet their needs.

✔ **Human resources:** People are as important as technology to the success of social collaboration, and HR should have a role in the workplace design element of the project. HR may also have concerns about aligning the collaboration environment with employee policies (or policies may have to be adjusted to fit the new possibilities).

✔ **Legal and compliance:** Particularly in regulated businesses such as banking, legal issues and regulatory compliance can sink a social collaboration initiative if not properly addressed. Get these groups on-board early so you can show how their concerns can be mitigated: for example, by archiving social communications for regulatory review.

✔ **Corporate communications:** Corporate communications teams sometimes initiate social collaboration as a replacement for traditional employee newsletters or e-mail communications. In other organizations, the communications group may be a laggard, while other groups (like Training) take the lead. Even if corporate communications doesn't immediately embrace the platform for its own purposes, you will want its help promoting the launch of your collaboration network.

✔ **Corporate training and professional development:** Social collaboration can complement formal training and education programs, extending the learning after the course is over and covering a broader array of topics than can be addressed through traditional company education programs. Social learning will be more successful if treated as an explicit goal of the collaboration network.

✔ **Community managers:** Even at the earliest stage of planning and piloting social collaboration, you should have at least one person charged with building and nurturing the online community. This role includes coaching and training employees on productive use of the platform, as well as the ability to intervene as a moderator in unproductive online interactions or remove inappropriate content from the site (a rare occurrence on most networks).

Large successful collaboration networks often have a team of community strategists, community managers, and system administrators overseeing the overall collaboration network, plus part-time community managers who have administrative rights for specific workgroups. Try to envision the structure you will require in the long run and put some basic scaffolding in place from the beginning.

✔ **Community advocates:** You need people who believe in what you're trying to do with social collaboration. You need as many of them as you can get, particularly within the groups where you plan to establish your first beachhead for social collaboration. These people may or may not have any official community management duties. Their more important role is to be active users of the collaboration platform: the people who will talk it up to their peers and show how it can be used effectively.

✔ **Skeptics:** As much as you need advocates who instinctively grasp the potential of social collaboration, you also need to acknowledge the skeptics who say it will never work. Your best tactic may be to ignore those who are habitually negative, but you may also consider trying to enlist those who are raising well-reasoned objections in working on how to overcome the obstacles they have pointed out.

Former skeptics who change their minds can be your best advocates.

✔ **Social media marketing specialists:** Although not all tactics that work on public social media translate to an internal collaboration network, many do. Before you can make your people productive on the platform, you have to get them to use it. Enlist the people who handle your firm's external social media in suggesting imaginative ways of engaging the employee population. Social media marketers know a lot about how to get people's attention and get a conversation started.

✔ **Designers and web developers:** Even if you can't harness quite the same level of budget and effort that would be lavished on a customer-facing site, steal whatever attention you can from your web developers and designers to make sure your collaboration network is good looking, easy to navigate, and highly usable.

Organizing advocates

One of the most important elements for the successful launch of social collaboration is an aggressive program for recruiting community advocates. You want to find the people who will believe in the online community before it really exists. Some may be social media enthusiasts or habitual early adopters of technology. Others may have had positive experiences with previous generations of collaboration technology or social collaboration environments used by former employers.

These are the people who you give early access to the collaboration platform so they can test it out and give feedback. You may ask them to play around with more than one environment at the product selection stage. Then after you make your pick, get their recommendations on the early decisions for the design and configuration of the environment.

You also want them to help you "cheat" on pre-populating the collaboration environment with content and conversation starters, so it looks like there is already something going on in the community even on what (for everyone else) is day one. Project managers can try to come up with their own list of content to use when "stocking" the environment. If you have organized advocates from all the business units you are targeting for the launch, you will have a much better chance of including what people from those businesses consider truly important.

At launch, your advocates become the friendly, familiar faces within those business units whom employees will turn to for coaching. They are the people who post regularly and try to draw others into participation in the online community.

Advocates extend the reach of the core community management team, relaying messages and amplifying them by relating them to the needs of the department or the local office in which they work. In a geographically distributed organization, you want to have local (or at least regional) advocates to spread the word.

Typically, advocates perform all these duties in addition to their regular jobs. To keep them motivated, project leaders need to dole out both planned and spontaneous recognition and praise. Be sure they know what they are doing is important (because it is). If a success story emerges from their work, make sure they get a generous dose of the credit.

Borrowing freely from consumer innovations

In the configuration and design of your collaboration network, it makes sense to leverage the innovations and conventions of consumer social networks and websites where possible. Although familiarity isn't a cure-all, you may as well take advantage of it where it makes sense.

For example, on many social software platforms, you can customize the labels on different features. Having said that, resist the urge to out-clever yourself and reinvent the wheel. For example, but if you have the option of renaming a Like button as something new, you should probably stick what the tried-and-true that most everyone knows and accepts instead of coming up with some other novel name. More importantly, wherever possible, features of your collaboration environment that mirror the functions of Facebook or Twitter should behave the way those consumer tools have trained your employees to expect.

For example, when pasting a link to a YouTube video to a status post, you'd expect a collaboration environment to generate an embedded preview — and be disappointed if it's displayed as a link only. If that's not the default behavior of your collaboration platform, I'd ask the vendor why it's not. Maybe you can set a configuration switch or use a plug-in that will make it so.

You want your employees to understand that social collaboration is different from participating in public social networks, so the software *should* function a little differently. The distinction I'm trying to make here is that having it be different (more businesslike) should not mean having to settle for less. You don't want to promote clunky software that looks just enough like a social network to be frustrating because it doesn't act like one.

Branding the network

Just how much you can shape and mold your collaboration network will depend partly on the platform you select, but most environments will allow you to add a logo and change the color scheme.

You want to take ownership of the collaboration environment and make it reflect the image your company projects to the world. Give it a name of its own. In many companies with successful collaboration networks, the average employee couldn't tell you what the underlying software was. They collaborate on "The Hub," not knowing whether the underlying software is Jive (as it is for UBM's The Hub), Tibbr (of KPMG), or Socialcast (the SAS Institute version). At Red Robin Gourmet Burgers, employees interact through Yummer (powered by Yammer), which is a play on the company jingle lyric, "Red Robin! Yummm!"

Publicizing the launch

Before your collaboration network becomes a big success, you need people to use it, and first you have to make them aware of it. That can be a challenging project all its own in a large organization.

Before the big launch, when the collaboration implementation isn't ready for prime time, some organizations start with a *soft launch,* which is a quiet launch, made known only within select circles of early enthusiasts and testers. Other employees who find out about it and are curious may be able to establish an account and pull in their co-workers, as long as they understand that the design and configuration are not final.

A real launch is louder and more aggressive. You may have one company-wide launch or a series of launch events targeted at different departments or constituents. Regardless, whatever the audience, you want to get as many as people as possible to try the software because in social collaboration, activity begets more activity.

You may want to build a company event around the launch or time it to coincide with a company meeting that you know a lot of people will attend. Launch with a public endorsement from the CEO and other top company leaders, if at all possible. Launch with early success stories from any pilot projects you've run and suggest how to build on them.

In terms of mass communication, sending e-mail blasts and reminders is an obvious first step, but you can certainly get a lot more creative.

In his book, *The Collaborative Organization* (McGraw-Hill), Jacob Morgan cites the example of Yum! Brands (the parent company of KFC and other restaurants). Morgan is the principal and co-founder of Chess Media Group, which consults on what he prefers to call "emergent collaboration," and he provides this example of a clever way to promote a new social network. When Yum! introduced its collaboration network, branded iCHING, it accelerated adoption using an elaborate internal marketing campaign featuring decal stickers for elevator doors and bathroom mirrors. Because of how the capital H in the logo was styled to look like two people shaking hands, the company used that letter alone on the elevator doors. Every time the doors closed, the decals created an image of people coming together. Meanwhile, the bathroom mirror decal was styled as a representation of a social profile with a clear area where the profile photo was supposed to go. While standing at the sink, employees would see themselves as they would appear on the social network.

Elevators also factored into KPMG's enterprise social network launch. When partners from the firm gathered for an internal conference, the organizers had arranged to have videos promoting the collaboration platform playing on the video monitors in the elevators.

Addressing Enterprise Requirements for Social Collaboration

In information technology, *enterprise* is a code word for big, sprawling, and hideously complicated. In reality, enterprise information technology systems don't have a monopoly on technological complexity. Consumer social networks and consumer websites are backed by some very complex systems, except that ordinarily consumers don't worry about any of that. They're presented with a simple experience, and that's all that matters to them. What is really different about large enterprises is their scale and the complexity of the legal and regulatory burdens they face.

Enterprise technology managers worry about a lot of things, including consumer technologies being used for business purposes. They work an environment that's not just technologically but organizationally complex. Multinational organizations with thousands of employees are the classic example, but even very small organizations may have enterprise concerns if they operate in complex businesses or have aggressive growth plans.

If your organization is a ten-person web development firm, you may want to skip this section or skim lightly over it. On the other hand, organizations with a few dozen or a few hundred employees have their share of enterprise concerns, particularly if they have been around for long enough to have a list of legacy technology and business processes to take into account, rather than starting from scratch.

Ensuring security and balancing trade-offs

No corporate network is triple-secret secure. Individual applications may be accessible only from within the firewall, but they are accessed by employees whose computers are also connecting to the Internet on a regular basis. Being able to connect to the outside world is important, so the prudent approach is to make some practical compromises while still trying to take reasonable steps to protect data and systems.

Many social collaboration platforms take this compromise another step further. Many of the most valuable scenarios for the use of these tools involve employees getting access from home, on the road, or from a mobile device. Other important collaboration scenarios involve connections to business partners who also need to gain access from outside the firewall. Usually, that means providing access via a simple web login form to whoever has a valid username and password.

This is why so many collaboration solutions are hosted, whether in a multitenant cloud or on a dedicated server. But it also means the collaboration system will be vulnerable to all of the problems that plague every other web-based, password-protected application, such as the tendency of users to employ the same login credentials on many websites.

Yes, you can set up your collaboration platform inside the firewall and require any external user to have virtual private network software to gain access to the application. Do this if you must to address some requirement for regulatory compliance, but understand that it will have its own trade-offs in ease of use and adoption.

More commonly, organizations that move forward with social collaboration work to make its security strong enough for everyday use, while deciding that some subset of data or business processes are too sensitive to be managed on the platform. Considerations for this process include

- ✔ **Data classification:** Categorizing types of data by the regulations or policies they are governed by or by the sensitivity or proprietary nature of the information.
- ✔ **Data ownership:** Determining who is responsible for a given class of data and can make the call on whether or not to trust it to the collaboration network.
- ✔ **Risk management:** According to the National Institute for Standards and Technology's Risk Management Guide for Information Technology Systems, "The principal goal of an organization's risk management process should be to protect the *organization and its ability to perform their mission*, not just its IT assets." In other words, this is not just an IT function but a judgment call. The key question is whether the value to the

> organization and its mission outweighs the risk, and the answer may be different for different classifications of data and processes.
>
> ✔ **Risk mitigation:** In addition to ruling certain data out of bounds, the risk assessment process may also lead to a mitigation strategy, which may include additional intrusion detection and prevention measures or a response plan to be implemented in the event of a security breach.

Archiving content for backup and legal discovery

In addition to protecting content, preserving it can be important. For example, many financial services businesses are required to archive all electronic communications for certain employees, such as brokers and financial advisors. Regulations originally crafted for e-mail and instant messaging are being applied to social collaboration tools as well. That means social collaboration data must be archived on a similar schedule if those regulations apply to your business.

Archiving may also be important for purposes of legal discovery in the event of a lawsuit. Content showing how an important decision was made may be important documentation for an organization's legal defense, or the organization may be compelled to reproduce it by the demand of an opposing legal team. In the absence of a system for archiving and indexing this content for e-discovery, an organization may still be required to produce it through a much more manual, labor-intensive process.

Integrating with existing portal and document management infrastructure

Typically, large established enterprises have previous investments in portal and document management systems that the social collaboration environment will need to integrate with, unless it will completely replace them.

At the product selection stage, this matters partly because a broad social platform like Jive or IBM Connections can be considered redundant with systems already in place. Some organizations choose to instead minimize the overlap with a social technology like Tibco's tibbr that emphasizes the social feed and tries to wrap that newfangled element of collaboration around the existing application using web frames and other integration mechanisms. Even if the decision should be that the social platform's document management meets the organization's needs as well as or better than prior technologies, that would imply the need for a mass migration of content from one to the other.

Otherwise, if some documents will be managed on the social platform and others will be managed on some other document management platform, at a minimum, there ought to be a strategy for what goes where and why. If there is a rational strategy — perhaps based on an information classification scheme that dictates legal documents should be managed outside of the social platform — the division can make perfect sense.

On the other hand, where collaboration platform users have a reasonable expectation that the content ought to be easily accessible to them, seek opportunities for integration: for example, cross-platform search across document repositories.

Linking to corporate directories and HR systems

Employee social platforms also benefit from integration with (or at least periodic synchronization with) other sources of employee data, including human resources information systems, network directory servers, and web-based "phone book" directories.

You want accounts to be created when employees join the organization and deleted or suspended when their network and e-mail accounts are removed.

In addition, you can make it easier for new members of the collaboration network to set up their profiles by importing data such as name, e-mail, phone number, educational records, and placement in an org chart.

If any corporate system includes a standard employee photo, such as a security badge photo, you may want to consider importing it into the employee profile at system startup. Part of what makes social collaboration feel warmer and more human is seeing people's faces, and that requirement is not met by a generic placeholder icon. A security badge photo may not be an employee's favorite image of himself, but if not, having it in place on his profile will be good motivation to replace it with another photo.

Layering social connections onto existing applications

One of the goals of many social collaboration initiatives is to "put social in the flow of work" by integrating it with the applications employees use every day to do their work. In other words, an accounts payable clerk should see some sort of social sidebar on every screen of an invoice processing application, making it easy to send a question to a co-worker that includes an embedded reference to that specific record. This becomes more practical in a workplace dominated by web applications for every business function (albeit not so practical if your payable clerks continue to use old fashioned terminal software connected to an AS/400 system).

The Jive Anywhere browser add-on takes advantage of the proliferation of web applications for business by making it easy to share any record that is represented by a unique web address. Not all web applications follow this convention, but for those that do, no integration is required beyond integration with the browser. On the other hand, this mode of integration doesn't run any deeper than link sharing.

The other common pattern is for a social stream to be embedded within a business record. For example, a customer record in a CRM system from Salesforce.com, SAP, or Microsoft's Dynamics may have a social feed embedded within it, showing the most recent comments on that record. Users can also easily post a link to that record into the social stream. Typically, the most intimate connections between the social environment and the application arise where both are provided by the same vendor: Chatter and Salesforce.com CRM, Jam and SAP CRM, or Yammer and Dynamics CRM.

However, other social collaboration vendors have every incentive to achieve whatever level of integration may be possible with popular products, even those from competitors. For example, Jive says that its Jive for Salesforce module enables bidirectional data exchange so information about opportunity, account, and case information is visible in Jive, and relevant Jive information is also visible in Salesforce.com.

Similarly, Moxie Software has crafted an integration for its collaboration environment, which is geared toward use by customer service and support teams, to link to the Salesforce.com Service Cloud suite of applications.

Connecting multiple social applications

Besides connecting social collaboration to business applications, at some point, you will likely want to connect social software products to each other, particularly if you work in a large organization.

Despite the ambitions of social software vendors to put themselves at the center of the social collaboration experience, as the platform everyone else will build on — or the universal *social layer* — none has secured overwhelming dominance. Commonly, different parts of the same organization will choose a different social software product or service: say, the sales folks use Chatter, HQ uses IBM Connections, and R/D use Socialcast. At the same time, the activity feed format of social applications has become popular as a user interface for all sorts of applications. The latest upgrade to your business intelligence software may arrive with what looks like a social feed for commentary on the latest reports published out of the system, even though that feed isn't connected to any broader social platform. Products for social media marketing or monitoring may include their own team collaboration tools, without being tied to your collaboration network.

For a consistent social experience, you would like to be able to aggregate feeds and present user profiles in a consistent way. When you click someone's name or photo, you should be taken to a profile where you can see all their activity and content across all the social collaboration tools used by your organization. Is that too much to ask?

Actually, it probably is too much to ask, at least at this stage of the market.

Some standards are emerging for connecting and combining social experiences, which I cover in more detail in Chapter 11. As these continue to mature, and vendors forge partnerships or produce prepackaged software for connecting to each other's products, the possibilities for integration at a reasonable cost will expand. As of this writing, I'm starting to see more options for integrating Chatter and Yammer streams into other platforms.

Certainly, you have to consider the cost and effort required for integration and decide whether you can afford a perfect solution (if you find one that's "perfect"). Users who work primarily with one social application and within a team of people who also use that application may not care much that they aren't linked to the broader enterprise. They may still appreciate the social user interface convention as a way of interacting with the system. They may feel comfortable hopping between different social applications that follow some common design conventions, even if they aren't integrated at a deeper level. If your business users aren't complaining that lack of integration is a problem, maybe you shouldn't make it into a problem.

Recommendation: Pay attention to (and try to moderate) the proliferation of islands of social collaboration. Build bridges between those you do have, where practical.

Putting Social Collaboration in Context

The market for social software for business is broader than the enterprise social networking products I cover in this book, which focus on internal employee social collaboration, as well as online collaborative work with business partners.

Some of the other ways social software is being put to work include

✔ **Public-facing enterprise social communities:** These include communities for customer service and support, as well as company-sponsored social sites for special interests that include some soft-sell marketing. Jive Software, IBM, and Telligent provide social community platforms that can be configured for internal or external use.

Other products like Lithium Technologies and Get Satisfaction focus exclusively on public-facing communities. They are enterprise products, but not for internal social collaboration.

In customer support and technical support scenarios, one of the advantages of the community format is that customers will often answer each other's questions, lightening the workload of support employees. Figure 3-1 shows the Jive Community, a public website aimed at Jive Software customers and sales prospects. It functions much like an internal implementation of the software, except that in this case anyone can sign up for an account rather than only employees and other authorized corporate users.

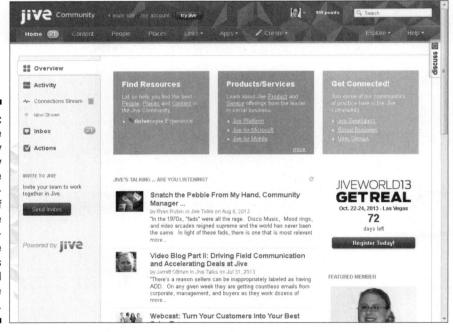

Figure 3-1:
The Jive Community is a publicly accessible implementation of the same social software Jive provides for internal corporate use.

✔ **Social media monitoring and analytics:** Capturing mentions of companies, brands, and products (yours or those of your competitors) on public social media websites. A lot of the innovation here is in semantic analysis to detect positive or negative sentiment or summarize common themes appearing in social posts.

✔ **Social media management:** Publishing content on Facebook, Twitter, and other websites and responding to the public.

✔ **Social CRM:** Products for connecting with customers through social networks or social customer service websites. This category overlaps with public social community products but also includes tools like Nimble, a social contact manager for sales and support teams for cultivating contacts on public social networks. Nimble has some collaboration capabilities, meant to be used in the context of the application, but isn't intended as a general-purpose social collaboration platform. See *Social CRM For Dummies,* by Kyle Lacy, Stephanie Diamond, and Jon Ferrara for more information.

If you're engaged in a broad social business strategy, part of planning for social collaboration is figuring out how it fits in. For example, if you are gathering market intelligence via social media monitoring, how will you share that information internally? Is there a need for technical integration between the monitoring platform and the collaboration platform? Are the users of the monitoring tool a good target community of a social collaboration pilot or showcase example?

Often, the different elements of a social business strategy aren't coordinated as well as they may be because they are managed by different parts of the organization. In that case, you may wind up with a social media marketing strategy, a social CRM strategy, and social collaboration strategy, but little to no synergy between them.

A more holistic social business strategy needs to be coordinated by a cross-functional team or leader who pulls together the puzzle pieces.

An alternate vision of workplace software

So, can we be so sure that the future of the digital workplace is social?

Critics of the concept of enterprise social networking often take issue with the use of the word *social,* arguing that business is not social. Business is business. Therefore, any system set up to encourage social interaction between employees is more likely to be a drag on business than an accelerator of it.

Ironically, a couple of the most prominent advocates of this position entered the workplace software world straight from Facebook: Dustin Moskovitz and Justin Rosenstein, co-founders of Asana, which makes a slick web tool for organizing teams that looks rather social, but which they say is all business.

Moskovitz was one of the co-founders of Facebook, the original engineering team leader starting in the days when the website was a Harvard dorm room project. One of Rosenstein's claims to fame is that he came up with the idea for the Facebook Like button as a quick way for people to signal affirmation to each other without having to take the time to write a note. Their product for organizing projects, tasks, and teams grew out of a side project they started at Facebook to help Moskovitz organize a fast-growing, fast-moving engineering team for the social networking site.

Still, they insist that Asana is not social software and express no interest in integrating with, let alone imitating, the likes of Yammer and Jive. "The first time I looked at Yammer, I thought I was on Facebook," Moskovitz told an interviewer from *The New York Times.* "Work is not a social network, with serendipitous communications and photo collections. Work is about managing tasks and responding to things quickly."

Asana does have some of what I would consider social software characteristics, including comment streams and profile photos or avatars for users, and even a "heart" button that functions much like a Like. However, its developers treat those as basic elements of a modern web design, not an attempt to create a social network.

Instead of posting random status messages, Asana users create and assign tasks and update their statuses on tasks they have been assigned. You can't put much of anything into the system that's not assigned to a task. The pictures are there to remind you who you are working with, not so you can follow those people, and profiles don't run any deeper than name and photo (although you can click someone's photo for a view of all the projects and tasks he's working on).

So Asana is really quite anti-social, in the sense of discouraging any interaction that's not task focused. When employees log in to Asana, they can focus on what they need to get done. If they want to socialize, there's always Facebook.

My take: Asana has won friends among project teams that find its focused approach valuable, but that doesn't make it the only valuable approach to collaboration. Asana does nothing to address the more unstructured aspects of work and management that involve discovering, sharing, organizing, and enriching organizational knowledge. Asana may be ideal for an engineering team working heads-down toward a product launch, but it wouldn't be the right tool for brainstorming ideas on marketing strategy or seeking expertise within the organization.

There is no reason these modes of collaboration can't coexist, and in the long run, I expect that they will.

Part II
Organizing Work with Social Collaboration

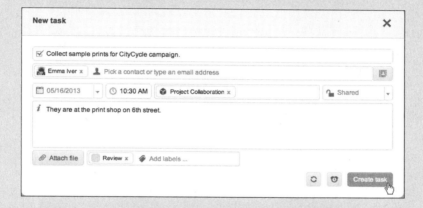

Read more tips on making professional contacts on an internal social network at www.dummies.com/extras/socialcollaboration.

In this part . . .

- ✔ Find out how and why to write a status post, plus other things to share such as documents and videos.
- ✔ Expand your professional social network inside the company.
- ✔ Organize projects and track progress.
- ✔ Collaborate on documents and other content.

Chapter 4

Everyday Sharing on a Social Network

*W*hen you sign in to a social collaboration system, you expect to be welcomed by the smiling faces of co-workers, collaborators, and people you follow. You also expect the software to make it easy for you to share news, questions, links, documents, photos, and videos. This is what puts the "social" in social collaboration.

Any collaboration system that wants to call itself "social" must meet a few basic expectations laid down by Facebook, Twitter, and LinkedIn. At the same time, any social system aimed at business collaboration must meet those expectations in a way that helps get work done. That means that in an enterprise setting, you expect to be able to share documents and business records (such as sales leads), not jokes and cat pictures.

If you're an experienced user of public social networks, a social collaboration system should be relatively easy to learn and use, but the expectations for behavior and the applications of social networking techniques are significantly different in a business context, as I discuss in Chapter 2. This chapter guides you through the basics of what to share and how, regardless of your level of experience with social media.

Sharing and Targeting Posts

In most social collaboration platforms, you can send a private message, which works more or less like e-mail. That's not the point of social collaboration, however. The point is sharing with larger groups, if not the entire organization. From an organizational standpoint, the goal is to widen exposure to knowledge, streamline the discussion of ideas, and get everyone thinking about how to improve processes, products, and services. Organizations that embrace this concept encourage their employees to share as widely as makes sense. And within this understanding, workers send private messages or e-mails for things that really need to remain private.

You can see that effective social collaboration requires thinking about what to share and whom to share it with. Here are some questions to ask before you post:

- ✔ **Focus:** Should this message be posted for everyone to see, or should it be shared within a focused community, project, or discussion group?

- ✔ **Targeting:** Are there specific users or groups who should be mentioned in and get notification about this post?

- ✔ **Classification:** What tags or categories can I add to increase the odds of it being seen by people with the most knowledge about or interest in my topic?

Posting a simple status message

Sign on to the social collaboration tool Yammer, and one of the first things to welcome you is the What Are You Working On? text entry box. Most other social collaboration systems want to know the same thing (your *status)* although the wording may be different. I can't help but think of getting caught whispering in the back of the class, prompting the teacher to ask, "Mr. Carr, do you have something you'd like to share with the group?"

A social network status message invites you to share more broadly, rather than whispering in cliques. And in a way, an e-mail exchange between two or three people is the equivalent of whispering. Although many social collaboration systems include their own mechanisms for private or small group messaging, a public social post is the equivalent of raising your hand and boldly proclaiming your thoughts or asking your questions to the entire class. Figure 4-1 shows a simple status message in Jive.

Users see each other's posts in the social collaboration platform's activity stream, a combined listing of messages and updates from contacts, as well as feeds they have subscribed to by joining a group or asking to be notified when a document is updated.

Figure 4-1:
A simple
status mes-
sage is a
standard
element of
social col-
laboration.

The status post format encourages brevity although business collaboration systems typically don't enforce anything as severe as the Twitter 140-character limit.

A common pattern is to make the post a concise announcement of a topic discussed in more detail in a blog post, with a link to that resource embedded in the post. Some of the more comprehensive social platforms, like Jive or IBM Connections, include their own blogging and document collaboration tools for that longer content.

Broad social collaboration platforms, such as those from IBM and Jive, include blog and wiki (collaborative document editing) tools that can be used to create web-native documents that go beyond the limits of a status post. For example, a lengthy strategy document with multiple embedded images would be more appropriate to create as a blog post. The author would typically share a status post announcing its publication and inviting feedback.

Executives who participate in social collaboration networks often use an internal blog to share company updates. Project teams often use wikis to prepare and update project planning documents, which are shared in a format that allows any member of the team to make edits. That's a basic difference between a blog and a wiki — a blog typically has one author, while a wiki has many.

Knowing your audience

A status post isn't as intrusive as a group or company-wide e-mail. When you post your status, you're speaking for the benefit of anyone who wants to listen. You're not presuming to know everyone who may benefit from your message. Instead, you leave open the possibility of being pleasantly surprised when someone you've not previously collaborated with turns out to have a great suggestion or the answer to your question. Too, you're not clogging the inboxes of people who may find your message irrelevant. Think of it this way: You are speaking up, not shouting.

Here's a trade-off, though: There is no guarantee that everyone you meant to reach with your message will receive it. Unless you specifically tag or mention another user, or take other steps to ensure certain people are notified of your post, it may scroll past on their personal news feed when they're out of the office or busy with other things. (I tell you how to tag another user in the upcoming "Tagging other users to get their attention" section.)

Also, in many organizations participation on the corporate social network is optional, whereas checking your e-mail is mandatory. This is one reason why e-mail, for all its faults, still has a healthy future in the corporate world. Again, if you'd like to direct a message to a specific person, tag that colleague.

Here's a second possible trade-off. Particularly in a large enterprise with thousands of employees, posts to the company-wide or even a departmental feed may scroll past so quickly that it's impractical to go back and read every message that you may have missed. Sure, you've probably missed messages in your e-mail inbox, too, but on a social network, there is not the same expectation that you try to read everything. Instead, workers browse for what looks interesting and filter for topics and people of interest to try to find the posts most relevant to them and their work.

Also, in many organizations participation on the corporate social network is optional, whereas checking your e-mail is mandatory. This is one reason why e-mail, for all its faults, still has a healthy future in the corporate world.

Sharing with the entire organization

Most social collaboration tools allow you to post or share with the entire organization. Whatever you share on a social network, a key implicit decision is whether to share broadly or with a more focused functional, departmental, or interest group.

Share news, announcements, and resources on the company-wide news feed when you believe they are of company-wide interest. Likewise, share a question on the company-wide news feed when you don't know who may have the answer.

For example, here are some reasonable company-wide news feed posts:

> ✔ *Anyone who is getting questions from customers about our new branding should review this <u>blog post</u> from Chief Marketing Officer John Smith.*

> ✔ *Does anyone have a good suggestion for how to respond to questions from customers who are confused by our rebranding?*

Sharing with a group

Not every post is meant to be company-wide. Often, you collaborate with a smaller group in your department, members of a project team, or people with whom you share a common interest. In a social collaboration application, a *group* is an area that's separate from the main activity stream where group members can share ideas and materials.

Here's an example from my own work. Because all the basic features of Yammer are enabled even in the free version of the product, I created a *Social Collaboration for Dummies* Yammer network (a group with both internal and external members) for friends, family, editors, and early reviewers for this book, as shown in Figure 4-2.

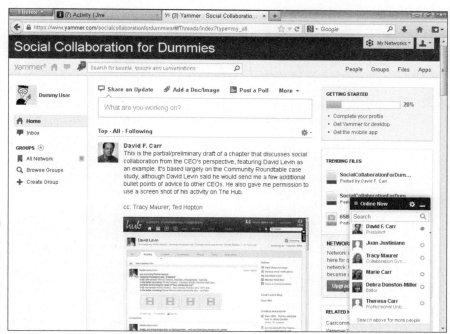

Figure 4-2:
My Yammer network for collaborating on this book.

As I mention in Chapter 2, groups can be configured to be open to anyone who wants to join, or they can be *closed,* meaning that every member of the group must individually be granted admission by the group manager or administrator. Groups can also be secret and invitation only, with their existence and all the content associated with them invisible in search results.

Groups add structure to a social collaboration network. Often they are organized around

- ✔ Departments or other organizational structures
- ✔ Functions, such as customer support
- ✔ Products or product families
- ✔ Project teams
- ✔ Common roles or disciplines of the participants
- ✔ Communities of practice, specifically geared toward promoting excellence in a process or discipline
- ✔ New employees
- ✔ Support of the collaboration network itself, particularly for new users
- ✔ Groups for off-topic or non–work-related discussions (if these are allowed), meant to build camaraderie, if not productivity

When you join a group, make sure you understand the level of privacy and confidentiality associated with that group. Most likely, you'll gain membership to multiple groups with various membership requirements. If you aren't sure whether the content you'd like to post is appropriate for a particular group, ask the group administrator for clarification on who can join that group.

Joining the appropriate groups for your role in the company is important to effective social collaboration. Or you may want to create your own groups, which is a great way to contribute as long as you know what you are doing. Often, the group owner is expected to play a community management role for that particular group, keeping content organized and discussions productive. You may or may not be required to get approval prior to creating a group (the process varies according to both platform capabilities and company rules). Most social collaboration strategists recommend making the process as streamlined as possible. If you're creating a group to support collaboration on a new project, this should be straightforward. For a group organized around a topic or a professional community of practice, first do a thorough search to make sure you aren't duplicating something that already exists. I address community and group management issues in more detail in Chapter 13.

The terminology for "group" varies from one social collaboration environment to the next, so you may see social discussions associated with groups, communities, places, projects, activities, and networks, depending on which social collaboration tool you're using.

Some of these are roughly synonymous, where one platform's "group" is another's "community." But there are also functional distinctions. For example, on IBM Connections, an Activity may include social posts and discussions, but it also provides a set of tools for project, task, and schedule management that aren't enabled for a Community, which is a more general-purpose social collaboration and discussion group. Yammer calls an internal discussion group a Group but also supports the creation of groups that can include external collaborators, known as a Network. (See Chapter 14 for details on engaging external collaborators.)

Learn the vocabulary of your chosen social collaboration environment to understand the available options for segmenting discussions.

The time to share with a group (instead of the organization's main activity feed) is when what you are sharing is mostly or exclusively of interest to that group. Pose your question to a group when the members of that group are most likely to have the answer. Example: The question *How flexible is the deadline for Chapter 4?* would make more sense to post to a project group including the editors for this book, rather than to all employees of my vast, worldwide empire. Posts to a group may or may not be private — that is, in the sense of being visible to only the members of that group. In some cases, your messages may be primarily targeted to group members but also show up in public feeds and search results. This depends on the ground rules of the social networking software or service as well as the administrative choices of the group organizers or administrators.

Users must understand whether they can entrust sensitive or proprietary information to a group discussion. This ought to be self-evident from the user interface but may also need to be addressed with training.

Again, the exact mechanics of group posting vary from platform to platform. However, groups can typically be configured as open or invitation-only, with multiple options for privacy and security for group content. Users may also be able to tag specific posts for broad or limited visibility, depending on the nature of their content.

Getting attention for your posts starts with being a good member of the online community who posts interesting and useful information. Beyond that, there are specific techniques social collaboration users need to know about how to get the attention of specific people and groups of experts, and I tell you about those techniques in the following sections.

Social content that is properly tagged and classified gets more attention when it is posted and is also easier to find later with a search of the social stream.

Tagging other users to get their attention

Most social collaboration platforms incorporate some variation on the @mention tagging functionality familiar to Twitter users, where you embed a reference to a user in your post, and the user is notified that you've done so. You @mention people to give them credit for an idea, direct a question to them, or simply get their attention. When you tag a user this way, he is notified that you mentioned him, making it less likely that he will miss your message.

Although the idea came from Twitter, the way an @mention typically works on social collaboration products is more similar to Facebook's implementation, meaning that you don't have to know the other person's username. Social collaboration tools typically recognize the @ symbol as a reference to another user.

After entering the @ symbol in a post, just start typing your colleague's name, and you should get a drop-down list of choices from your network, including their names and profile pictures. Figure 4-3 shows how that works in Jive. When I started to enter a message tagging "Tony," as soon as I typed **@Ton**, Jive offered a matching list of users.

Figure 4-3:
Using an
@mention
in Jive.

Many social platforms let users use the @mention mechanism to reference communities, discussion groups, or workspaces, in addition to individuals.

Classifying posts with hashtags or formal taxonomy

Another concept imported from Twitter is the *hashtag,* an informal way of classifying a post by including a keyword preceded by the # sign. For example, #socbiz as a common shortcut for social business. When you embed a hashtag in a post, it will be rendered as a link, allowing people to click that link to then see all the other recent public posts that include the same hashtag.

Some social collaboration systems also support more formal taxonomies for assigning content to categories and subcategories. This is the more traditional approach for creating neatly organized content or knowledge management repositories.

Spontaneity is the strength and the weakness of hashtags and other ad hoc schemes for tagging content. You can add a hashtag to a post at your own discretion, without needing to get past a gate keeper responsible for protecting the company taxonomy. This means you can start a topical discussion with everyone interested in the #mynewthing hashtag almost instantly.

On the other hand, the new hashtag you create may be redundant with last month's discussion on #youroldthing. Spontaneous tagging is by nature not as organized as a taxonomy overseen by someone with training in library science or knowledge management.

One way how hashtag systems are starting to address this is with recommendations that steer the post author toward standard tags. For example, as soon as a post author starts to type **#soc**, the system may suggest #socbiz as the commonly used tag before the author has a chance to create a redundant #socialbusiness tag.

Figure 4-4 shows the suggested tags displayed for the hashtag #Accounting in a NewsGator activity stream post. To make your posts reach the right audience, you will want to use standard tags whenever possible and invent new ones only when posting about something truly novel.

Figure 4-4:
Suggestions make it easy to see what standard tags have been associated with a term.

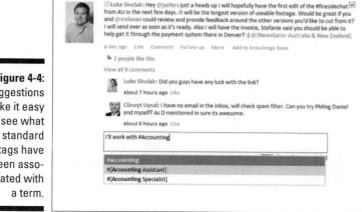

Choosing Types of Posts Useful for Social Collaboration

Varying the types of posts you make to a social network is one way of getting more attention for them. Choosing the right type or format for a post makes it more likely that you'll communicate in the most effective way and get the response you're looking for.

The classic status post is informational: *Here's what I'm doing now.* (That's the origin of all those jokes and complaints about people posting their breakfast cereal choices on Twitter.) In a business, a status post answers the question, *What are you working on right now?* One of the virtues of sharing this information on the social network is it can eliminate the need for the dreaded status report meeting, which consists of going around the table and having every member of the project team share a quick summary of their progress. When team members share their statuses regularly in a social workspace, they keep tabs on each other's progress on an ongoing basis.

However, a steady diet of status posts can get boring. Effective collaborators make use of other post types, including questions, polls, and thank you/recognition messages.

Asking a question

One of the most useful things you can post to a social network is a question. Questions start discussions, and active discussions make a social feed more lively, interesting, and useful. Posting a question to a social network is particularly valuable when you don't know who may have the answer. You can post your question to the company-wide feed or to one or more groups related to your topic, and often get back an answer much more quickly than would be possible through any other means.

Posting a question is a sort of search, just one in which the intelligence for returning an answer comes from people, not software. Instead of putting your energy into composing the perfect search query, you must take care to properly tag your post and consider what community or social stream to publish it into.

Some social platforms, such as Jive, treat questions as a separate content type from standard status posts, as shown in Figure 4-5. This allows Jive to track whether your question has been answered. Employees seeking to show off their expertise can browse for unanswered questions and respond to them.

Figure 4-5:
Track
whether a
question is
answered.

Polling the organization

For quick feedback on a question that has a limited number of answers, consider formulating your question as a poll.

Yammer makes it easy for anyone to create a poll question followed by a series of possible answers. The poll answers are then displayed as a multiple-choice list, with a chart of user opinions created interactively as members of the social network vote on the question. Figure 4-6 shows a Yammer poll.

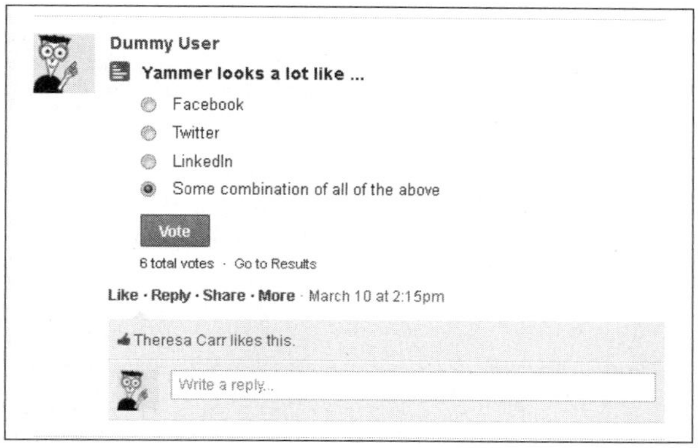

Figure 4-6:
Ask a question in a poll.

Creative problem solving

Gloria Burke, director of knowledge & collaboration strategy and governance at Unisys, tells the story of how the team in a UK office responsible for getting good professional profile photos for every employee stretched its budget by posting a question about whether there were any photographers on staff. The NewsGator Social Sites software Unisys uses allows employees to include a series of Ask Me About topics in their profiles, so the question tagged "photography" immediately came to the attention of a colleague who previously had worked as a professional photographer for the Royal Air Force for more than 20 years. As a result, employees in that office wound up with some of the best profile photos in the entire company.

Thanking people and recognizing employees for achievement

A social network is a great place to thank and recognize the people who help you get your work done. A social post is a way of publicly acknowledging their contribution in front of the whole company or a group of their peers.

Social recognition is so powerful that some social-minded organizations (such as Facebook) have incorporated recognition given by co-workers as well as supervisors into their formal framework for employee performance evaluations. Work.com, from Salesforce.com, is based in part on Facebook's relationship as a customer and design partner of Rypple, a startup that Salesforce.com acquired. Used in combination with Chatter, Work.com is a *social performance management application,* meaning that it encourages employees to share their goals and achievements on the social network and allows for peer-to-peer recognition of good work. Figure 4-7 shows this activity displayed in the Chatter iPad client.

Social recognition approaches often let users award "badges" to each other to signify the type of recognition granted and make recognitions stand out from other social posts. See an example in Figure 4-8 from Yammer.

Figure 4-7: Work.com makes achieve-ment and recognition visible in a social context.

Figure 4-8: Use badges for recogni-tion posts.

Sharing Files and Media

One of the distinguishing features of social collaboration systems for business is the ability to share files. Most public social networks will let you share a photo or a video but not a PowerPoint or Word file. They make it easy to share multimedia experiences but not to collaborate on a proposal. Social collabora-tion systems offer the photo- and video-sharing tools that you would find in social media, along with the file sharing tools that you need for business.

Sharing files and documents

In social collaboration, a document or file can appear as an attachment to a post in the social stream of an individual or group. Most systems also allow you to view the stream of comments associated with any given file.

Sharing a file on the social collaboration network rather than sending a copy of it to multiple users by e-mail saves network bandwidth and storage and offers these additional advantages:

- ✔ **Comments in the activity stream:** Document collaboration takes on a different flavor when combined with a social feed. Instead of collaborating on the document itself by editing it or adding comments, you may want to page through it using a web-based viewer and add a simple comment like *Looks good to me!* or *Can you add some more realistic examples for Chapter 4?*

- ✔ **Version control:** Online document collaboration also avoids the confusion that can arise when different versions of a spreadsheet or proposal are being e-mailed around, and no one is quite sure which is the most current version. Sure, multiple versions of a document will wind up being passed around the social network, but at least the most recent one is likely to be associated with more recent messages in the news feed.

Common file sharing capabilities include the ability to upload and download files and preview standard file formats within the browser. The linked or attached resources are often rendered as a preview of the web page, document, image, or video. In the case of a web page, the preview can be generated based on the HTML title and description tags for that page, plus any rich media information that can be extracted about images or videos embedded in the page.

More advanced features, present on some social platforms and not others, include document management features, such as the capability to check in and check out documents (to prevent multiple people from editing them simultaneously), web-based document editing, and version tracking. I tell you more about that kind of collaboration in Chapter 7.

Working with collaborators on a business record

Beyond the main company activity stream and various group streams or feeds, many business applications are sprouting activity streams. For example, an accounting system may have a stream showing unpaid client invoices, with comments on the status of collection efforts.

Enterprise software products of all sorts increasingly incorporate the notion of the social feed as another user interface element. Meanwhile, social collaboration platforms compete to show how they can function as a "social layer" that can be embedded in, or wrapped around, any other web-based business application.

Part of the point of the feed format is to make it easy to see the most recent activity within the system. Meanwhile, the social network can provide the means to work around gaps in transactional systems.

Where these features are available, take advantage of the opportunity to build social collaboration into the flow of work.

Sharing images and video

Sharing images and video in the social network or feed is just as big of an attention-getter on a private social network as on a public one. When users are scanning an activity stream, posts with multimedia content stand out more.

Ideally, this content should be useful, but there's no reason it can't be fun. If customers are lined up around the block for your company's new product, photos of the crowd will be exciting news to everyone involved. If some photos feature cute kids in the crowd or people making funny faces, that's okay. Posting random photos of cute kids absent the business content, however, would be less appropriate for a business social network. When you post a photo or other image, the interface then displays a preview of that image in the activity stream. Video handling is a little more variable. When you post a link to a YouTube video on Yammer, it's displayed in the feed as a thumbnail image, and viewers can play the video without ever leaving the feed. In other words, it works much like posting a YouTube video on Facebook. Some other collaboration systems display a link to YouTube content as a link but not as embedded media content.

A few platforms offer more elaborate functionality. For example, NewsGator offers an add-on module with which you can set up your own "private YouTube," with software to convert between video formats and stream video from your own servers. Enterprise platform players like Cisco, IBM, and Microsoft with video capture, videoconferencing, video streaming, and web conferencing products in their portfolios can embed those multimedia experiences in the social stream — if you have licensed the right assortment of products or cloud services from them, that is.

Responding to Another User's Post

Posting and sharing your own content is great, but effective use of a social network is not all about self-promotion. You must listen to what others say and think about what you can add to the conversation. Each post in the activity stream of a social collaboration application is accompanied by a Like button (or similar opportunity to express your approval) and a space where you can type a reply. This part of the interface looks a little bit different in each application, and some applications also provide other tools, such as a Share button.

When you see a post that interests you, you can respond to it in these three ways (among others, depending on the platform):

- ✔ **Like:** This is a quick sign of approval, the equivalent of a nod and smile or even a "Good job!" "Liking" a post on a collaboration network means pretty much what it does on Facebook and other public social networks that employ a similar mechanism. Sometimes the terminology is a little different: maybe a thumbs-up, or a system for awarding points. The idea is the same, though — to give a quick vote in favor of a piece of content. This one-click feedback mechanism doesn't even require writing a message.

  If you're in a hurry, or if you have little to say beyond *I like this,* just clicking the button is enough. Such feedback may be quick, but it's still helpful, letting the author know that someone else found the content useful. As a post accumulates likes and comments, it becomes more visible to more people on the social collaboration network, perhaps showing up on a list of trending topics or most active conversations, which, in turn, attracts more likes and comments.

- ✔ **Reply:** Some interfaces include your avatar and space to type your reply below each post. Others require you to click Reply to access the field in which you can type your reply. Either way, responding to a post in the activity stream is fairly straightforward; you simply type your message and press Enter or click the button that sends the message.

- ✔ **Reply with more info:** Sometimes you'd like to direct a colleague's attention to another resource, or bring another colleague into a discussion. You can do that by replying to a post and including a link, uploaded document, or tag, as discussed elsewhere in this book.

- ✔ **Share:** Give the post a broader audience by sending it to a colleague or a collaboration group, along with your note about why it's significant.

Social collaboration platforms keep track of the Likes on each post, as shown in Figure 4-9. You can see that Salesforce.com Chatter users particularly like to Like progress toward sales goals.

Like

Figure 4-9:
Likes and comments on a sales chart.

Sometimes you may want to do both: Click Like and also write a comment, saying more about why you think the post is interesting or useful.

Answering the right question can make you a hero, not only to the person who posed it but to others following the discussion. Or, maybe you don't know the answer to the question being posted, but you know who would. Write back, tagging the expert who ought to be part of the conversation in your message.

If you think what others are saying is wrong, try to set them straight — politely. When a conversation bubbles up around a topic that you had seen discussed previously, provide a link to the old discussion so it can inform or maybe eliminate the need for the new one.

Jive users, community managers, and administrators answer each other's questions about best practices for social collaboration on the Jive Community website (shown in Figure 4-10), which is itself a social collaboration community.

More updates by Tracy Maurer

Tracy Maurer posted 3 months ago

Hey 🔲 Ryan Rutan - any possibility you guys would consider having a frame or something for Jive Employee's avatars so that it was much more obvious who they were in the JC? I have an example where a Jive employee replied to a case posted by another Jive employee, and it was obvious from context that he thought he was talking to a customer. Would love to see you get creative here! :)

3 Comments

Ryan Rutan 3 months ago

Its a topic of much discussion. With the Bunchball plugin installed, status levels are hidden. I'll bring this up again and see what we can figure out =)

👍 Like (1)   ⚠ Report Abuse

David F. Carr 1 month ago

Do either of you mind if I use a screen shot of this discussion for the Social Collaboration for Dummies book I'm working on? Tracy, I'd also like permission to use a screen shot of your profile from this system.

👍 Like (2)   ⚙ Delete

Tracy Maurer 1 month ago

Sure thing, David!

👍 Like (0)   ⚠ Report Abuse

Comment   @

Figure 4-10:
Social collaboration lets users answer each other's questions.

Chapter 5

Working Your Network

*B*uilding your network for social collaboration has a lot in common with building your network on LinkedIn, the public social network for professional networking often associated with recruiting and job hunting. A social collaboration network is another tool for professional networking, but the goal is to make you more effective in your current job.

Within a social collaboration network, you build connections to keep yourself informed about what's going on within the company but also to meet people who can be helpful in the future (or who may need your help). In both contexts, you want to project a positive, professional image.

Making and Cultivating Connections

LinkedIn founder Reid Hoffman says the best way to build a professional social network is to start with your allies — the people you turn to regularly for advice and guidance. This may include old college friends and respected former co-workers. Digital collaboration may be the least significant aspect of your relationship with these people because they are true friends whom you get together with in person whenever possible.

Within a corporate social network, your natural allies may include co-workers, peers in other departments, your supervisor, and subordinates. Regardless of whether they are friends outside of work, they are people you know well and work well with. You use the digital network to work with them on shared documents and team projects because they are your most frequent collaborators, but you also interact in many other ways.

Where social collaboration becomes more important is with the maintenance of weaker, more casual connections.

A note on making new connections

In general, internal social communities don't offer the kind of profile privacy settings you find on public social networks. The entire collaboration network is generally "private" in the sense of being inaccessible to outsiders, but any employee can see basic contact details or send a message to any other employee. Employees can keep specific documents and messages private to themselves or to a group of collaborators, but their profiles are generally accessible. If the option to hide profile details is available at all, community managers invariably counsel using it sparingly. You might imagine that the CEO would want to limit the availability of certain contact information, such as a cellphone number, to a specific circle of advisors.

Takeaway: There is almost always a way to contact someone directly through the social network. It's not like on LinkedIn, where contact details and even the name of an individual discovered through search results may be hidden for all but first-, second-, and third-degree contacts (the exact mechanics vary based on account type). However, whenever you *do* have a contact in common with the person you are trying to reach, it often makes sense to take advantage of that. If the common contact is someone who respects you and will put in a good word for you, you have a head start on establishing a working relationship with the new contact you're seeking.

Here's how that may work: You meet someone interesting, in person or online, start "following" them (essentially, subscribing to their social collaboration updates), and wind up connecting with other people from their network. You find a document that's highly relevant to your work and follow the link back to the author so you can keep tabs on anything new he posts on the subject. Over time, you may converse with these people online, connect with them in person as the opportunity arises, and turn them into closer connections.

The extended connections you establish beyond your circle of close friends, co-workers, and allies are known in social networking theory as *weak ties*. Weak ties are important because you can have a lot more of them, and digital social networks allow you to keep track of many more of these people than you can in your head. Even if we don't remember each other at first glance, our respective social profiles are packed with reminders, including the mutual contacts who can vouch for us. These aren't people who would lay down their lives for you or stake their reputations on your reliability. Still, they have enough nodding familiarity with you to do you a casual favor or make an introduction to someone who can help you with your project or cut through layers of bureaucracy. You, of course, would do the same for them.

Professional social networking is about knowing people who know people as much as it is about knowing people with specific technical knowledge. Even when they don't know the answer to a question or the solution to a problem, people with extensive networks know where to turn. They understand the organization and its politics. They know how to get things done.

You may or may not be able to turn yourself into one of those people, but if not, you want to be connected to people like that. Here are some guidelines for getting connected:

- ✔ **Start with your existing connections.** The best way to build your network is a little at a time but steadily. In the beginning, you'll probably start with a handful of network connections. Some systems will automatically assign you a starter set of digital relationships based on a company org chart. If that's not automatic, start by making sure you have the appropriate connections to your supervisor, subordinates, and the co-workers you collaborate with more frequently.

- ✔ **Watch the activity stream.** Watch for patterns of interaction between others on the social collaboration network, looking for those who are well connected or well informed about the business in general or specific facets you're interested in.

- ✔ **Search for people with specific knowledge or skill sets.** If your collaboration network includes a good search tool, use it to find content on the topics you care about and trace it back to the author or authors. To the extent that people have fleshed out their profiles and tagged them properly (which they don't always), you may find experts and other good connections that way.

  Try to think ahead to the connections you may need someday, based on the sorts of work you're doing or planning to do, as well as your career path and ambitions.

- ✔ **Seek introductions.** Most social collaboration network profiles allow you to see who your connections are connected to, and some of those people should probably be your connections, also. Browsing contacts lists on profiles is one way of finding potential connections. Following the stream of social interactions from your contacts will also let you see who their best contacts are.

Be polite, but don't be shy. The point of a social collaboration network is to build connections throughout the workforce. Colleagues are unlikely to object to you following them or reaching out to make a connection, particularly if you show yourself to be a productive member of the community who helps others as you would like to be helped.

Returning the favor

Typically, employee social networks don't require reciprocal connections where a contact is established only if both parties agree to it in the mode of Facebook friendship or LinkedIn professional connections. The IBM Connections social collaboration software does support the concept of inviting other users to join your network. If they agree, the effect is similar to you following them and them following you back. But you can also follow people, rather than sending a connection invitation.

Even when they aren't enforced by the platform, reciprocal behaviors are still a good idea in the world of network building. If someone follows you, you should follow her back, more often than not. In addition to doing this as you go along, you may want to periodically review your network to see who is following you whom you may want to follow in turn. Figure 5-1 shows how you can browse a listing of your followers in NewsGator.

If someone shares or comments on your content, look for opportunities to return the favor. However, don't be phony about it. If you're clicking Like and Share in response to content that you don't actually like and that members of your network are unlikely to want to have shared with them, you can hurt rather than help your online reputation.

Beyond returning the favor, you should proactively offer help to the people in your network — helping others as you would like to be helped. Again, that can mean liking or sharing the content they post. It can also mean answering their questions or introducing them to someone who would be likely to have the answer.

By being a good citizen of the network, you build your online reputation and political capital for the day when you're the one who needs questions answered or messages spread throughout the organization.

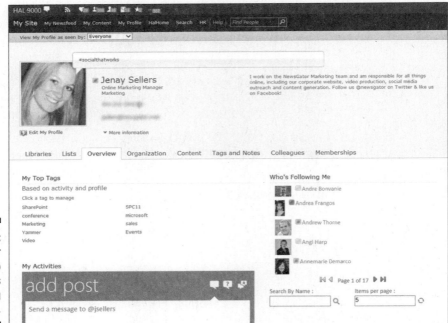

Figure 5-1: Review your network to see who is following you.

Cultivating connections

Good connections deserve to be cultivated. You cultivate your network of connections by keeping it growing and healthy.

- ✔ **Eliminate gaps.** Pay attention to the mix of connections you have as well as whether there are gaps, such as new co-workers whom you've not yet connected with online. Perhaps they need you to show them what the collaboration network is good for.

- ✔ **Reinforce casual connections.** If you build an extensive social network at work, you won't be tightly connected to all those people. Remember that part of the point of an online social network was to allow you to establish more weak ties, or casual connections.

  Even casual connections need to be reinforced, however, or they wither away to nothing. In everyday use, the social software environment gives you the tools to keep in touch with those more casual contacts. When they post something, you can Like it or share it (when appropriate) just to stay on their radar.

- ✔ **Build stronger connections with your best allies.** There may be other contacts you want to cultivate more actively: say, people you work with or would like to work with but don't see every day. Even if they haven't posted lately, find an excuse to mention them in your posts or send them a message. Ask their advice, showing that you respect their opinion. If you don't work in the same location but have an excuse to visit, consider asking them to lunch.

Throughout this chapter, I make several references to connecting with people who share your expertise or interests. One of the ways how a social network can be most valuable is in helping you connect with expertise you lack and answers to questions you didn't even anticipate you'd need.

This is where having a sizable and robust network becomes very valuable. You can ask your own network of contacts the big question, and maybe you'll get lucky and have someone who knows the answer already connected to you.

Maybe a search of the social network will turn up someone with the right expertise. Often, though, the human social network is more powerful. Post your question to the social network stream, and you may get (if not an answer) an introduction to someone who probably knows the answer. What works even better is reaching out to the people you know — the people whose relationships you've cultivated — until you know a little bit about what and whom they know.

With a strong network, even if you don't know who to ask, you will know who would know.

Looking Professional Online

You should dress up your profile the way you dress yourself for success in the workplace. At a bank or other traditional organization, a man's profile picture may include a suit and tie (or at least, a dress shirt and tie), but it may be perfectly appropriate for a software developer at a startup to be pictured in a T-shirt and jeans. In most any business, it would be inappropriate to post photos of yourself half-drunk or half-naked. (Does that even need to be stated?) Employees shouldn't use their corporate network as a platform for their personal partisan political beliefs (disconnected from the company's interests in regulation or policy). Of course, it's always possible to think of exceptions (such as the lad mag publisher who celebrates immaturity or the activist at a partisan political consulting firm). The point is that you need to make yourself look professional according to the standards of your industry.

The things to avoid ought to be obvious, but you can boost your professional profile within the company by doing a few other things right.

Fleshing out your profile

Along with your account on the collaboration network, your profile may have been prepopulated with some basic data: your name, title, e-mail address, phone number, and place in the org chart according to corporate personnel records. The picture from your employee security badge may be your default profile photo. Personnel systems may also provide some details about your level of educational attainment and any internal training courses you may have completed.

Or your profile may start as a blank slate, with only your name filled in. You want your profile to be more than the bare minimum details, though. Just as you want to be able to find people within the company who have specific experience and expertise, you want to make yourself easy to be found by others when you have something to offer them. If you can then tag your profile, in addition to offering a narrative description of your background, others can then find your profile through the same taxonomy they would use to locate other kinds of content.

Figure 5-2 shows a well-rounded, employee social profile, with a good photo, full contact info, a brief bio, and a list of keywords for topics of expertise.

And your photo should be good enough that those who connect with you online will also recognize you if they pass you in the hallway.

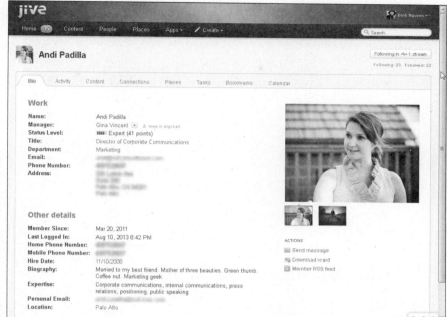

Figure 5-2:
A good
employee
profile
shows
personality,
areas of
expertise,
and contact
info.

Answering questions

If you want to establish yourself as an expert or authority on any topic, pay attention to relevant questions and provide knowledgeable answers. In addition to making a good impression on whoever posted the question, your answers help build your reputation as a go-to person for questions on that topic. Anyone who searches on that topic will see the trail you've left.

One nice feature of the NewsGator platform that assists in this process is automated matching of tags associated with questions and tags associated with profiles. If you include a tag on your profile, you will automatically be notified when someone asks a relevant question, making it easy for you to jump in with the answer.

Other platforms support keyword-based or tag-based filtering of social feeds, which can be another way of identifying questions on a topic where you often have the answers.

Sharing useful information

Just as on public social networks, you don't necessarily have to generate a ton of original content to be a valuable member of the community. Often, some of the people who add the most value are those who share interesting news articles, opinion columns, or videos, adding a few sentences of their own commentary. If the articles are relevant to your business, the market it operates in, or the professional development needs of your colleagues, they will thank you for sharing. If the analysis you offer, however pithy, seems accurate, you will get credit for your understanding. This can also be the jumping-off point for a broader discussion of business strategy or market strategies.

Share what you find interesting and useful. Be sure to include a note or a question making clear why it is relevant to your business. Those who have chosen to follow your posts will probably agree. At a minimum, they will find out more about what interests you and will share more relevant content with you.

Joining the right groups

Your network includes groups of people as well as individuals. Terminology varies (groups, communities, spaces, workspaces, projects), but often the subcommunities are more useful for many purposes than the company-wide community.

Membership in some groups may be automatic or required based on your participation in a project or your job role. Others are optional, topical groups. For example, my company has a group where website editors, production, and IT people share tips on the use of search engine optimization (SEO) and social media to connect with readers. Other groups are dedicated to sales strategy, time management, and "Exercisers in Need of Motivation" (a self-help group for employees).

Groups provide an opportunity to connect with people with similar interests or expertise, as well as teams focused on specific projects, functions, or initiatives. In addition to interacting through the group, you may decide to connect with some of its members individually, and they may seek to connect with you.

You find groups by searching for them or by paying attention to the group memberships of your best contacts.

If you search for an interest group that ought to exist but doesn't, consider starting one. Depending on the rules laid down by community managers and IT administrators, you may need advance permission to start a group. Even if you don't, ask for advice on how to go about it. For one thing, you want to confirm that there's not an existing group that does what you have in mind — or, if there is a similar one, that you can articulate the distinct need your proposed group will fill. The uncontrolled proliferation of groups can create chaos in social collaboration networks, so you don't want to add to it unnecessarily.

Assuming you can make a good case for a new group, positioning yourself as its founder and owner can be a good way of raising your professional visibility within the company — and, ideally, contributing to its success.

Having fun while showing respect for the workplace

Even at work, social networking ought to be fun. Just how much fun it should be, though, is a subject of some debate.

Some businesses in more traditional or conservative industries will field an enterprise social network only on the understanding that all conversation on the network should be work-related. *Period.* Posting a joke or a link to a review of the movie you saw over the weekend probably wouldn't get you fired, but it would be frowned upon. Other organizations allow the occasional, casual post that is purely social on the main company feed or as an off-topic post within a workgroup. Typically, these are the same firms that allow the formation of non–work-related groups on the network on the theory that they give employees experience using the social software, while also building personal connections between employees that pay off by creating a more cohesive organization and supporting stronger teams.

I lean toward the more permissive philosophy, which many organizations have applied successfully to build more vibrant communities while still focusing the overall effort on getting work done. This is an issue for community managers, discussed in Chapter 13.

However, if you're trying to work within the rules rather than being in a position to make them, you should not only read the official policy but also "take the temperature" of the environment and pay attention to what others can and cannot get away with in practice.

Show respect for the norms of your workplace, whether you agree with them or not, but try to be engaging within that framework.

Here are some guidelines that should apply to most organizations:

✔ **Show enthusiasm for work activities.** In all cases, showing enthusiasm for your work is a good thing, as is giving praise to subordinates or peers who do a good job.

✔ **Take a natural, casual approach.** Behave like a human, not like a machine that cranks out links to sales reports. Humanizing the workplace can be a pleasure all on its own. Many of us who have been trained by the public social networks find discovering new connections and having other people discover us to be a fun thing, so even in the most straight-laced organizations, you've got that.

✔ **Use good judgment.** Posting pictures of your team having fun at work or celebrating their achievements at an after-work party is probably a good thing, if the photos are in good taste. Follow cues from co-workers and leaders in deciding what counts as good taste in your organization.

✔ **Look for opportunities to show you have a sense of humor.** As I mention earlier, some collaboration networks will frown on posting jokes. For the most part, that's not even what I'm talking about. Often, what you really want to do is slip a bit of observational humor into the end of a post or a comment on someone else's content.

Humor in the online workplace

Humor makes you more interesting and engaging and will help you build your network. The best public speakers know that even when addressing the most serious topic, fitting in a moment of humor keeps the audience's attention while also relieving tension. Humor is a currency that can purchase attention for your more serious points. Of course, you have to calibrate your sense of humor to be appropriate for the workplace and not a bar room.

There is always a risk in humor, starting with the chance that no one will find your remark funny. Worse, you may unintentionally offend someone, in which case you will have to apologize. It should go without saying that you should never *intentionally* be giving offense. Don Rickles should not be your model for humor. (For those

readers who are too young to remember Don Rickles, just know that if something is intentionally shocking or offensive, it's off-limits.) The best uses of humor in the workplace make a point about human nature as it relates to work and how we can work together better.

The fun you have at work should be in the service of building a stronger workplace. You can't be having so much fun on the collaboration network that it distracts from getting work done, but being boring is often a bigger danger. To build a better network, have a little fun with it.

You want people in your network to take you seriously, but that doesn't mean you should be serious all the time.

Chapter 6

Managing Projects and Tasks

. . . .

. . . .

*C*entral to the promise of social collaboration is changing how we work for the better. Otherwise, social collaboration is just social networking within the organization — truly "Facebook within my business" but nothing more. Thus, one of the most active frontiers in social collaboration is finding better ways to organize tasks and projects through the network.

In this chapter, I discuss several approaches to organizing work in a collaboration network, from relatively loose, social mechanisms to more structured ones that nevertheless take advantage of the social network.

To make this a little more concrete, I examine two specific products:

✔ **Podio**, a cloud-hosted social platform used by businesses large and small and known for its innovative approach to organizing tasks and information

✔ The **Activities module** in IBM Connections, one of the leading social collaboration platforms for large enterprises

At the end of this chapter, I discuss some of the advantages and trade-offs to consider for the different approaches to task management. You should think about these aspects of task management if you're the person charged with choosing and/or implementing a social collaboration system.

Sharing Progress Reports as Simple Social Posts

At a basic level, every social collaboration tool that allows you to post a status message has the potential for improving your coordination of tasks and projects. Happy users of enterprise social networks often celebrate cutting down on meetings, particularly the dreaded "status report" meeting where the participants in a project sit around a conference table and report their progress and obstacles. When team members post their statuses online, the need for the status meetings is reduced and may go away entirely.

Supervisors and project managers can also make course corrections announced as status posts or targeted messages.

At a web design firm, for instance, the scenario may be something like this:

> *Joe:* I just got the artwork for the landing page in from that new freelancer. It looks good, but I'll probably need another day to tweak the layout to match and make some copy revisions.
>
> *Bill* (Joe's manager): We really need to hit our Thursday deadline. @Mary, can you help Joe out on this?
>
> *Mary:* Sure. Joe, why don't you let me work on the layout? And you can focus on the copy.

An exchange like this, most likely within a project workgroup, is social networking as a communication and coordination tool for keeping projects on track, which is valuable in its own right. Projects can also be accelerated through sharing planning documents, using the collaboration tool. Some social platforms have decided to emphasize social sharing and not venture into task or project management. The last time I checked, Yammer didn't offer have any explicit task management functionality, although that can be added through integration with cloud software partners, such as Sparqlight.

For small organizations and simple projects, project coordination through the status line may be all you need. Or you may have another tool, such as Microsoft Project, that you use for more formal project management, with social collaboration playing a supporting role. Social task management is somewhere in between — more structured than status messages and discussion threads but looser and more flexible than traditional project management. That's what I discuss in the following section.

Understanding social task management

Social task management is one of the areas where competition and acquisition activity among the social tool vendors is most intense, seeking to position themselves as providing essential tools for the "future of work."

Even as the social collaboration platform players seek to subsume task management as a feature, stand-alone products in this category are proliferating. Stand-alone products like Do.com (from Salesforce.com) and Asana (founded by former Facebook engineers, including its original chief technology officer [CTO]), as well as products like Wrike that can be used stand-alone but also integrate well with enterprise social platforms like Jive.

Of the major social collaboration platforms, IBM has strong task management functionality in its Activities module. Jive recently acquired a social task management startup called Producteev, which will be incorporated into an update of the task management features in Jive. Constellation Research analyst Alan Lepofsky, who tracks this product category, is also impressed by Podio, a social collaboration tool acquired by Citrix in 2012, that emphasizes task management and provides an easy-to-use App Builder for organizing work.

Many of the task-focused startups have focused less on traditional enterprise qualities (such as scalability and integration) than on the kind of simplicity that would appeal to consumers or the small-to-midsize business (SMB) market. That includes Asana as well as Do (created by a team that Salesforce.com acquired and has allowed to operate relatively independently).

"The way they've explained it is it's not so much SMB versus enterprise as that they're going after small usage, by which I mean a typical project will have 10 to 25 people," says Alan Lepofsky, a Constellation Research analyst who follows this market. In other words, a company may have thousands or tens of thousands of employees, but the scale of collaboration around a task or project will still tend to be a relatively small, tight group.

On the other hand, another way these tools differ from traditional project management tools is that membership in the collaboration group need not be limited to those who are assigned tasks related to a project. "You might have a dozen people assigned tasks, but then other people put into that workspace just to monitor," Lepofsky explains. For example, salespeople may use the tool to monitor the progress of an engineering team's work on a new product. "That's a really neat thing and very different from traditional task management," he says.

Using More Sophisticated Social Task Management

Social task management tools explicitly manage deadlines, assignments, and relationships between tasks. They distinguish themselves from other task and project management applications with social-style interaction. At the same time, they distinguish themselves from purely social tools by helping employees get work done, rather than merely talking about work. Here are some typical features:

✔ **Create and view tasks.** You can easily create tasks as personal to-do items and see a list of any tasks been assigned to you. As Figure 6-1 shows, tasks feature prominently in the Podio activity stream. In addition to the My Tasks listing on the right, there can be tasks attached to comments, embedded in projects, or associated with Podio Apps (explained later in this chapter).

✔ **Assign tasks to colleagues.** You make assignments to your connections on the social network as easily as you might @mention them in a post.

✔ **Set deadlines.** Keep work on track by putting them on a schedule.

✔ **Receive notifications.** Users are notified of assignments through the social activity stream and often also by e-mail. Additional notifications may be generated when a deadline is approaching or a task is past due.

✔ **Get to know the team.** Every task is displayed with the names and profile pictures of the people associated with a task, including the person who created it and those assigned to complete it, with links to each of their profiles.

✔ **Add comments to a task.** You can comment on tasks, so that a post asking, for instance, whether the deadline for a task is realistic appears in the context of the task itself.

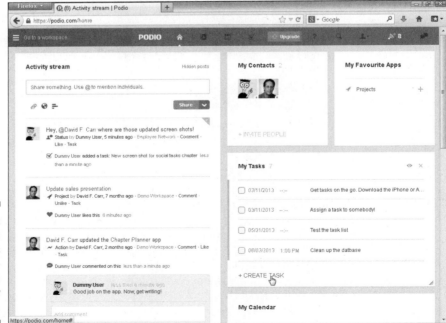

Figure 6-1:
Tasks and projects can be represented in the activity stream.

I discuss the basic elements of tasks, assignments, and deadlines here.

Creating a task as a social object

The breadth and depth of a social platform is defined in part by the content types, or types of objects, it can manage.

Making a task a *social object* means you can share it, comment on it, and otherwise interact with it as you would a status post or other object on the social network. I'm speaking in generalities here because (of course) product details will differ. The point of making a task a social object is so you can connect it to the rest of the features of the social network and make your collaborations more productive.

By making tasks a distinct object type, we can make them behave differently from ordinary posts. For example, we can give a task a deadline, assign it to one or more people, and allow the assignees to mark it complete when they have performed the task. In addition, by putting tasks in a social context, we can interact with them as we would posts, images, or documents by sharing or commenting on them. So instead of just seeing that a task is done or not done, we can follow a comment stream with progress updates that give a better idea of whether a deadline is likely to be met.

Assigning tasks to other users

Part of the point of social task management is to assign tasks through the *social graph* — the network of connections between people in an online system. You may start with a long list of tasks that you have mapped in a larger project, but as you start to prioritize you will want to start assigning tasks to specific people who will be responsible for getting this done. Doing this in a social context makes it easier for everyone to see who is responsible for what.

Also, in a social collaboration environment, you aren't just typing names into a spreadsheet but linking to the profiles of specific individuals to whom the system will then send automated notifications and deadline reminders.

You pick your team by mining the directory of profiles, which includes not only names but photos and other information to help distinguish between people with the same or similar names. Better yet, the system knows a lot about your relationships with these people: whether folks are in the same department, whether you follow them, and whether you interact with them frequently or rarely. Particularly in a large, international corporation, being able to see your closest connections at a glance rather than looking through the entire directory is a big plus.

The rules for making assignments vary among software platforms and organizations. Some egalitarian systems allow everyone to assign tasks to anyone else, with the option for the assignee who is too busy with other things to decline to accept it. On the other hand, given a profiles directory that reflects the organizational hierarchy, you could make a rule that supervisors can assign tasks to subordinates but not the other way around.

Tasks can be assigned to one or more individuals, or to a group where whoever gets the task done will mark it complete.

Setting deadlines

There is nothing particularly "social" about deadlines, but clearly deadlines are an important element to making sure work gets done. Once deadlines are set, those assigned tasks will send persistent reminders and alerts. Exposing deadlines in a social context also allows peers to see who is on schedule, running behind, or in need of help.

Some systems also include the possibility of setting an overall deadline, plus intermediate deadlines associated with subtasks, or setting intermediate milestones on the path to completing a task.

At the risk of being a little simplistic, the main points of setting deadlines are to keep to a schedule and know when you are falling behind. And here's how using social collaborations tools can help:

- ✔ **For an individual:** Social task management tools provide a listing of tasks and their deadlines, often with past-due items shown in red or otherwise highlighted.

- ✔ **For the group:** Making peer performance compared with deadlines visible creates positive social pressure to keep projects on track.

- ✔ **For the project manager:** The social stream can be a valuable source of intelligence on which people who have been assigned tasks are running ahead or behind schedule. In addition, social task managers provide a dashboard for seeing an overview of which team members have missed deadlines. Some tools may also display a percentage of work complete statistic, as reported by the person responsible for completing the task.

If a project comes in late, or fails to achieve the expected results, the discussions surrounding tasks and deadlines will also come in handy for a postmortem analysis of what went wrong and lessons learned for next time.

Exploring additional social task management options

Other task management features, which social collaboration tools may address to a greater or lesser extent (or not at all), include

- Organizing tasks into larger units of work, such as projects
- Providing project planning and monitoring tools to help allocate units of work across a team without overloading any one individual
- Project monitoring tools and visualizations (such as Gantt charts), to show overlapping tasks assigned to individual teams plotted on a timeline
- Managing *dependencies* between tasks, where one cannot be started until another is completed
- Orchestrating tasks into a workflow or business process management framework, where the completion of one task kicks off the initiation of the next one in a sequence.

Structuring Work in Podio

Podio is cloud-based, social collaboration product with all the basics features you would expect for status posts and group discussions, but it also provides a couple of important facilities for organizing work:

- An App Builder for structuring information and processes
- Tasks as distinct social objects, which you can add from anywhere and associate with anything

This section is all about accessing and using these tools.

Introducing Podio apps and tasks

In the social, mobile generation of computing, the word "app" connotes a little, focused application. The underlying technologies for delivering an iPhone app or a Facebook app are different, but you expect an app to be slick, colorful, and modern — not dull, corporate, and outdated.

In Podio-speak, an app is a simple application, one you can build yourself or adopt and modify from its App Market.

Podio's agile tools

Podio co-founder John Froda often talks about wanting to match the easy organization of information that makes many workers gravitate to Excel because they can put almost any textual or numeric information into it, adding columns as needed to track additional information. Spreadsheet programs like Excel are really intended for tracking numbers like budgets and calculating formulas, but people use them to plan projects, organize lists of contacts, and function as ad hoc databases that don't require IT support. Arguably, the uses of the spreadsheet have been stretched too far when it comes to tracking business data.

Instead of creating a web-based spreadsheet, however, Podio has tried to create a comparably flexible tool for the social web, with the ability to mash up other resources. For example, the App Builder form designer makes it as easy to add a Google Maps component as a more standard text entry field. A contacts widget, used for purposes like assigning the editor for a book chapter, is smart enough to pull contacts from the social network or allow a user of the app to manually enter contact information.

The Podio App Market is stocked with apps users have created and shared, all for free.

Creating a Podio app doesn't require learning a programming language or database design. The App Builder is really a drag-and-drop form designer, which automatically creates an underlying structure for storing the data people will record when they use the app. As I mention earlier, you can use a Podio app someone else has already created, or you can also put together an app that includes only the tools you need.

From within any Podio workspace, click Add App and click either Go to the App Market or Go to the App Builder, as shown in Figure 6-2. (I tell you how to design your own app in the next section.)

The Podio App Market is well stocked with apps for common business purposes, such as a Customer Relationship Management (CRM) app for tracking sales leads and customer support. The advantage of creating an app or finding and modifying one for your own purposes is you can track exactly the information you need to track — and no more.

Here is some key Podio terminology associated with the tools available in that platform:

- ✔ **Apps:** The apps let you do structured work within social collaboration. Say, rather than posting a status item about a customer complaint, you fill out a form to make sure you don't forget the details. Apps also work together with the Podio task management tools to organize and track work.

✔ **Workspace:** In Podio, every app exists within a workspace — what other social tools may term a *group* or *community* — often dedicated to a particular project or business function. Podio also provides a sample app (Projects) to record the project owner, members of the project team, start date, and end date, with a slider widget for indicating progress toward completion.

✔ **Tasks:** They're everywhere in Podio. For example, if someone posts a complaint to the activity stream, assigning a follow-up task related to that item is as easy as clicking a link beneath the post. In other words, creating a task is as easy as clicking Like on a post. Your task description can then be as terse as *Please follow up on this,* with a deadline, because the task will be linked back to the original post.

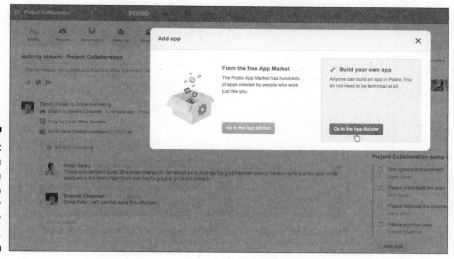

Figure 6-2:
Choose an app from the Podio App Market or create your own.

You can create a task as a standalone item or within a workspace — as a task for a particular team — or associate it with an app, or with a specific record being tracked in that app.

For example, a task connected to an app may be *Check all these records for duplicates,* and a task associated with a customer record in a sales tracking app may be *Check with these guys to see whether they are ready to reorder.*

Here is a walkthrough of some of the key app and task creation options in the Podio environment.

What Podio's customers say

Podio's approach is only one example of how to structure work in a social environment, but it is well thought-out. As a relatively ad hoc environment for organizing work, it may not have all the controls that a conservative enterprise may expect. That's why I also talk about IBM Connections in this chapter.

However, Podio does have some large customers. One fan is Amy Lyons, senior manager of support operations at CCH, a tax and accounting software division of Wolters Kluwer, an international software, information, and services firm. She says she fell in love with Podio after being introduced to it by her contacts at Citrix, maker of the GoToAssist product her firm uses for remote software support.

Traditional project management software tends to be "a lot more cumbersome" and require a lot more training to use, she says. "I needed something everyone could jump right in and adopt." More than competing with project management software, Podio is an alternative to the informal task and project tracking typically done through e-mail, she says. Managing tasks through Podio is a lot smoother because collaborators are notified when she assigns a task, and she is notified back when they complete it — and can track which tasks are or are not complete through the tool. "I don't have to go back and dig through e-mail for any of that," Lyons says.

Besides structuring everyday tasks within the support operation, she has used a Podio app to track activities like recruiting on college campuses.

P.J. Quesada may be more typical of Podio's user base. He introduced it at Ramar Foods, a family business based in Hawaii that distributes Filipino foods. As a third-generation owner who leads the firm's marketing and operations, he likes how Podio lets him structure processes, such as tracking the development of graphic design for advertisements or product packaging. Although he has no real formal training in computer science, he has been able to create the apps himself. "Tasks can be generated based on how you structure the app. By having tasks distributed to the appropriate parties, you can get things done a lot faster," he says.

Building a Podio app

One of the fundamental tools Podio provides for organizing work is its App Builder. Here is how you use the App Builder to define basic web apps with associated databases. Apps let you store, organize, and receive all sorts of data, with tasks as one of the basic data types.

1. **In a workspace, click the Add App icon.**

2. **Click the Go to the App Builder button.**

3. **In the App Builder, give your app a name — for example, *Design Approval* — type the name of the single item that would be created in the app — for example, *Design* — and then choose a relevant icon.**

4. **Drag and drop the building blocks on the left side of the screen into the app based on what business function you would like your app to perform, as shown in Figure 6-3.**

   For example, if the work to be managed with this app is time-sensitive, you want a Date field to be able to set deadlines with. If you will use this app to delegate work, use a Contact field and rename it something like *Responsible Person.*

5. **When you have all the building blocks you need, click Save.**

   You now have a functioning app and can begin to add new business records using this structure.

To change the app at any point in the future, click the wrench icon in the upper right of any screen within the app and then click the Modify App button.

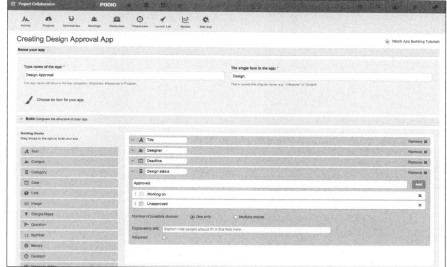

Figure 6-3:
Drag and drop building blocks in the Podio App Builder.

Creating a task

You can create Podio tasks that are associated with an app or a workspace, but you can also create stand-alone tasks. Here is how to create a task as simply as posting your status.

1. **Click New Task or press T on your keyboard to start creating a new task.**

   The task editor is shown in Figure 6-4.

Figure 6-4:
Entering
task details
and assign-
ments.

2. **Enter the name and a description of the task.**

3. **Assign the task.**

   You can assign tasks to your contacts on the private social network. Alternatively, you can assign a task to someone outside the organization (such as a contractor) by entering an e-mail address. That person will get an invitation to join as Guest User with access to one specific workspace.

4. **Set the due date and time for the task.**

5. **For best results, associate the task with a workspace.**

   This helps teams understand who is working on what, reduces the chances of duplication of work, and enables feedback for a better end product.

   If you created your task from within a workspace, the name of that workspace will be filled in by default. Otherwise, the field will display a prompt: "Attach this task to any item or workspace." Click on that field, and begin typing the name of the workspace. Podio will present the matching workspaces you can click to select.

6. **(Optional) Change the task's privacy status from Private to Shared to make it visible to all members of the workspace.**

7. **Click the Create Task button.**

If you assign the task to someone other than yourself, that colleague receives a notification about the new task. The task also appears in that colleague's Task list. You will be notified whenever the task is interacted with: for example, when it's marked as complete.

Creating related tasks

Tasks in Podio are most commonly used in relation to app items. For example, you may relate a task to a lead in your Podio CRM app asking a member of your sales team to get in touch with that prospect.

Related tasks are shown in context to the work they are dedicated to and save time for users because they can clearly see, instantly, what this task is for.

1. **When looking at an app item (a record managed by a specific app), click the New Task button in the right sidebar, as shown in Figure 6-5.**

   In this example, we are using the sample Projects app, which is only one of many ways to structure work activities in Podio. The record we're viewing is for a marketing campaign with a project manager assigned, specified start and end dates app and associated documents. Two tasks are already associated with the project, and we can see that one has already been completed (checked off and crossed out). We can add any number of additional tasks required to get our work done.

New Task

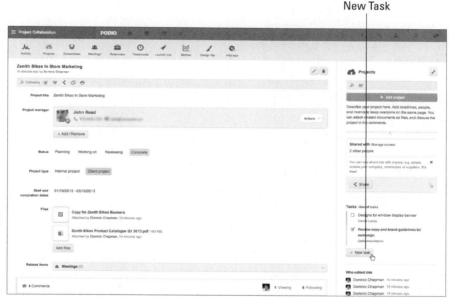

Figure 6-5:
Add a task to an app item here.

2. **Fill in the task details.**

   Fill in the name, description, and deadline, just as you would for a stand-alone task.

3. **Assign the task to whom you would like to do the work.**

   Those people will be notified. They will see that the task is referenced to an item and be able to click the reference to go to the full item. Figure 6-6 shows a task (a request to review copy) associated with an app item (in this case, a project planning record).

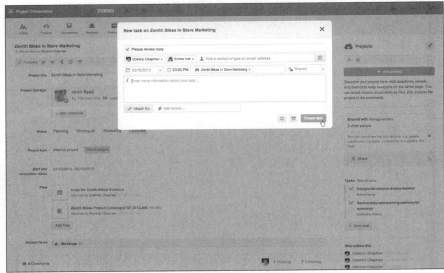

Figure 6-6:
A Podio task associated with an app item.

The task will appear in the right-hand sidebar when you look at the app item.

If the task is marked as private, it will be visible only to the person who created the task as well as the person(s) to whom the task is assigned.

Tasks that have been completed will show in the same right-hand sidebar of the app item, with a strikethrough effect on the text. Select the check box next to any task to mark it complete.

Managing Activities in IBM Connections

IBM Connections is delivered to customers as a social collaboration portal with a series of apps, with the Activities app presented on the same level as the wiki and blog modules.

When the Activities app is enabled, it functions as a sort of special purpose group for organizing lots of related tasks and supporting information. While IBM Connections also supports looser forms of collaboration organized around discussions and information sharing, the Activities app adds project-oriented structure. The outline view of an activity shown in Figure 6-7 includes tasks that can be checked off when complete as well as related documents.

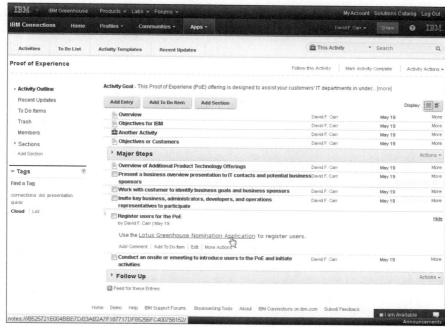

Figure 6-7:
The Activi-
ties app
in IBM
Connections.

The process for using the Activities app is pretty simple:

1. **From the Apps menu, choose Activities.**

2. **Click the Start an Activity button.**

3. **Outline your activity.**

   The elements you can add, each associated with a button at the top of
   the screen, are

   • *Add Entry:* Add content, including a title, content formatted in a
     rich text editor, and (optionally) file attachments.

   • *Add To Do Item:* Add a task, which optionally can include a dead-
     line, a priority rating, an assignment to a specific member of the
     collaboration network, and a rich text description.

   • *Add Section:* Add an organizational heading to the outline. Entries
     and To Do items assigned to that section will appear indented
     under that section headline.

4. **Save your work.**

Activities as social project coordination

Using the Activities app in IBM Connections isn't necessarily the kind of formal project management you may use to manage building a bridge or designing flight control software for a jet fighter. However, this app is something that IBM has found useful internally — and IBM, after all, is a multinational organization that plans some pretty big activities. One of the virtues of IBM Connections is that it originated as a collection of apps used to run a large, complex, global organization — IBM itself. For example, IBM personnel use IBM Connections Activities to organize all the major and minor planning, logistics, marketing, and public relations tasks associated with putting on its major user conferences.

Sure, the Activities app isn't the *only* way a large organization like IBM manages projects, but it's a convenient tool for lightweight management of related activities within the social collaboration environment.

Comparing Approaches to Social Task Management

Designers of social task management products and modules within larger social collaboration platforms typically stop short of calling what they do "project management," which is a term associated with formal, rigorous planning and management of teams. Instead, these designers put more emphasis on agility: that is, the ability to coordinate work activities flexibly and change plans on the fly.

And these "agile" techniques and tweaks have attracted attention from the makers of project management software as well as workflow and business process management software, which represent other ways of organizing work. Many of these products are sprouting social software extensions.

One of the reasons why social task management has attracted so much attention is that every software developer — and certainly every development team manager — has to juggle tasks and meet deadlines, inspiring many programmers to pursue their own visions of a better way to organize work.

Those visions of a better way to organize work often reflect the influence of *agile software development* methodologies, which emphasize organizing work into small increments and adjusting plans frequently to produce the best results. Social task management can be a supporting tool for bringing an agile approach to software development and other sorts of work.

The following sections cover some of the advantages and trade-offs to consider for the different approaches.

Building social features into project management tools

To integrate projects with social collaboration, should you start with the collaboration part or with the project part? If your organization has a need for formal project management, project management software that includes social features may make the most sense.

An example is AtTask, which Gartner Inc. classifies as one of the leading cloud-based project and portfolio management software solutions. A couple years ago, AtTask added a social module called TeamHome (`www.attask.com/stream`).

Ali Dekan, staff program analyst for a major electronics manufacturer, uses TeamHome to coordinate the activities of thousands of engineers around the world. Although social collaboration does not replace the more intense project planning that she does with the core application, it's very complementary, she says.

"It gives us a way to sell accountability to people who are busy doing other things," Dekan says. Project managers need to know what everyone is working on and the progress they have made, but everyone other than the project manager sees filling out progress report forms as tedious make-work. Thus, the need for periodic meetings where everyone around the table must give a status report. TeamHome can eliminate some of the tedium and a lot of those meetings by fitting into something more like the Facebook status-posting metaphor, where people post their activities and check out what everyone else on their team is working on.

Another project management tool to consider is Wrike (`www.wrike.com`), a cloud software startup that incorporates social collaboration concepts. Wrike can be used standalone but also integrates with social collaboration platforms, such as Jive and IBM Connections.

Adding tasks to a social platform as a social object type

The integrated approach in Podio, IBM Connections, and other social collaboration platforms is to make tasks an integral element of the platform.

This approach takes full advantage of the network of relationships between collaborators and presents users with a more consistent user interface for sharing and commenting on tasks.

One of the advantages of a social collaboration strategy built on SharePoint is that it inherits all the task management and project workspace capabilities that SharePoint has evolved over several generations of the platform.

The question I always have about independent applications that incorporate their own social features is how well they integrate with platforms that seek to provide a company-wide, social collaboration experience. You may decide that this isn't critical for some teams, if that one application — whether for project management or any other purpose — is the main application employees will interact with to get their work done and the main social collaboration they will require. Just understand that if the social experience of that application isn't linked to a global social profile and global feed, you may be giving up some opportunities for cross-functional social collaboration.

For the most consistent social task management, look for either an integrated capability from your social collaboration platform of choice or a third-party application that offers high-quality integration back to that platform.

Or, you may decide that social task management is your most important usage for social collaboration, so that a product like Asana, Do.com, or Sparqlight becomes your core platform instead of in addition to another social collaboration platform.

Coordinating activities through informal social sharing

Finally, you may decide all these approaches are overkill. Maybe the simplest way for your teams to coordinate their activities is through better communication through a social stream. This is the digital equivalent of project management by shouting across the room to someone in another cubicle. But, if you find that is the best way to get your work done — and the work is in fact getting done — there is nothing wrong with keeping things simple.

Chapter 7

Collaborating on Content

In This Chapter

▶ Sharing documents and files

▶ Writing and editing documents together

▶ Keeping content under control

*M*uch as social networks are associated with broadcasting status messages and blog posts, another sort of content is more important to true collaboration: namely, the content that people create together. Members of a collaboration network work in teams to create all sorts of group documents. Sometimes the document itself is the work product: for example, the draft of a new vacation leave policy that members of the human resources team may edit, update, and add to over a period of weeks or months before publishing it to the wider organization. Just as often, if not more so, collaborators work on planning documents or budgets that are part of some larger project or initiative.

Content collaboration takes many forms, but one convenient breakdown is to look at sharing files — typically, business documents, such as Microsoft Word, Excel, or PowerPoint files — as opposed to working with web-based documents.

The content collaboration features of social platforms range from simple to sophisticated — something I discuss in the context of product selection in Chapter 8. In this chapter, my focus is on how to use the common content collaboration features effectively. Also, because one of the side effects of making online content creation easier, I address how to avoid cluttering your social collaboration network with disorganized content.

Sharing Document Files

File management capabilities vary between social collaboration platforms, but as a rule, this is an area where the designers of these platforms tend to favor simplicity over sophistication. In other words, social sharing of a file attached to a status or blog post or posted to a group should be as easy as possible.

On a social collaboration platform, you can share a file in various ways.

> ✔ **Upload it to the activity stream or a group or workspace.**
>
> ✔ **Share a document that someone else has uploaded with your colleagues.**
>
> ✔ **Include a link to the document in a status post or comment.**

The point of file collaboration in a social environment is to take advantage of the social dimension through the ability to discuss or share files in the social stream in addition to collaborating on the files themselves. When a file is posted to an enterprise social network, it also carries with it links to the profiles of the document authors. That supports a core virtue of social collaboration: the ability to find content through people and people through content.

The interface for each social collaboration application is slightly different from the others, but they typically provide most of the document-sharing tools and features that I discuss in the following section.

Uploading and downloading

Sharing documents obviously starts with the ability to upload and download them, which is something every social collaboration environment supports, and often in more than one way. Here are a few common patterns for sharing document files:

> ✔ **Basic:** Click a button labeled something like Upload and use the browser's file choosing dialog box to select one or more files.
>
> ✔ **Drag and drop:** Drag one or more files from a folder on your computer onto the social collaboration user interface, and the upload starts as soon as you hit the correct drop region on the page.
>
> ✔ **Desktop file system integration:** With the addition of a desktop software component (such as the IBM Connections Desktop Plugin for Windows), users can right-click a file in any Windows folder and get a menu of commands that includes an option for sharing the file on Connections.
>
> ✔ **Desktop app integration:** Microsoft Office is the most common target for plug-ins that simplify the process of publishing documents to a collaboration platform directly from within the app. An example is Jive for Office. In this case, the integration is at the level of the application rather than the file system.

Following a successful upload, a link to the file will be displayed on the collaboration network with either the name of the file or a title provided by the user.

File synchronization apps and plug-ins can also automate the process of keeping the local desktop copy of a file in sync with the latest version in the collaboration environment.

Previewing in the browser

A handy alternative to downloading a file is the ability to preview it in the browser. Jive, IBM Connections, Yammer, and others provide built-in file viewers for this purpose. Figure 7-1 shows a document preview in Jive. This makes sense for anyone who wants to read the file but not necessarily edit it or save a copy to his computer. You may also want to preview a file first and then download it after you confirm that it contains the information you need. Or you may give feedback through the comments associated with the file, based on what you saw in the preview.

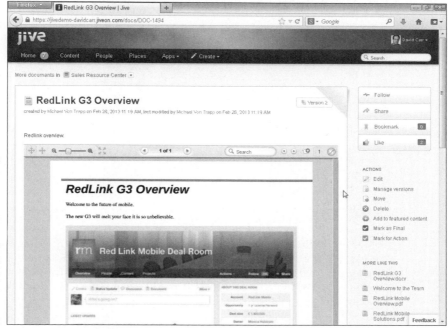

Figure 7-1:
A web-based preview lets you see the contents of a document without needing to download it.

A few browser-based apps go beyond previews to support web-based editing of files, a capability first seen in Google Docs (now part of Google Drive). IBM has a similar app, IBM Docs, which can be used with IBM Connections. Both allow editing Microsoft Office files in a browser-based editor.

Note that web-based editing is probably most appropriate for relatively simple documents, such as memos. For more heavily formatted documents, you'll incur some risk of the web-based editor failing to preserve the original formatting. Preview apps generally do a good job of approximating the formatting of the original file, and even if the preview is imperfect, at least the underlying file is unaltered.

Checking in and checking out

In general, *collaborating* on a document file means downloading it, using desktop software to edit it, and uploading a new version. Document management systems traditionally avoid confusion over who is editing a file with a *check-in/check-out* mechanism:

- ✔ **Check-out:** When a collaborator checks out a downloaded file, it is locked for editing, and only that person can upload a new version to check in as the new, official copy. An administrator can also remove the lock, if necessary (for example, if someone locks an important file right before going on vacation).

- ✔ **Check-in:** When a new version of a file is checked in, it becomes the official current copy, but older versions are preserved in case you need to go back to them.

One of the virtues of SharePoint-based solutions like NewsGator Social Sites is they inherit all the document management capabilities of the underlying platform.

Sharing documents as social objects

IBM Connections supports file check-in/check-out and other basic document management functions, but many social collaboration tools take a simpler approach, relying on coordination among collaborators through the feed. In other words, they handle documents like other social objects, such as links or images, that are shared in the activity stream or a group discussion. Someone who revises a document may simply upload a new version as an attachment to a status post describing the changes, and the newest version that shows up in the activity stream (or in a search) is presumed to be the most current version.

Sharing files through the activity stream leaves some room for confusion, as versions of files proliferate. Make sure you understand how sharing is managed on your social collaboration platform, as discussed in the following paragraphs.

Arguably, file sharing via a stream is still an improvement over sharing files via e-mail because the shared files are stored centrally in the collaboration tool, rather than being buried in e-mail inboxes. Ad hoc file sharing may also be simpler for users who find more advanced document management systems confusing or who would tend to subvert them anyway by uploading an independent instance of a file rather than checking it in properly to replace the old one. In addition, sometimes creative teams will create alternate versions of a file in parallel as competing drafts toward a final product, rather than working in the linear fashion implied by a respected check-in/check-out file management approach.

Some social collaboration platforms have evolved their own methods of tracking document versions. For example, Jive automatically creates a web-based document associated with every file uploaded. The web document includes a headline and a text body, just like any other post, and you can comment on it just like any other post. Revisions to that document are then tracked, so that the most recent is shown by default, but it's possible to go back to an earlier version as necessary. That includes revisions to the attached file. So one way to maintain order on the Jive platform is for collaborators to make sure they upload a new version of a file as a replacement for the one posted previously.

Supplementing built-in document management

Here are a few strategies I see organizations using when their document management needs go beyond what their chosen social collaboration platform of choice provides:

✔ Find a document management product that integrates with your social collaboration platform of choice.

✔ Manage important documents through a separate document management system but link to those resources through the social collaboration tool.

✔ Use the social platform for the early stages of brainstorming and collaboration, but post every document that graduates to a more official status to a separate document management system.

For example, professional services firm KPMG uses Tibbr for social collaboration processes including formulating proposals to potential clients, but the actual contracts it negotiates must be stored in a document management system with more rigorous controls. KPMG has a detailed content classification policy that governs what documents can be stored where.

What's published to the activity stream in this case is a notification that the document has been updated, plus any comments the author may have added about changes in the new version.

Writing and Editing Documents Together

Uploading and downloading files are, in some sense, unnatural acts for social collaboration, where the ideal would be to do everything — such as writing, revising, commenting, and editing — within a browser. In some cases, working with files offline makes perfect sense and may be the only option. No web-based editor truly matches the capabilities of an offline tool.

On the other hand, many basic business documents can be created on the web, for the web. If colleagues intend to publish a document on a social platform anyway, it makes sense for them to create it in an environment that eliminates the need for uploading and downloading, while simplifying the process of linking to other online resources. This is particularly true when a document has multiple authors and editors.

In this section, I tell you about the ways that you can collaborate on creating a document.

Collaborating on content, wiki-style

Wiki software allows any authorized user to create and edit articles in a web-based editor that simplifies the process of linking between documents. Most people are familiar with the web's masterpiece of collaborative writing and editing, Wikipedia, which is an encyclopedia produced by a worldwide team of volunteers, working under the supervision of editors employed by the Wikimedia Foundation. Many social collaboration platforms include wiki or wiki-like software although they may not use that terminology per se.

The base concepts for wiki software go back to 1994 when Ward Cunningham introduced his WikiWikiWeb, taking the name from the Wiki Wiki Shuttle he had run into at the Honolulu International Airport. (*Wiki* is the Hawaiian word for "quick.") Early wiki software simplified the coding of web pages, but it depended upon users entering the correct codes into a basic text editor. This remains true for some open-source products such as MediaWiki, the software that powers Wikipedia.

Most commercial wiki software now comes with a *rich text editor* — a web-based word processor for writing and formatting pages — although some of these still provide advanced users with the option of tweaking the underlying HTML or wiki formatting and linking codes. Figure 7-2 shows the wiki editor in IBM Connections, which is used to create and edit shared community content. An "About Us" article is shown here in a rich text editor, but tabs across the top of the editor allow you to switch to an HTML source view or a preview of the final result.

Figure 7-2: Wiki software allows any authorized user to edit web content.

To add a link, the user clicks a button and gets the option of choosing a resource on the social network to link to (such as another blog article or wiki entry) or an independent web address. Figure 7-3 shows the pop-up search screen in Jive that allows you to find and link to any other existing page or resource in the social collaboration environment.

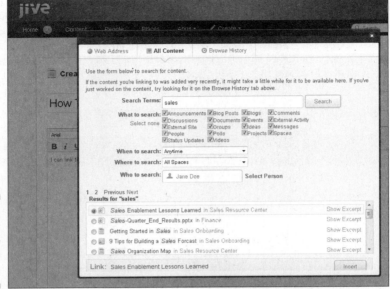

Figure 7-3:
Linking to
another
page within
Jive.

A wiki by any other name

Wikis are outgrowing their roots as tools that required coding skills, but the concept of collaborative web editing lives on.

Atlassian's Confluence is one social platform that still proudly calls itself a wiki, even as its developers continue to refine its rich text editor and round out its other social collaboration features. IBM Connections includes a wiki as one of the major apps that make up the platform. To maintain wiki-style structure, IBM Connections has users add pages as child pages or peer pages in a hierarchy with existing articles.

Meanwhile, Jive Software no longer uses wiki terminology, but Jive Documents with wiki-like collaborative editing features can be created by any user. Yammer provides Yammer Notes, a basic rich text editor that omits the option of letting users edit the underlying code.

The trend is for social collaboration platforms to provide essentially the same rich text editor for multiple types of content: blog and discussion forum entries as well as wiki-style articles.

When you edit a wiki article, the system retains all the previous revisions, making it possible to retrace exactly what was changed, when, and by whom. If a user inserts errors or deletes correct information, an editor with the right administrative privileges can revert the article to an earlier version (or lock it to restrict further edits). Figure 7-4 shows the version comparison utility from the IBM Connections wiki.

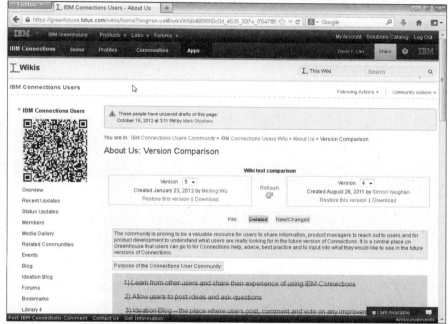

Figure 7-4:
Wiki version tracking makes it possible to track additions and deletions or restore an older version if necessary.

This is how wikis prevent their democratized vision of open content creation and editing from devolving into chaos. When users abuse their editing privileges by vandalizing a page (not uncommon with celebrity and political articles on Wikipedia), the editors can revert to an earlier version and restrict editing rights to a smaller group of trusted users.

On a corporate social network, the risk of this kind of mischief is minimal. For peace of mind, company leaders may be wise to restrict editing rights to official documents (think vacation or travel reimbursement policies posted on the collaboration network). However, employees are unlikely to make unauthorized changes, knowing that every edit will be tracked. Just as fears of employee misuse of the activity stream and discussion forums tend to be misplaced, the risk of intentional damage to wiki documents is small. Version tracking is more often a lifesaver in the case of unintentional errors, such as when an employee mistakenly deletes large blocks of important information, and you need to get it back.

For most routine work purposes, the ideal is to share editing rights broadly rather than narrowly and lock wiki documents against editing only in rare cases. The harm of denying users the access they need to fix an error or add information is almost always greater than the chance of something going wrong. Collaborative editing systems are often configured to notify the other authors whenever a document is updated, providing them with the opportunity to catch any errors that may have been introduced and correct them.

An alternate pattern — and one that can work even for documents locked against editing — is to provide a comment stream associated with the document and discuss changes or additions that may need to be made there. A designated editor can then implement the corrections, time permitting. Meanwhile, readers can scan the comments for additional information that may not be in the document itself.

Editing simultaneously, à la Google Docs

An alternate model for collaborative editing is Google Docs, the web-based office suite provided with every Google account along with Gmail and the Google+ social network. Now part of Google Drive, the suite includes a web-based word processor, spreadsheet, and presentation program. The Google Drive word processor in particular, with its feature of allowing multiple authors to work on a document simultaneously, has influenced the design of Yammer Notes and other products. IBM offers IBM Docs, an enterprise equivalent of Google Docs, as another element of its collaboration platform that can be used as a companion to IBM Connections.

The Google word processor is derived from Writely, a service Google acquired in 2006 along with its parent company, Upstartle. Google developed the spreadsheet and presentation modules itself.

Google Drive is a related file sharing utility. When you upload Microsoft Office file types (Word, Excel, and PowerPoint) into Google Drive, the service allows you to view or edit them in Google's equivalent office productivity tools.

Google doesn't claim complete functional parity with Microsoft Office documents or the ability to perfectly preserve their formatting. Microsoft has gone farther in the direction of creating feature complete web-based editors for Word and Excel. Users of SharePoint, Office 365, or Microsoft cloud services (such as SkyDrive) can use these web-based editors as an alternative to downloading and editing files.

As I mention earlier, IBM offers IBM Docs as its version of a web-based office suite that can be used with IBM Connections.

Because Google provides application programming interfaces for integration with Google Drive, other social applications can use it as an embeddable component for document management. Bitrix24, one of the upstart collaboration vendors trying to gain more attention for itself, recently added integration with Google editing tools as an alternative to its integration with Microsoft Office. Google itself has talked about developing Google+ into a cloud-based enterprise social network that would compete with the likes of Chatter and Yammer, with Google Drive as the file management and document collaboration components of the platform. Google+ accounts that are linked to Google Apps accounts for business can already share messages and documents with only the circle of users who have accounts on the same domain.

By default, Google Drive documents are private unless the author chooses to share either viewing or editing rights with a larger audience.

Web-based document editors have some characteristics in common with wikis. For example, they have the same goal of simplifying the creation and editing of web documents. However, they are more focused on replicating the capabilities of desktop office productivity tools than creating rich sets of interlinked documents.

One of the eye-catching features of the Google Docs editor is support for real-time collaborative editing. Instead of locking a document for editing, Google Docs allows multiple people to access it and make changes at the same time, each seeing their collaborator's changes appear as they are made, with a different-colored cursor showing where the other person is working. The collaborators can exchange text chat messages in a sidebar at the same time, or they may talk on the phone as they work together. The idea is to simulate the kind of collaboration on the draft of an article that may occur between two employees sitting side by side and taking turns at the keyboard.

Real-time collaborative editing is a tricky technical feat, requiring rapid exchange of asynchronous messages from a JavaScript app, relayed through the service to the other user's browser. This capability has since been duplicated in a number of other products, including IBM Docs and the Notes feature of Yammer.

Figure 7-5 shows simultaneous editing of a Yammer note, with the text entered by the remote user highlighted. (What you can't see in this black-and-white figure is that the text is highlighted in the same color as the collaborator's username on the right.)

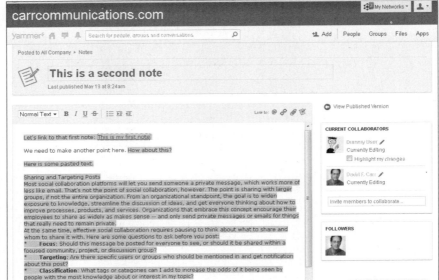

Figure 7-5:
Collabo-
rators can
simultane-
ously edit
a Yammer
Note.

Keeping Content under Control

The potential downside of making it easier for employees to upload files, create online documents, and share this content left and right is that you can wind up with a tangled web of information. If your social collaboration content is no better than the maze of file shares it was supposed to replace, and searching for the most current version of a document is as hard as ever, employees may well ask, "So what's the point?"

From a knowledge management perspective, the ideal situation would be for every document to be carefully classified according to a formal taxonomy and maybe reviewed by someone with a degree in library science prior to publication. The social collaboration approach is far more ad hoc, aiming to make it easier to create and share everyday work documents. However, here are some ways that social collaborators can keep content under control so that it's easy to find when colleagues need it:

- ✓ **Classify content when you post it.** Content creators are encouraged to do a bit of classification — if nothing more than a few informal tags — when they upload documents.

- ✓ **Provide clear titles and descriptions.** Give each document an unambiguous title so that the context is as clear as possible when it turns up on a list of search results. For example, something like *UBM-UK Vacation Schedule 2014* as opposed to *vsked2014*. The social collaboration platform may use the filename of an uploaded file as the default title, but most systems will allow you to change it to something more intelligible.

✔ **Comment for clarity.** The social comment stream associated with a document can help add more context.

✔ **Assign content curators.** Community managers, knowledge managers, and subject matter experts can play the role of curator, finding and highlighting the most valuable content on the collaboration network. For example, a community manager working with the human resources team can fine-tune the tagging and categorization of the vacation, expense reimbursement, and ethics policy documents, in addition to creating a page that links to the current version of each.

In other words, you can take some of the knowledge management discipline that you skip up front and add it on the back end.

Ideas for corralling content

When I placed a query on the Jive Community forum for users of that platform about combating content sprawl, I received an interesting response from Lexmark Enterprise Knowledge Architect Dennis Pearce. He suggests that the perception of disorder is really a side effect of moving from departmental and functional "silos" to a more open environment. "I think silos provide a kind of 'pseudo-organization' of content. It is still a mess at the enterprise level, but it's not noticeable to most employees because they have only a narrow, restricted view of all the content," he writes. "I try to remind our users that we are not making a new mess; we are making the existing mess visible; which is a good thing. The first step to cleaning up the mess and organizing is knowing that it needs to be cleaned up."

As UBM's Community Systems Manager Tracy Maurer explains, "The way that we have approached getting naming and tagging to be more consistent is:

✔ Having community managers that update tags and/or consult on content title procedures.

✔ Any time someone complains about not being able to find something, we educate them on both searching and tagging/titling steps.

✔ Also encouraging those who don't easily find things to add tags to content once they do find it.

✔ Holding training workshops specifically for people who will be regular content contributors (HR people, product managers).

Doesn't always work, but word gets around."

Part III

Exploring the Social Collaboration Software Market

Don't want employees collaborating in the cloud? See "Running Cloud-Free Social Software" at www.dummies.com/extras/socialcollaboration.

In this part . . .

- ✔ Find out how to choose a social collaboration platform.
- ✔ Explore the major social collaboration products.
- ✔ Consider the cloud — heavenly match or vaporous trap?
- ✔ Find tips on how to survive shifting standards.

Chapter 8

Beginning Your Search for a Social Collaboration Platform

*T*echnology alone will not make an online community successful or improve the quality of the collaboration between employees within a company. Success depends upon strong leadership and day-to-day management of the social community, combined with an accumulation of success stories that encourage more experimentation and more success. Making the right platform choice doesn't guarantee any of those things; however, the *wrong* platform choice will undercut the best leadership. For example, if the system that employees are encouraged to use proves unreliable or frustrating to use, it will fail to deliver on the leader's promise of a tool for improved productivity.

"Picking right" isn't as simple as choosing the market leader or the product with the strongest recommendations from a technology analysis firm (such as Gartner, Inc.). You're not just looking for the best product, but the best product for *your* organization. The right choice for a global consulting organization with thousands of employees probably wouldn't be the right choice for a 20-person ad agency that wants to build a simple workspace into which it can invite clients and contractors.

In this chapter, I outline the steps involved in choosing a social collaboration platform, help you evaluate the needs of your organization, give you an idea of what different types of vendors you'll encounter, and offer one last bit of advice on making this decision. In the next chapter, I give you more details about the merits of specific vendors. Some of the selection criteria that make the most difference to the CIO, to HR and talent management, or to the sales organization also are addressed in Chapters 16, 17, and 18.

Developing a Plan for Choosing a Social Collaboration System

It's easy to imagine a small business owner choosing a cloud-based, social collaboration product on the advice of a friend, creating accounts for himself and a dozen employees, and never looking back — or casually switching, a year later, to a product he likes better.

Larger enterprises would never select a collaboration system that casually, nor should they. When you offer social collaboration to hundreds or thousands of employees, you are asking them to adopt a new way of working and communicating with each other. You want to make a good choice and one you can stick with. Smaller firms, too, can benefit from picking right the first time.

Here are some guidelines for organizing the selection process.

✔ **Set a cut-off date for looking at new products.** If your selection process takes more than a few weeks, don't be surprised if some exciting new social software startup appears in the news or another vendor starts banging on your door, claiming to have the perfect solution to your needs.

And maybe it makes sense to stop everything and look at a new option. In general, I'd recommend that it makes more sense to keep to a disciplined schedule. Do the best review of the options on the market that you can, but set a cutoff date after which you will move on to the next stage — narrowing your list of choices, rather than adding to it.

✔ **Define must-have requirements.** Before making a product selection, be sure to not only identify your requirements but prioritize them. Which features can you simply not live without?

For example, if your organization makes heavy use of SharePoint for project management, document sharing, and other forms of collaboration, SharePoint integration is mandatory. In fact, the quality of the SharePoint integration offered by a particular social platform will likely be a deciding factor.

If your organization absolutely, positively will not consider doing business collaboration in the cloud, the ability to deploy the collaboration software into your own data center is a must-have requirement.

✔ **Outline nice-to-have features.** Many other social collaboration features may be attractive but optional.

For example, your organization may value a social platform that integrates with the company information systems for human resources and corporate training, automatically enriching employee social profiles with a digital org chart and data on an individual's professional certifications. Maybe having that would be nice, but not essential. A product that had that feature would enjoy a slight boost in your ranking of the products but not enough to overcome shortcomings in essential features.

✔ **Narrow the choices.** Even though the number of software and cloud providers who claim to hold the keys to productive social collaboration can seem a little overwhelming, you can probably eliminate some of them right away. (I give you lots of details on the various vendors and platforms in Chapter 9, so go to that chapter when you're ready to start crossing options off your list and investigate others further.) If yours is a small organization with simple needs, you can cross complex and expensive products off the list. Goodbye, IBM and Jive. If yours is a multinational corporation, you probably won't consider Podio as your company-wide social platform (although it may have a role to play as a productivity tool for smaller teams within the organization).

The process of elimination should leave you with a more manageable list of choices deserving a closer look.

✔ **Examine the candidates.** After compiling a list of vendors to contact, you want those vendors to provide analyst and reference customer contacts, preferably including references from organizations similar to your own.

✔ **Choose your pilot project or projects.** Large organizations typically venture into social collaboration with a pilot project before embracing it on a grand scale. Still, this project must be large enough and serious enough to both exercise the capabilities of the software and have a chance to show business results.

✔ **Make your choice and go for it.** Throughout this book, I present patterns for successful social collaboration, but none of that is any good if you don't get started.

Identifying Key Distinguishing Features

Beyond the base level of social collaboration features like content sharing and social networking, you may find your choice is ultimately driven by other distinguishing features that make one choice more useful than another. Here are some:

- **Mobile software:** Making social collaboration as available from a smartphone as it is from a PC.

- **Search:** Once you have made it easier for employees to create content and share knowledge, you want to make it easy to find again. Perhaps even more importantly, you want to make it easy for people to search for and find each other.

- **Document and content management:** If document management will be integral to your social collaboration platform, the strength of that feature may be decisive. Alternatively, the social platform's ability to integrate with other content management systems can be the critical feature.

- **Innovation management:** Whether as a built-in feature, an add-on module, or a specialized product that can be integrated, software to organize ideas for new products or business improvements may be an important part of your social collaboration strategy.

I explore each of these in more detail in the following sections.

Mobilizing for results

Workers have been checking e-mail on their phones for many years now, but the latest smartphones and tablets allow them to do much more. Social networks like Facebook and Twitter now see more activity coming from smartphones than PCs.

Social collaboration for business is moving in the same direction, but probably more slowly than many employees would like. To be fair, collaboration software must address challenges like enterprise security and interaction with business documents that Facebook doesn't have to worry about in the same way. Creating mobile apps that meet those requirements while still satisfying ease-of-use expectations set by consumer products is a challenging software development and user experience design problem.

Mobile access is important enough that it ought to be a major selection criterion. Arguably, it should also be included from the beginning in your implementation of social collaboration — if not for everyone, at least as part of a substantial pilot project.

For buyers, key criteria include

- Availability of apps for the iPhone, iPad, Android, and Windows mobile platforms.
- Quality of mobile web support: that is, the capability of the app to function in the browser on a phone or tablet.
- Range of collaboration features available through the mobile app. Is it limited to viewing and posting to the application stream? Does it provide access to all the features? Does it simplify access to the most commonly used functions?
- Intelligent use of the mobile mode of application access: for example, by taking advantage of GPS tagging of social posts so a salesperson doesn't need to type the name or address of a business he's is calling on, just update his visit with that customer or sales prospect.
- Offline capabilities, such as synchronization of shared files that can be viewed or edited on the mobile device.

Many companies I have spoken to begin by implementing social collaboration as a web application first and then add mobile access later. But there is a good argument for making mobile access from the beginning.

Searching for the best social search engine

One important purpose of social collaboration is to make it easier for employees to connect with the people, knowledge, and content they need to get their jobs done.

The applicability of this section varies between social collaboration products, depending on whether they include document and content management features or only lightweight social streaming. Some lightweight products still try to address the search requirement using federated search techniques in which a search query is sent to multiple databases and content repositories, and the results are aggregated. People-search capabilities also vary from simple name-based search to more sophisticated search by areas of expertise.

The challenges of social search

Workers are often disappointed that the search engine experience on the company intranet falls short of what Google and Bing have trained them to expect. This is often true even when the enterprise has implemented a product (such as the Google Search Appliance) for indexing internal company content. Public search engines take advantage of an extreme mass market of user behavior, determining relevance according to links from blog posts and the aggregate behavior of users clicking some search results more often than others for a given query. Internal enterprise search engines rely more on indexing the text of the documents themselves. However, links, likes, comments, and other social collaboration activity that points to a document can provide additional context to highlight documents that are frequently referenced for useful information. Search keywords not present in a document may appear in a comment about that document, providing an alternate way to find it.

Another important dimension of social search is that it provides access to knowledge that may not be codified in any document, existing only in someone's head. Or maybe the knowledge is documented but not categorized in any way you would ever think of looking for it. Find the right person, and you've found your answer.

Finding specialists throughout the organization

In any organization, the ability to find people with specific knowledge, expertise, or experience depends on a few things:

- The quality of the search engine
- The availability of structured, standardized information about each employee in a social profile
- The volume of social posts and documents linked back to the employee profile containing relevant clues

    Find the content, and the employee's social profile is just a click away.

Some social platforms will seek the right person to answer a question on your behalf when you can't think of whom to ask. For example, if you post a question to NewsGator Social Sites and classify it with standard tags, the platform will send an alert to everyone who listed that subject as a subject in which they have expertise.

Finding information in content

The more traditional online search is a search for content, which in social collaboration can mean status posts, comments, documents, and discussions.

If possible, try to get a peek at the search experience of an instance of the software that has been running for years and talk to longtime users about how satisfied employees are (or are not) with the search experience. Find out whether they can search by content type and limit a search by date.

On a busy corporate social network, a search for a frequently discussed topic — say, "expense reimbursement policy" — can easily bring back hundreds of hits other than the official policy document you may be looking for. A good search experience would allow you to narrow your search by content type: for example, only documents about the policy, not status posts and discussions complaining about it.

Limiting a search by date can also be a good tactic for finding current information: say, this year's expense reimbursement policy, not the one from four years ago.

Lacking human common sense, a search engine may conclude that the old document is more relevant than the new one because of the links to it and discussion about it, which the new version hasn't had time to accumulate.

This is the sort of long-term concern about search quality that's difficult to assess based on a pilot project or limited-time trial of a social collaboration platform, but you can find out a lot by talking to others who use the product.

Discovering people and content through predictive recommendations

Social collaboration platforms incorporating predictive technology never stop searching for people you should connect with and content you should view. In general, predictive technologies work on your behalf without you explicitly asking for their help. By analyzing your social network and information you disclose about yourself (such as the professional interests listed on your profile), in combination with observations about the content you view and interact with, the platform tries to identify patterns. It then tries to match those patterns with everything it has to offer, from, "If you like Jim, you'll like Jane" or "Because you've been studying the second-quarter sales figures, you may want to view the new third-quarter stats."

Like search, predictive analysis thrives on very large volumes of data that can be subjected to statistical analysis — meaning, it's not necessarily as effective in a social intranet with a limited employee population.

However, even if predictive analytics is counted as a frontier bleeding-edge capability for social collaboration, meaning that it may not always be accurate, the suggestions it makes to employees can be counted as a positive if they even occasionally lead to productive new working relationships or spark ideas that lead to new products.

Also, because friend recommendations have become so common on consumer social sites, a product for business that matches that capability may do a better job of meeting employee expectations for social software.

Managing content beyond the status post

A key decision in the selection of a social collaboration platform is whether you will use it as a primary enterprise document management and content management platform. The alternative is to limit social collaboration to managing social content, such as status posts and discussion threads. If you have an established, document management system, selecting a social platform that also emphasizes document management could be redundant. At a minimum, it would require you to give users clear guidelines about what to post where, under what circumstances.

In general, social collaboration tends to emphasize simplicity over sophistication. Requiring users to fill out a form with a description of the document and a dozen check boxes to precisely categorize it may be the ideal for knowledge management — but if the user interface is a hassle, users tend to fall back on the relative simplicity of sending e-mail attachments.

You want to make it as easy as possible to post a file with a short note, and let the software do as much of the work as possible of suggesting tags and categories, while generating a description and document preview. More elaborate document management can be reserved for processes where it is critical, such as tracking contract revisions.

Most, if not all, social collaboration platforms let you post a note with a file attachment, but not all platforms include more sophisticated file management capabilities such as version tracking. Similarly, some platforms support wikis or other tools for creating and editing web-based documents, while in other cases the vendors decide that's not essential.

Jive and IBM Connections are relatively full featured by this measure, while Yammer, Chatter, and tibbr are lightweights. But a lightweight product may be just what you need if you already have satisfactory document and content management systems.

Social collaboration platforms can coexist with established, document management systems. For example, you can use IBM Connections in combination with the IBM FileNet enterprise content management platform. That is helpful for existing FileNet customers, but to make the platform more useful to other customers, IBM has been enhancing Connections to add more file management functions on a stand-alone basis. Jive offers basic file management as part of its platform but has also partnered with Box, a cloud-based file sharing service with strengths such as the ability to synchronize files between PCs and mobile devices.

Meanwhile, social software that integrates with Microsoft SharePoint, including NewsGator Social Sites and Microsoft's own Yammer, can take advantage of SharePoint file and document management facilities.

A great way to narrow the field of potential choices for a social collaboration platform is to decide on content management strategy first.

File sharing and the cloud

Social collaboration products overlap somewhat with the new generation of cloud-based products for file sharing and multidevice synchronization, such as Box, Dropbox, Google Drive, and Microsoft SkyDrive.

For example, Box has won the business of major enterprises such as Procter & Gamble as a means of secure file sharing both inside and outside the firewall that is accessible to employees from home or on the road, as well as external collaborators such as creative professionals at ad agencies.

On a standalone basis, Box provides social-style commenting on files, which may be all the social collaboration functionality some organizations care about. On the other hand, Box offers an integration with Jive to make its service function as an extension to the enterprise social network. Most social collaboration platforms offer the option of integration with one or several of these cloud file collaboration products.

The explosion of interest in cloud-based file sharing products from their singular focus on doing one thing well — or at least a small number of related file management tasks — through a streamlined user interface.

Motivating behavior with gamification

Gamification refers to a set of user interface elements interaction styles, derived from computer games, intended to motivate and reward behaviors. Gamification is as much about behavioral science as it is about games, but the idea is to take advantage of some of the same dynamics that make computer games so engaging and addictive. For example, computer games do a good job of on-boarding users (orienting them to how the game works), gradually introducing them to more complicated challenges, motivating them to improve their skills, keeping score, and recognizing levels of achievement. Similar techniques can be applied to on-boarding employees into the company or training employees to use a complicated piece of software by introducing the simplest elements first and progressing to the more complicated features.

Gamification techniques are being incorporated into social software platforms as a means of on-boarding new users and also as a way of recognizing the most active participants. Gamification can also be applied to motivating specific business outcomes, such as increased sales.

A few of the common elements of gamification include:

- **Keeping score:** Users are awarded points for desirable behaviors.
- **Badges:** Icons associated with a user profile that recognize specific desirable behaviors, such as creating a group or closing a $100,000-plus sale.
- **Leaderboards:** A ranked list of the individuals with the highest scores.
- **Guided missions:** Users are guided through a series of activities and they get points for performing well. This can be useful for training activities, where concepts are best learned in a specific order.

Gamification is an increasingly common feature of all sorts of software, including social collaboration platforms, but it has also given rise to independent cloud services from specialists like Bunchball and Badgeville. Through their application programming interfaces and user interface widgets, they add gamification features to all sorts of web applications, including social collaboration. Because gamification services can be integrated with social collaboration and also other applications, they have the potential to track and reward a broader variety of work behaviors.

These gamification services also become more powerful when they are integrated into social collaboration, adding the power of peer recognition. As users earn badges or advance in rank on a leaderboard, their achievements can be recognized in the social activity stream and on their profiles. For example, in addition to recognitions for social collaboration activities, their profiles may display badges for sales wins or excellent customer service.

Gamification is another factor to consider in the product selection process, both in terms of the quality of the gamification features built in to a social collaboration platform and that platform's ability to integrate with external gamification services.

Supporting innovation and ideation

When CEOs and other executive leaders embrace social collaboration, it's often because they hope to make their organizations more innovative. By connecting people across the organization, they hope to spark ideas for new products or process improvements.

There are a few social software features that can occur either in social collaboration platforms or in complementary products that may influence your product choice.

One is to organize idea generation, or ideation, campaigns challenging employees to help solve specific problems within a specific timeframe. You start by gathering as many ideas as possible. Then voting and rating systems make it easier to whittle a long list of ideas down to a manageable number. Overall, this can be a very effective way of focusing on the goal of innovation.

Since good ideas do not always arrive on a schedule, you also can use your collaboration network as a suggestion box where ideas are welcome at any time. Employees can post their ideas to the company-wide stream or share them within the most relevant group for that idea.

The Jive platform provides an ideation module that can be enabled to create a separate "ideas" content type. Figure 8-1 shows the Jive ideas module at work. Instead of creating a blog post, or starting a discussion, you can classify your post as an idea. This adds just a little more structure. For starters, an idea is displayed in the activity stream with a light bulb icon next to it. Others can comment on your idea, as they would with any other sort of post, but they can also vote it up or down. This makes it easy to see which ideas have received the most votes. Ideas also can be marked "under review" or recognized as graduating into an active project for implementation.

I've most often seen this used for suggesting routine software or process improvements, rather than breakthrough innovations.

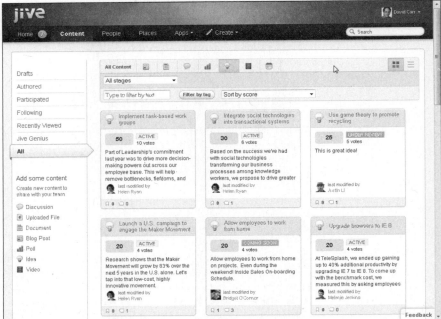

Figure 8-1:
Jive ideas
module.

Choosing Software to Organize Ideas

Successful online innovation initiatives often revolve around a specific challenge to the community, with responses to be submitted by a definite deadline. This helps create a sense of urgency.

Often, the more successful users of open, social innovation employ an innovation management application that adds structure to the process rather than relying on the discussion features of a social platform alone.

Some of the best-known innovation management software and cloud services providers include Spigit, BrightIdea, and HYPE Innovation. These are social software products by nature, in the sense of inviting contributions, comments, and voting from a broad community of people. The leaders I've mentioned also offer some level of integration into popular social collaboration platforms. For example, Spigit plugs in to Jive as an app so users will not need to sign in with a separate password, and content from ideation sessions also is integrated with Jive search.

IBM has built a whole consulting practice around hosting "innovation jam" events, and it offers an Ideation Blog component as part of its IBM Connections enterprise social network, shown in Figure 8-2. You can see that idea submissions are formatted roughly like posts in a blog but with the number of votes each has received displayed next to it. Entries can be sorted chronologically, or by the number of votes or number of comments they have received.

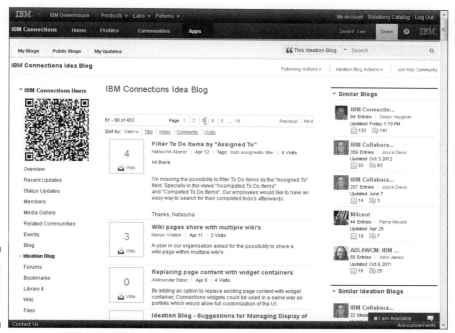

Figure 8-2: An Ideation Blog in IBM Connections.

NewsGator also has an optional ideation module for its social software, which runs on top of SharePoint. NewsGator ideation is shown in Figure 8-3. It lets you organize idea-gathering campaigns around specific corporate needs, inviting employees to submit ideas and vote on each other's proposals. The system identifies the most popular ideas and calls out the most commonly occurring tags used to classify the ideas, which hint at recurring themes.

Figure 8-3:
A
NewsGator
ideation
campaign
invites
employees
to submit
and vote on
ideas.

Understanding the Different Types of Vendors and Products

After you identify your organization's needs, the next step is to make basic choices about what sort of software you want and whom you will trust to deliver it. For many other organizations, this entails striking a balance that meets necessary requirements for sophistication without encompassing unnecessary complexity.

The following discussion about the types of vendors and products available can help you make those choices. If you aren't familiar with many vendors, don't worry; I cover a few dozen vendors in Chapter 9.

Comparing established system vendors versus startups

One good starting point is to compare the advantages of major enterprise systems vendors — including IBM, Oracle, and Microsoft — against the dozens of social software startups that would like to win your business.

Here are some key differences between startups and enterprise systems vendors:

- **Startups:** Can be great sources of innovation, competing aggressively with other startups who all want to prove they have a unique approach to reinventing the workplace.

- **Enterprise systems vendors:** Take more of a plodding approach to refining their products, but they address a much longer list of requirements including compatibility and integration with other elements of their product lines.

Here are some reasons for choosing a systems vendor over a startup:

- **Corporate stability:** A major systems vendor is less likely to go bankrupt or to be acquired.

- **Depth of consulting and support services:** You know you will be able to get the help you need (at a price, anyway).

- **Compatibility with related products and technologies:** If you already have chosen a systems vendor to provide other technologies, that vendor may also offer a compatible and easily integrated social collaboration product. For example, if your organization has an existing intranet and web applications based on IBM WebSphere, IBM Connections would be a natural choice for adding social networking.

- **Experience creating platform-level products:** Deep knowledge of operating systems, databases, and middleware ought to translate into better platform architecture, meaning more reliability and flexibility in the long run.

- **Understanding of large enterprise requirements:** Vendors with years of experience serving global corporations and government agencies tend to do a better job of anticipating and meeting requirements for the scalability, security, compliance, and integration requirements of large organizations.

Now for the flip side. Here are some reasons for choosing a startup over a systems vendor:

- **Agile, rapid product development:** Software improvements are unimpeded by bureaucracy or a large installed base of legacy technologies.

- **Independence:** A vendor less tied to one particular *technology stack* (such as a family of products from Microsoft or Oracle) may be better able to deliver a solution that works in diverse environments. This flexibility is important for enterprises that have grown through acquisition or that acquired technologies in a decentralized fashion.

- ✔ **Leapfrog innovation:** A startup may be quicker to match and sometimes improve upon innovative features that appear in other social collaboration products or in public social networks.

- ✔ **Less bound by convention:** A startup can be more likely to come up with an approach that is radically different — and maybe better.

- ✔ **Personal connection:** Smaller organizations may be more willing to listen to your suggestions about changes and improvements to the software.

- ✔ **Simplicity and convenience:** Most new social software products come to market as cloud applications, delivered over the web on the basis of a monthly or annual subscription.

- ✔ **Price:** Startups often charge less although you have to be careful about judging the total cost of any solution (including indirect costs like training and integration) versus value to the business.

Seeking simplicity

"Simple" is generally a good word in the software world, and one of the selling points for social collaboration is ease of use and the simplification of common business tasks. Small businesses in particular tend to value simple and affordable software rather than complete but overwhelming enterprise software packages. Big businesses would like to keep things simple, too, where practical.

Here are some of the desirable dimensions of simplicity for social software:

- ✔ **Ease of use:** Some businesses may require a social collaboration product that is so simple and familiar that people can start using it with little or no training.

- ✔ **Ease of navigation:** Your goal is a friendly UI with features you want without being cluttered with a lot of buttons and menus you will never touch.

- ✔ **Extendibility:** You also likely want apps, plug-ins, or other add-ons that let you add new features as needed.

- ✔ **Built-in support:** You might want the software as a cloud service, thus requiring little or no support from IT.

- ✔ **Compatibility:** And you probably require that the software co-exist with the productivity tools your employees already use, such as Microsoft Office or Google Apps.

The trick is figuring out where to draw the line between simple and overly simplistic solutions. A simple solution may meet your requirements at first but fall apart as more complex social collaboration scenarios and business requirements emerge.

Going lightweight

A related but not identical decision is whether to prefer a lightweight tool over a comprehensive platform. In software, *lightweight* means streamlined, elegant, and just perfect for one specific purpose. Think in terms of a light-weight backpack for long-distance hiking, which may be very sophisticated in terms of its materials and construction but is still easier to lug around than an old Army backpack.

A strategy of choosing lightweight products for your digital workplace may mean picking a social cloud service that is tightly focused on providing an activity stream for collaborators. Just as the champion backpacker may choose the best equipment from several manufacturers, one championship strategy for social collaboration may be to augment that social stream with other lightweight products for other modes of collaboration such as file shar-ing and video chat.

Lightweight social collaboration products encourage this approach with apps for integration, as in the Box file sharing app for tibbr shown in Figure 8-4.

Figure 8-4: Tibbr provides a social col-laboration layer that can wrap around other web-based tools, such as file sharing utilities.

In addition to accessing Box through this embedded app screen, tibbr cre-ates activity stream stories for shared files pulled from Box and the com-ments about them, as shown in Figure 8-5.

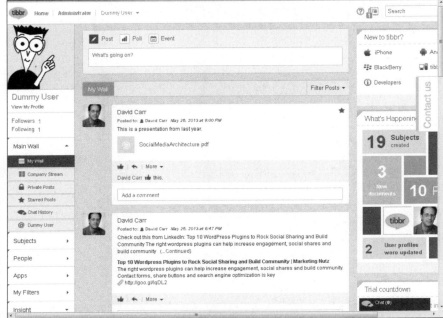

Figure 8-5:
A shared file managed by an embedded app appears in the tibbr activity stream.

A lightweight social collaboration strategy also may make sense for an enterprise with established solutions for other modes of collaboration, which the organization wants to supplement rather than replace.

For example, the statistical analysis software company SAS Institute uses Jive for public customer support communities but picked the more lightweight stream-centric Socialcast for internal use. By the time SAS adopted social collaboration, it already had established internal blogs, wikis, and content management systems, so those aspects of Jive would have been redundant for the social intranet.

Insisting on sophistication

Large enterprises tend to have a longer list of requirements for social collaboration. Of course, some smaller businesses also have sophisticated business models or operate in regulated environments. And by "sophisticated social collaboration features," I mean

- Iron-clad security
- Traditional on-premises software, at least as an option
- Contractual service level agreement guarantees of reliability, performance, and security for cloud or hosted options

✔ Compliance-related features, such as archiving of social streams for legal discovery or review by regulators (or integration with compliance platform products)

✔ Integration with other enterprise software products such as enterprise content management, workflow, web portal, Customer Relationship Management (CRM), and Enterprise Resource Planning (ERP) systems

✔ Ability to add custom software extensions to the platform and change the UI

✔ Support for enterprise standards for integration, security, and authentication

✔ Functionality as a platform on top of which developers can build social apps

When you insist on sophistication, social collaboration becomes more complicated and expensive. However, complex businesses often have no choice. Either they use a sophisticated platform, or they won't be able to engage in this form of collaboration at all.

When you need it all

The comprehensive social software strategy is to include many major modes of collaboration available through one platform, maximizing the opportunities for them all to be used together. For example, the activity stream in Jive or IBM Connections includes updates and comments from the integrated blog, wiki, and discussion tools as well as simple status posts.

Those tools also present a very similar rich *text editor* (a visual word processor for writing and formatting web content) for creating a blog post, web document, or discussion group post. That's a simpler environment for training or self-service learning than one where the social post, blogging, discussion, and wiki tools all have different user experiences.

A single social platform also makes it easier to present a user profile linked to all the user's content, while also providing a navigation path from the content to the user's profile.

Weighing Trade-Offs

In the end, every business software product selection comes down to trade-offs: lowest price versus premium features, simple versus complex, lightweight versus comprehensive; perfect versus good enough.

Getting started trumps perfection

Product and platform choice is only part of social collaboration success — and not necessarily the most important one. Or, it may be more correct to say that technology is a limiting factor. If you choose a platform that's a poor fit for your current requirements or that can't easily be adapted to fit new requirements as they emerge, that choice could doom your social collaboration initiative or force you to start over on a new platform.

Don't get mired in the mindset that that there is only one right choice for your organization. Maybe several could be a good fit.

And you may want to dodge the potential battle of finding a single standard that works for the entire company. Perhaps different social tools work better in different parts of the company. Ideally, your organization would provide some guidance at the corporate level on when each tool is appropriate and perhaps investigate technical strategies for integration between them.

The best way to succeed at social collaboration is by collaborating and learning from experience what strategies work best for connecting employees and engaging them in the work the organization needs to get done. So, job one is to get started, rather than getting caught up in the evaluation process as a theoretical exercise. If you aren't confident that your initial choice will be a lasting one, run a pilot project where employees use it for some practical purpose and report back on what did and did not work. (I tell you more about pilot programs in Chapter 9.)

Trusting future features

Every social software product is a moving target. Hockey great Wayne Gretzky has been quoted saying the secret of the game is to skate not to where the puck is but to where it is going to be. Choosing a social software product means making some predictions: for example, whether your chosen vendor will keep up with the competition, leap ahead, fall behind, get acquired, or go out of business.

When mapping specific product features, often you must judge whether the "road map" of features to be delivered in future versions is reliable. Should you make your decisions based solely on what a product can deliver today? Or should you be willing to overlook a few gaps in the current feature set if the road map shows those issues being addressed? Is there reason to believe the forthcoming, promised features will actually leapfrog the comparable existing features in shipping products?

These decisions are as much about judging the character of a company and the strengths of its leaders as they are about assessing technology. For established technology companies, it should be possible to look at the vendor's track record of following through on promises and doing so on a predictable schedule, versus running behind schedule or changing course mid-stream.

One example, discussed at length in Chapter 9, is judging how Microsoft's acquisition of Yammer will change the roadmap for other collaboration products, such as SharePoint.

For another, consider the changing relationships between Jive and its integration partners. In 2011, Jive introduced a sort of app store built in to its platform (the Jive Apps Market) with the intent of building an ecosystem of apps (mostly cloud-based). Part of the rationale was to let partners offer a range of choices for different business applications that customers could plug in to the social platform. At the same time, Jive is continually reevaluating what features need to be part of its base platform and what add-on features it needs to offer itself. For example, the Wrike social task management product became one of the first apps partners, taking advantage of Jive's relatively weak support for task management. Then Jive bought a social task management product called Producteev, which it plans to incorporate in its core product and as an add-on module.

The exact shape and quality of the result remains to be seen. At this writing, the only definite thing Jive has announced is a free version of Producteev being introduced more as a sales lead–generation tool for the vendor than as the final product for large enterprises. As a prospective Jive customer who saw social task management as an important application, you would have to make some judgments, asking yourself:

- Should I wait and see what Jive delivers before making a platform decision? Is this a critical feature or a "nice to have" in my selection criteria?

- How well do the task management features provided by Jive through partners or promised on its road map stack up against what's already being delivered in IBM Connections, with its Activities feature?

- Do I like the features in an add-on app like Wrike better than what Jive is promising? Is Wrike the more complete tool for managing projects instead of just tasks? And is that what I really need?

- Will the business and technical partnership between Jive and Wrike remain healthy enough so that I can bet on the combination of the two?

As Yogi Berra said, "Prediction is very hard, especially about the future." The real prediction you have to make is which social collaboration platform maximizes the chances of future success for your firm.

Chapter 9

Charting the Products and Vendors

*N*ow it's time to consider some leading social collaboration products and platforms.

The nature of book publishing means that this overview captures only a snapshot of a rapidly changing market. I do my best to provide updates on the *For Dummies* website. Of course, I also encourage you to keep tabs of the coverage on *InformationWeek Social Business* as well as other news and analyst reports.

This is the chapter where I help you sort out the crowded social collaboration vendor market and narrow your choices to a short list. I also tell you how you can try some programs for free, start a pilot program, and evaluate some of the major players. Because so many companies use SharePoint, I tell you how you can incorporate it (or not) into your social collaboration plan.

Examining Selected Social Collaboration Vendors

This section includes all the products listed in Gartner, Inc.'s 2012 Magic Quadrant review of "Social Software in the Workplace" plus a few additions Gartner didn't consider or excluded for not meeting its criteria.

Because it is consistently ranked as a leader in this space by Gartner, Jive sponsors free access to the full report through its website, www.jive software.com.

Gartner categorizes vendors with this terminology:

- ✓ **Leaders:** Rank high on both "completeness of vision" and "ability to execute"
- ✓ **Challengers:** Have the ability but are judged less complete
- ✓ **Visionaries:** Have the vision but lack some other strengths
- ✓ **Niche players:** Aren't as complete or as strong

To keep these rankings in context, consider that a so-called *niche player* that addresses a need important to your organization could be a more appropriate choice than an enterprise product from IBM or Jive that would be overkill for your needs. On the other hand, those vendors would argue that the cloud versions of their products provide room to grow for a small but fast-growing company.

I used Gartner's categorization to pick the leaders listed below, but the same firms also rank high in the analysis of other market research firms.

Reviewing the leaders

Vendors will come and go, and some will merge, and product names will change, but I feel confident saying that Jive, IBM, Microsoft (with SharePoint and Yammer), and Salesforce.com will still be among the market share leaders in social collaboration.

The question is which of them, if any, is the right choice for your organization.

The first three I will discuss are available as on-premises software as well as cloud or hosted solutions.

- ✓ **IBM Connections:** This is one of the most comprehensive social collaboration platforms, including activity stream, discussion group, task management, wiki, and file management modules. Connections can support both public and private social communities. Connections is a comprehensive product that also integrates with other IBM portal, collaboration, and content management products.

  Consider this solution if the credibility, support, and consulting services offered by IBM help make the sale to management. Connections also makes sense if you want a comprehensive collaboration platform, rather than one focused on the activity stream alone.

- ✓ **Jive:** Jive Software's social collaboration solution is rivaled only by IBM as a comprehensive social collaboration platform used by large enterprises, including tools for discussion, blogging, file sharing, and wiki-like web content management. Like Connections, it can be configured to support either public or private social websites. Jive gained additional credibility and financing with a December 2011 IPO.

Jive may be the right solution for your organization if you want a comprehensive social platform used by major enterprises. The cloud edition makes Jive more accessible for smaller businesses and teams within larger firms.

✔ **SharePoint:** Because Microsoft provides this product, it's ubiquitous in large companies, and SharePoint 2013 made it into a more complete social collaboration platform. Microsoft's 2012 purchase of Yammer opens new possibilities, particularly for users of the Office 365 cloud edition of SharePoint. SharePoint is often paired with social software add-ons like NewsGator.

This may be a good choice for your organization if SharePoint already is being used effectively for internal collaboration, particularly if your organization is also a "Microsoft shop" for other collaboration tools, such as Lync unified communication.

These leading social collaboration platforms are available in the cloud only:

✔ **Salesforce.com products:** Salesforce.com offers multiple social products, including Chatter, Work.com, and Do.com.

 • *Chatter:* Chatter can be used independently as a stream-centric social collaboration platform, but it's best known and most used as a companion to the Salesforce.com cloud software for sales, marketing, and customer support. Major enterprises often employ Chatter with their sales teams even if they use other social collaboration products for other functions. A basic version of Chatter is included for free with Salesforce.com CRM.

Two other significant products are

 • *Work.com:* Used for social employee recognition and continuous performance reviews. Can be used in combination with Chatter.

 • *Do.com:* Used for social task management.

Consider these options if you use other Salesforce.com products, particularly if your key social collaboration scenarios revolve around sales, marketing, and customer support.

✔ **Yammer:** Microsoft's Yammer came to market as "Facebook for business" yet it is also an increasingly credible enterprise collaboration platform for businesses large and small. In addition to a Facebook-like central newsfeed, Yammer supports collaboration groups, including the capability to include external participants. Yammer doesn't include blog or wiki modules per se, but its rich microblogging tool and the notes module in Yammer groups can be used for similar purposes. Synergies with Microsoft SharePoint and Office are emerging and should become a stronger selling point over time.

Yammer may work best for your organization if you want a familiar Facebook-like social environment for collaboration. The free version of Yammer includes all its major features, with the exception of enterprise account administration tools. Meanwhile, Microsoft is pricing aggressively for Yammer Enterprise and Yammer in combination with other cloud software like Office 365.

Let me emphasize again that I'm not saying these should be the choices at the top of your list, only that they are big, credible players. Read on for more options.

Collaborating in the cloud

Like Yammer and Chatter, many social collaboration products are offered exclusively in the cloud. I discuss the advantages and tradeoffs of cloud-based collaboration software in Chapter 10.

✔ **Box:** Box primarily focuses on cloud-based file sharing for business but does provide social commenting as well as integration with Jive.

Consider Box if file sharing with mobile workers or external partners is your main concern. I don't think of Box as a complete social platform, but it is a serious file and document collaboration player with enterprise appeal.

✔ **Google Apps and Google+:** Google has all the elements for social collaboration, both inside and outside an organization, but the barrier between the two is more permeable than with other solutions. Google+ Circles make it possible to share only with a specific group of people, and Google Apps account holders can limit the sharing of a post to only members of their e-mail domain.

Consider Google if your organization is going all-in with Google services.

✔ **Huddle:** Huddle is a software as a service (SaaS) product that falls somewhere between Box and Yammer, emphasizing internal and external file collaboration but more complete as a social collaboration platform than Box.

If file collaboration with employees and external partners is important to your strategy, along with social discussion, consider Huddle.

✔ **Igloo:** Igloo Software markets its product as "a modern intranet," including activity streams, commenting, and private blogs, as well as file sharing.

Consider Igloo if you want a simple, streamlined cloud collaboration solution.

✔ **Moxie Collaboration Spaces:** Collaboration Spaces is part of the Spaces by Moxie Suite focused on web customer service (chat, knowledgebase, and self-service), where internal collaboration is positioned as a tool for delivering better and faster answers to customers.

If your most important collaboration scenarios revolve around customer service and support, this may be a good application for you.

✔ **Podio:** Citrix bought Podio in 2012, adding the innovative cloud startup to the family of products that includes GoToMeeting. Podio combines social software concepts with an emphasis on task management and user-designed apps for structured collaboration.

This solution can be a good choice if you value Podio's approach to social task management and structured web collaboration to replace inappropriate uses of spreadsheets.

✔ **SAP JAM:** This cloud-only social collaboration platform is based on a social tool from SuccessFactors (a cloud-based human resources and talent management service that was acquired by SAP) as well as elements of an SAP social workflow product called StreamWork. SAP is integrating social feeds with its business applications in addition to providing a social workspace.

This option is a good choice if you have a commitment to SAP or SuccessFactors that makes JAM the most natural choice.

Cloud, hosted, or on premises

These products are available as traditional enterprise software that you can install on your own servers or host on dedicated equipment. Each also offers some option for a subscription-based cloud deployment option.

✔ **blueKiwi:** According to Gartner, blueKiwi "was one of the first products to base the user experience on activity streams. In 2012, blueKiwi was acquired by Atos, Europe's second-largest IT services provider."

Consider this option if you want a stream-centric social platform with a reputation for being easy to implement.

✔ **Confluence:** The Confluence wiki first gained a foothold as a platform for software documentation, dovetailing with Atlassian's bug-tracking software for developers. Since then, Confluence has grown into a broader social software platform for many applications.

Consider this option if wiki-style content management is an important aspect of your social software strategy. Confluence is also a relatively affordable product, accessible to small-to-midsize businesses.

✔ **Drupal:** This free open source software has strong community backing and more than 10,000 add-on modules available. Acquia provides corporate support and commercial extensions. Social intranet is one of many possible Drupal web portal configurations.

Drupal will suit your organization if flexibility, customization, and cost advantages outweigh the complexities of working with open source software (which can be mitigated with Acquia hosting and consulting services).

✔ **Liferay:** Liferay is an open source, Java-based web portal platform with a Social Office module for social collaboration.

Liferay's social solution can fit into a broader open source strategy for your web content and applications.

✔ **NewsGator:** A favorite social add-on to SharePoint in the years when Microsoft support for social features was clearly incomplete, NewsGator retains a loyal base of customers who trust it to continue to innovate ahead of Microsoft. NewsGator is also developing social applications such as video publishing, ideation, and talent management that go beyond the base features of a social platform.

If you're committed to the SharePoint platform but not satisfied with its stand-alone features and unwilling to adopt Microsoft's cloud-only option (Yammer), consider NewsGator.

✔ **OpenText Social Communities:** OpenText is a solid enterprise software player best known for content management, process management, and search technologies.

Consider this option if you value integration with other OpenText products.

✔ **Oracle Social Network and Oracle WebCenter:** Oracle aims to offer social features integrated throughout its enterprise applications suite, which can be a good long-term strategy for making social collaboration more pervasive. However, Oracle has yet to establish itself as a major social software player.

If your organization uses multiple products from the Oracle applications suite or values Oracle's credibility as an enterprise option, you may also consider adopting an Oracle social collaboration platform.

✔ **Saba PeopleCloud and Saba Social Collaboration:** Saba's interest in collaboration software grew out of its products for corporate training and talent management, including videoconferencing and discussion boards for peer-to-peer learning. Saba has progressively broadened the social collaboration features of its traditional on-premises software, while also introducing a separate cloud-based Saba PeopleCloud product aimed primarily at new customers and smaller businesses.

This may be a good option for you if your approach to social collaboration starts with training, workforce development, and other human resources concerns, or if you already have a commitment to other elements of the Saba platform.

✔ **Socialcast:** Socialcast is a stream-centric social collaboration platform that started in the cloud, but caught VMware's attention partly by offering customers the option of on-premises deployment as a software appliance, hosted using virtualization technology. VMware acquired the company in 2011, making it the flagship of a social and productivity software division.

This may be a good option for your organization if you're seeking an enterprise solution focused on the social stream and discussion groups and don't require wiki or content management tools in the same platform.

✔ **Socialtext:** One of the earliest commercial social software products, Socialtext started in 2002 as an enterprise wiki and broadened to include more social software features. In 2012, it sold to Bedford, which also owns Peoplefluent, and began increasing its emphasis on HR and training scenarios for social collaboration.

This can be a good choice if you want a relatively simple product, suitable for a small to midsize organization, or you like the focus on HR and training scenarios. Like Socialcast, Socialtext takes a virtualization technology approach to providing an on-premises option for customers who prefer that.

✔ **Teambox:** Teambox, a social collaboration environment with a task management focus, is typically used by small firms or teams within larger ones.

If you want a streamlined social team workspace, Teambox can be a good fit.

✔ **Telligent Enterprise:** Along with IBM and Jive, Telligent is in the small club of social software players that offers a broad social platform that can be delivered in different configurations for either internal collaboration or public customer and partner communities.

If you want a broad social software platform, particularly if you value using the same platform both internally and externally, consider Telligent Enterprise.

✔ **Tibbr:** Tibco's stream-centric social collaboration tool is used by major global enterprises like KPMG but also accessible to smaller firms through the cloud. Tibco's heritage in integration middleware gives tibbr enterprise credibility.

If you want collaboration in the social stream, linking to rather than duplicating other content management and collaboration tools, tibbr may be the solution for your organization.

✔ **WebEx Social:** WebEx Social (formerly known as Cisco Quad) emphasizes integration with Cisco products for instant messaging as well as

Internet voice and video, making it easy to initiate a phone or video call through the social stream or an employee profile.

Choose this option if integration with other Cisco products is important to your organization. WebEx Social is available as a Cisco cloud service, through third-party hosting services, or as on-premises software.

But wait — there's more!

Despite a couple of dozen choices, the information already presented in this chapter is far from comprehensive. You can find dozens of others with different ideas of what social software should be, with new players emerging all the time. Here are other choices I would advise considering, depending on your criteria:

- ✔ **Social task management:** Consider Asana, Appian, Samepage, Sparqlight, Wrike, and Mindjet. Each takes a different approach.

  - *Asana* gets a little extra attention because it was founded by two Facebook technologists (including Dustin Moskovitz, a former CTO and onetime Harvard dorm roommate of Mark Zuckerberg), insists its app revolves around a "work graph" not a social graph.

  - *Appian* is a business process management tool sprouting social extensions.

  - *Samepage* also positions itself as a file sharing tool.

  - *Sparqlight* and *Wrike* are social task managers that can be used alone or integrated with other social platforms.

  - *Mindjet* applies mind-mapping techniques to the visual display of project and planning data.

- ✔ **Open source options:** I talk about Liferay and Drupal earlier in this chapter. Here are a few more:

  - *eXo:* The eXo platform is competing for attention as an open source portal with social features.

  - *Apache Shindig project:* This is the reference implementation of the OpenSocial standards. I've mostly heard about Shindig in the context of testing OpenSocial application scenarios (for example, in Ford's advanced IT lab) and as a foundation technology for other products, including eXo and Cisco's WebEx Social.

- ✔ **SharePoint social extensions:** Although NewsGator is the best-known social companion to SharePoint, there are others.

  - *Neudesic Pulse:* Neudesic Pulse is another Microsoft partner app, a separate application on the Microsoft platform that integrates with SharePoint.

> • *Sepulveda:* A product of the interactive design firm Blue Rooster, Sepulveda is a tightly integrated application that runs on top of SharePoint as a platform.

Social collaboration also overlaps with other technologies for managing documents, content, and knowledge. For a big-picture view, look at an analytic tool that The Real Story Group publishes for free, its vendor "subway map" available at:

```
www.realstorygroup.com/vendormap
```

The vendor map shows the relationships between many different content and collaboration technologies, showing where the overlaps are like junctions between the subway lines representing categories like Collaboration & Social Software and Portals and Content Integration.

Building a Short List of Candidates

In some organizations, one vendor will be the presumptive choice from the beginning. There are enterprises that embrace the label of being an *IBM shop* or a *Microsoft shop* (they typically follow that company's lead on social collaboration). And that loyalty can be the best decision, based on the depth of the relationship as much as the technology. Still, step back long enough to look at the alternatives seriously enough to judge whether the default choice is really the best choice. By this point in the process, you may already be talking with vendors, but you will be just gearing up to talk with a few of them more seriously.

Review your prioritized list of requirements, read the news stories, case studies, white papers, and whatever analyst reports your budget allows.

On the other hand, if you're still at the stage of experimentation, you may want to jump ahead to piloting a couple of products with small teams and seeing what works. This can make perfect sense given the availability of free trials and freemium products, but you still need a short list of things to try. Even if they don't cost money, pilots can be expensive in time invested.

For a methodical approach, you want your list to be narrow enough that you will not be wasting time on unrealistic options but broad enough that you don't prematurely eliminate good choices. Ask for a demo that not only showcases the product's major features but shows how they can be applied to your business.

Shortlist Builder

One research tool worth looking at is The Real Story Group's Shortlist Builder, a web-based assessment tool available here:

www.realstorygroup.com/Shortlist Builder

On the firm's catalog of evaluation reports, Shortlist Builder prompts you to fill in your platform, license, and functional requirements for a product. It then builds a customized report including The Real Story Group's evaluations of the vendors that match your criteria. For example, I ran a test using a broad set of criteria, and the tool came back with a list of 24 potential products for me to look at. I tried it again, the second time insisting that I needed a product based on Microsoft's .NET Framework and the availability of an on-premises deployment option, the Shortlist Builder came up with three matching products.

Downloading one of the group's reports costs at least a few thousand dollars for a one-time access or a bit more for an annual subscription that provides access to updates and, in some versions, consultation time with the firm's analysts. The group specializes in social, collaboration, content management, and related technologies, giving it a depth of expertise in this area. Also, The Real Story Group is structured to provide objective evaluations because it supports itself solely on fees from enterprise customers; it's not supported by vendors and has no divided loyalties. I know The Real Story Group President Tony Byrne as a regular speaker at the E2 Conference series and am impressed with his commitment to integrity. If you're making a major collaboration platform decision that you want to be able to stick with for years to come, subscribing to this service can be money well spent.

Tony Byrne of The Real Story Group talks about starting with "a longish short list" of plausible vendors and products that you will investigate in more detail. In your first round of research, your goal should be to eliminate most of these, whittling your short list down to those worth talking with more seriously. Before making a decision, he suggests you invite your top two or three picks to participate in a bake-off competition where they will implement a pilot instance of the software that addresses the specific business scenarios you have in mind for social collaboration.

Getting Started for Free

Consumers like getting stuff for free. Consumer social networks, along with other mass market web services, have trained us to expect to get a lot for free. Periodically, some spoil sport reminds us that we're paying for most of these things somehow, even if it may not be immediately obvious. That is, when you enjoy ad-supported media, you are the product. Or, to put it another way, consumers "pay" for access to a "free" service like Facebook with their attention and all the data about our behavior that the service gathers, mines, and uses to create products it can sell to advertisers.

Corporate technology buyers tend to be suspicious of free software and services, preferring the comfort of a contract. But often even they see the wisdom of doing some experiments for free before attempting to secure the funding for a more ambitious social collaboration initiative.

Taking advantage of freemium and free trial offers

Yammer and Podio are offered on a *freemium* model, meaning you can use them indefinitely for free. The premium features, though, aren't free. For example, Yammer reserves a few features for paying customers (notably, administrative tools that enterprise IT tends to consider indispensible). Podio limits free accounts to five users with full rights although they in turn can invite guest collaborators with limited access.

In both cases, the creators of these applications accept that some fraction of their user base will figure out how to use their tools productively without paying for access; the vendors write off the expense of supporting those users as a form of marketing. More often, organizations that find social collaboration valuable prove willing to transform themselves into paying customers. The ones who stick with free accounts tend to be occasional users, which means the load they put on the service is minimal.

If your organization is a small business or nonprofit with a shoestring budget and no exotic requirements, consider taking the free versions of these products as far as you possibly can.

The right way for an enterprise to take advantage of free or freemium services is deliberately, with a plan for how you will transition from free to paid accounts if that makes sense.

I discuss some of the pitfall of freemium cloud software in Chapter 10.

Calculating the cost of "free"

Freely downloadable open source software, such as Drupal, can be the foundation for social collaboration. The base Drupal technology may be free for the taking, but if you want it neatly packaged for use as a social collaboration platform, or if you want an official source of support when developer community discussion boards aren't enough, you will pay to get it from Acquia or another firm that offers expertise in Drupal configuration and web development. To quote Richard Stallman, whose Free Software Foundation spurred the open source movement, free software is free as in *free speech* and not *free beer*. If you want someone to tailor software to your exact needs, you're still going to have to pay.

Free cloud services aren't necessarily free, either. They may cost the CIO in gray hair. They may cost the help desk time and effort dealing with complications introduced by free services, even if they're not officially supported. A freemium product like Yammer can look to the unsophisticated employee like a corporate service, even if it's not, because everyone on the collaboration network is an employee of the same firm.

Meanwhile, by sticking with a 30-day free trial model and maintaining the expectation that its software must be paid for in the long run, Jive can afford to assign a "success coach" for every account, providing support to make the trial successful and convert trial customers into paying customers.

These cloud-based free trials are a relatively recent addition to the Jive business model, allowing it to reach a mass market of smaller customers and teams within larger businesses. Meanwhile, Jive continues to sell to larger customers on a more traditional enterprise sales model where the terms of any trial implementation or pilot project are open to negotiation.

Conducting a Pilot Project

Taking advantage of a free cloud service means using it as-is and with minimal support. Often, that's not good enough, particularly for large organizations with specific business applications in mind.

Planning the pilot project

Using a pilot project *bake-off* as a decision-making tool before committing to a social collaboration platform means having two or more organizations load your organization's content into the platform and work with some subset of your employees to put the collaboration platform through its paces.

The bake-off approach probably works best for large enterprises whose business is so desirable that vendors will jump through hoops to win it. Smaller businesses can instead experiment with free trial versions of a few products, applied to some real project or task, before making a bigger commitment.

Considering the cost

If you're asking vendors to spend weeks demonstrating how they would address your demanding requirements, they may charge a consulting fee to produce the proof-of-concept social network, knowing you can take the ideas regardless of whether you take their software.

You certainly can negotiate hard to get them to do it as inexpensively as possible, if they want to win your business. But paying for a proof-of-concept pilot project, or participation in a bake-off, can make sense if you can make a better decision as a result.

Designing a successful pilot project

Some experts point out that implementing a pilot program can be a mistake, if social collaboration starts off so tentatively that it has little chance of demonstrating its worth. For instance, Andrew McAfee, the business and technology strategist who coined the term "Enterprise 2.0" to describe the use of social technologies in business, made this argument in a 2010 blog post that's still widely quoted. Expressing his frustration over repeatedly hearing from large enterprises that had started with a small pilot project but where unimpressed with the results, he wrote:

> I believe these kinds of pilots are unintentionally set up to fail, or at least underwhelm. This is essentially because they contain too few people, most of whom know each other too well.

> The more I learn about and think about the value of emergent social software platforms, the more I suspect that the deep meta-benefit they provide is technology-enabled serendipity, defined as 'good luck in making unexpected and fortunate discoveries.' Serendipity is possible when we're collaborating with our close colleagues on a well-defined project, but that's probably when it occurs least often. It's much more likely during wide forays and broad searches, the kind that are so easy to do with current technologies.

You can read the rest at:

```
http://andrewmcafee.org/2010/04/drop-the-pilot/
```

The preceding is probably a better argument for paying attention to the design of a pilot project — and the assessment of the results — than for scrapping the pilot altogether.

For example, some companies who now boast about the success of their social collaboration initiatives started with a pilot that involved a relatively small number of people but from many locations and divisions. By giving these pilot teams a project to collaborate on for which the social platform was the best solution for a geographically and organizationally dispersed group, the designers of the pilot avoided competing with the type of collaboration that can best be accomplished by shouting across the office.

Generating buzz

Wim de Gier, the senior global project manager at LeasePlan, likes to compare the exclusivity of his firm's early pilot with IBM Connections to the early days of Gmail, when only a small fraction of Internet users had access to a treasured invitation to try Google's e-mail service. By restricting access, Gmail created pent-up demand. LeasePlan, a global vehicle leasing and fleet management company, was able to do something similar, enlisting a cross-functional team of 170 people in different business units to try the environment. When their co-workers got curious about the environment and requested access, he would tell them, "Hey, sorry, not allowed." And in the process, he created buzz for the social software platform. By the time he was ready to take his case to management for implementation of the social tool, he had a list of 1,000 "wannabes" based on all the people who had requested accounts.

Today, Connections is available to 6,000 LeasePlan employees across 40 subsidiaries and 30 countries.

Ensuring access to data

The collaboration strategists in the "kill the pilot project" camp argue that users have little reason to invest their participation, their knowledge, and their valuable content in a platform that the company doesn't seem to be committed to. Just as having too few people involved frustrates the chances of productive social networking, having too little content in a collaboration system undercuts the value of sharing and searching for information. By the same logic, it makes little sense to invest time in fleshing out your profile and establishing connections with other employees if the entire social network could evaporate at any time.

By this logic, you may limit any pilot phase to IT employees and other technology champions willing to test the environment, with the understanding that it's not necessarily permanent. Or, you may compensate for the uncertainty by committing to port as much content as possible from the pilot environment to whatever one you eventually land on. At least, you can promise to try to do that, technologies permitting.

Identifying Distinguishing Characteristics of the Leaders

According to Gartner, Inc., the leading social collaboration vendors are Jive, IBM, Salesforce.com, and Microsoft (SharePoint and Yammer).

These organizations are distinguished from the rest by the credibility they have gained from serving the social collaboration needs of some very large organizations, as well as their vision for the future of the technology. These may or may not be the leading contenders on your own short list: Issues of budget, licensing, and the applications you have in mind could drive you in a completely different direction.

Still, Gartner's selection of leaders have some very different offerings for different strategies.

Choosing a comprehensive platform

If you're in the market for a comprehensive platform that supports many modes of social networking and social media publishing (including blogs, wikis, file sharing, discussions, profiles, and social streams), you can narrow the list to Jive, IBM Connections, and Microsoft SharePoint.

Vendors like Jive Software fall somewhere between the newly minted start-ups and the global enterprise systems players. Founded in 2001, with its initial focus on providing public discussion board software for businesses, Jive has developed elements of a platform for enterprise social networking, including an apps market for other software products that can be plugged into the Jive environment. Jive has attracted dozens of major enterprise customers and continues to refine its products to meet their requirements. Jive's software can be installed on-premise or in dedicated hosting environments that appeal to enterprises that want to maximize control and minimize risk.

At the same time, Jive is trying to expand its appeal with a cloud edition of the platform that is easier for small companies and teams within larger firms to adapt with little or no requirement for support from an internal IT department.

Jive is a youngster compared with IBM, Oracle, or Microsoft, but has been successful enough to hire people with expertise in enterprise systems engineering, boosting the credibility of the organization and the quality of its software. Other broad social platform vendors not included as a Gartner leader would include Telligent Enterprise and NewsGator Social Sites (as a companion to SharePoint).

Focusing on the activity stream

Another strategy is to focus on the activity stream and modes of interaction that are unique to social networking, as opposed to previous modes of groupware collaboration. The products most focused on the activity stream (from the Gartner leader quadrant) are Chatter and Yammer.

Others to consider would be VMware Socialcast and Tibco's tibbr.

Supporting a specific application like sales collaboration

If your priority is improving collaboration for the sales team, or between sales and marketing, Salesforce.com's Chatter jumps to the forefront — if, that is, your organization uses Salesforce.com CRM. Part of Microsoft's strategy with Yammer is to deliver a similarly strong pairing with its Dynamics CRM product.

Other application scenarios may lead you to other products from outside the Gartner leaders quadrant. For example, both Saba and Socialtext emphasize the use of their products in the context of human resources and training. SAP JAM grew out of the enterprise application suite vendor's acquisition of SuccessFactors, which provides cloud applications for managing and motivating a workforce, and SAP is using JAM to embed social functionality in other enterprise applications as well, including CRM.

Managing tasks and projects

Over the past few years, a surge in interest in social task management has spawned startups such as Asana, Sparqlight, and Wrike, but some of the leading platforms have this functionality built in.

If managing tasks and projects through a social tool is an important selection criteria, IBM Connections stands out for its Activities app, created specifically for coordinating related tasks while using the social network as a medium for making assignments and tracking progress. Microsoft SharePoint also includes a robust task management system that social applications can leverage.

Among lightweight cloud applications, Podio is a social collaboration network with an emphasis on task management and other ways of organizing work.

I discuss social task management in Chapter 6.

Dealing with SharePoint

Speaking of SharePoint, Microsoft's portal software winds up factoring into practically every social collaboration strategy, regardless of whether it is at the center of that strategy.

At a minimum, every serious social collaboration tool for enterprise use must include some form of SharePoint integration, and the quality of that integration often ranks high among the selection criteria of corporate customers.

About 75 to 80 percent of the Fortune 500 are SharePoint customers. When the product was new, Microsoft made a practice of distributing a free version of the software with Windows Server, which became an easy option for departmental server administrators looking to provide basic intranet publishing. Today, there is still a free version called SharePoint Foundations 2013. When more demanding applications emerged, many organizations that got started for free paid for an upgrade. Microsoft has also successfully promoted SharePoint as a platform for file sharing and application development. The SharePoint 2010 edition added some basic social collaboration features, including status posts and MySite profiles.

In a 2012 *InformationWeek* article on "10 Enterprise Social Networking Obstacles," I included SharePoint as Obstacle #5 because it was so ubiquitous that major enterprises tended to gravitate toward it, even though at the time it wasn't terribly competitive. I based this charge partly on the lament of Dion Hinchcliffe, executive vice president of strategy at Dachis Group and social business enthusiast. In a blog post from about the same time, he had written, "SharePoint has often slowed down the move to more social tools for big companies in particular."

Since then, Microsoft has made itself a more competitive player in social collaboration with the release of SharePoint 2013 and the purchase of Yammer.

Assessing commitment to Microsoft's collaboration platform

Where SharePoint falls in your social collaboration strategy will depend on your commitment to the platform. Ask yourself these questions:

- ✔ Is SharePoint a core, strategic technology platform for your organization, filled to the brim with assets that will be critical to the success of the collaboration initiative?

- ✔ Has SharePoint been used casually, perhaps to host some departmental newsletters on an intranet but nothing terribly strategic?

✔ How satisfied are your employees with the SharePoint user experience? Have they been using it effectively, or are they frustrated?

✔ Would adding social collaboration around the existing SharePoint experiences make them more effective?

Finding the intersection of SharePoint and Yammer

As of this writing, Microsoft is promising a "converged experience," merging user interface elements of Yammer and SharePoint, arriving first in the Office365 cloud version of the product. Parallel features are expected in the on-premises version of SharePoint, but not at the same pace.

Questions for your Microsoft sales representative may include

✔ Will Microsoft continue to invest in the SharePoint social newsfeed? Will it be competitive with the features offered by Yammer?

✔ Will Microsoft ever provide an on-premises version of Yammer? (Probably not, but it doesn't hurt to ask.)

✔ What exactly is Microsoft doing to more deeply integrate Yammer with SharePoint? For example, how will the integration extend beyond the home screen news feed to encompass SharePoint document management, project management, and user profile data and functions?

Microsoft's acquisition of Yammer also raises a great many questions about the future of *NewsGator Social Sites,* an enterprise social networking product that works as an application running on top of SharePoint. Although NewsGator continues to race ahead with social networking features that go beyond those provided by even the latest edition of SharePoint, it is seeking other ways of distinguishing itself, including the addition of some of its own cloud-based extensions. At the same time, one of the things many SharePoint shops find attractive about NewsGator's software is that it does not force them to move to the cloud.

Because these products are interdependent, any further change in Microsoft's road map for SharePoint and Yammer could force changes in NewsGator's plans, as could competitive pressures from dozens of other players. That makes studying this matrix of plans like studying the roadmap of a region subject to frequent earthquakes and judging which branches in the road are most likely to crumble.

The example of NewsGator, SharePoint, and Yammer interweaving is only one example of the interplay between social software players and their shifting plans.

Here are some possible strategies for navigating this maze.

The evolution of Microsoft social collaboration products

The future of a product can also be affected by organizational changes. For example, at this writing, Microsoft is articulating a vision for the Yammer social interface becoming the standard for social interaction on SharePoint. Microsoft paid $1.2 billion to acquire Yammer in 2012 at about the same time that it was starting to preview the features that would be arriving in SharePoint 2013. Now, even though SharePoint 2013 expanded the social networking functions built in to SharePoint itself, Yammer is better able as a cloud-based product to keep pace with innovations in social technologies.

Although prior editions of SharePoint had introduced some social features, most organizations serious about creating internal social networks supplemented those capabilities with add-on products. And Microsoft has built more competitive social features into SharePoint, signaling that Yammer will be its flagship product for enterprise social networking.

In particular, users of Office365 (Microsoft cloud-based suite of collaboration applications that includes SharePoint) are being encouraged to use Yammer as an integral part of that suite. The path forward for social collaboration in on-premises instances of SharePoint (companies that run SharePoint on their own servers and networks) is less clear. Microsoft is encouraging using Yammer in those settings, too, but it also has to recognize that many customers who run SharePoint on premises do so partly because they're not comfortable doing corporate collaboration on a cloud-based system. Would they be any more comfortable with a hybrid scenario where assets such as shared documents are managed locally in SharePoint while social collaboration around those documents is handled in the cloud by Yammer?

Using SharePoint as your social platform

A couple years ago, calling SharePoint your enterprise social network would get you laughed out of a convention of community managers. Without heavy customization or the use of an add-on product, SharePoint simply wasn't competitive.

With SharePoint 2013, though, the product has done a lot of catching up in how it manages profiles, activity streams, and people searches, as well as offering an apps model for extending the platform.

Microsoft has also been talking about ways for SharePoint and Yammer to be used together (even though Yammer is a cloud product and most SharePoint instances run inside a corporate firewall).

So where does that leave those IT managers who don't want their collaboration apps to touch the cloud with a 10-foot pole? This is where understanding the product roadmap and judging how far to trust it becomes important. Will Microsoft continue to invest in social features for SharePoint itself, or will all that energy go into Yammer?

Extending SharePoint

Another option is to stick with SharePoint as the core but extend it with another product, such as NewsGator Social Sites. NewsGator is built as a SharePoint application, giving it the tightest possible integration with the platform.

I have spoken with many enterprises that chose to align with NewsGator when it was one of a very few options for making a SharePoint-based enterprise social network measure up. Even with the introduction of SharePoint 2013, those I've spoken with remain confident of NewsGator's capability to innovate with social features faster than Microsoft will.

Linking SharePoint to your social platform

The more common strategy among social collaboration vendors is to seek ways of linking to or embedding content from SharePoint into their platforms and vice versa. For starters, a SharePoint web page can be referenced with a link in the social stream just like any other web page. Another approach, which Yammer was leveraging since before the acquisition, is to provide a SharePoint Web Part UI component that pulls in a social feed, such as a Yammer discussion thread relevant to the topic of a particular SharePoint page.

Deeper levels of integration are also possible. For example, the Jive for SharePoint add-on module reconfigures Jive to use SharePoint as the content repository for file storage. In addition, activity feeds can be integrated between Jive and SharePoint (subject to some restrictions in the SharePoint security model), according to Jive.

Scrapping SharePoint

Another option is to replace SharePoint wholesale with a social collaboration platform if the social platform is really compelling and your commitment to SharePoint was never all that deep. Usually, when a social software vendor boasts to me about replacing SharePoint, I find that the product may have replaced one particular use of SharePoint, but hundreds of other instances of the software still rattle around the organization.

Even if you make a strategic commitment to social collaboration not based on SharePoint, it probably doesn't make sense to chase down every SharePoint instance being used as a glorified file server and rip it out. What makes more sense is to demonstrate the value of your social collaboration platform of choice, dramatically enough that employees and their managers will realize that's where all the important content needs to be, going forward. Over time, old SharePoint servers may wind up being decommissioned and their content transferred over.

Again, the point is not necessarily to deploy new technology but to prove the value of new ways of working, enabled by technology. Whether that goal is best served by building on SharePoint or scrapping it is up to you.

Chapter 10

Social Collaboration in the Cloud

Some of the most prominent social collaboration tools were born in the cloud, meaning they are offered as *software as a service* (SaaS), delivered over the web, rather than software you download or get shipped to you on a stack of CDs in a box. For example, no one besides Yammer runs its own server for social collaboration on Yammer: You get it as a cloud service or not at all.

Some products originally marketed as traditional enterprise software, such as Jive and IBM Connections, are also available in cloud editions and various other forms of application hosting.

In many ways, social collaboration is a perfect match for the cloud — an inherently web-based experience that needs to be available to employees at home or on the road, as well as in the office. Cloud products also tend to have a cost advantage derived from the extreme economies of scale achieved by cloud data centers. In this chapter, I tell you about the advantages of cloud solutions and help you decide whether they're right for your organization.

Cloud computing is still new enough that many traditional organizations distrust it or have legal and regulatory reasons to worry that it's unsuitable for business collaboration. I have some advice for overcoming that distrust and making it work for your organization.

Before you select a cloud platform, you should also understand what kind of leverage you have (and don't have) when you're negotiating a contract with a service provider. I tell you about that in this chapter as well.

Playing in the Cloud

The reinvention of business collaboration is driven at least as much by the rise of cloud computing and software as service products as it is by social media.

By definition, cloud software products are provided as Internet services rather than software for businesses to set up on their own servers. Companies like Salesforce.com have proven that important applications, such as tracking sales leads and coordinating sales activities, can be provided through a web browser. The point is not necessarily that the app is web-based, and not every web application should be labeled a cloud application. Cloud services sometimes have their own desktop PC clients and often reach mobile devices such as phones and tablets using apps rather than a mobile browser.

Rather than being defined by the user interface, a cloud application is one that you can sign up for online and begin using immediately (or very nearly so) and scale quickly by buying more capacity from the service provider. The customer isn't responsible for buying, renting, or administering a specific Internet server, and may in fact be getting services from several servers working in tandem. Instead of worrying about (or having tight control over) the back-end configuration details, the customer pays for access to the application and lets the service provider worry about the details. (This is also known as *software as a service,* or SaaS.) The cloud service provider, in turn, is supposed to provide more than enough capacity to accommodate new customers or new requirements from existing customers at a moment's notice.

In addition to software as a service applications, cloud computing includes more basic services like storage and web hosting from organizations like Rackspace and Amazon Web Services (a division of the online retailer Amazon.com). These provide large pools of raw compute capacity and network bandwidth that they can make available to their customers on demand.

Many collaboration technology startups now deliver their own subscription-based applications on a foundation provided by Amazon Web Services or one of its competitors, making it easy for them to scale quickly as demand for their applications grows. These infrastructure as a service cloud players provide very good (although not perfect) reliability. They also make it easier to deliver a service that can be available with good performance, from anywhere, because they operate multiple data centers around the globe.

This makes them a good match for collaboration apps, which are often fielded partly to support telecommuters and employees who spend a lot of time on the road, as well as workers who need to collaborate across geographically dispersed company locations.

In this section, I touch on some of the benefits of cloud computing and help you decide whether cloud computing may be a good fit for your organization.

Recognizing the innovation taking place in cloud computing

The advantages of the cloud are significant enough that leading social collaboration products like Yammer are available only as cloud services. You can't purchase a copy of the Yammer software and set it up on your own server or servers, not for any amount of money.

Yammer keeps its cost down by simplifying its operations, keeping the servers that run its software as identical as possible, all running the same version of the same software so they can be cloned as necessary to support the expansion of its user base. When Microsoft acquired Yammer in 2012, it was quick to assure the world that Yammer would be allowed to continue to maintain its singular focus on cloud-based software delivery.

One of Yammer's longtime rivals, Jive Software, started on the traditional enterprise software model of selling software, supporting on-premises installation of that software, selling periodic upgrades, and distributing bug fixes and software patches as necessary.

When Jive announces a new version of its software, many of its customers take a wait-and-see attitude before deciding that the upgrade is worth the money. This means that Jive must support multiple versions of its software that are currently in active use. Even some customers for whom Jive hosts the software on their behalf want it to run on dedicated servers and be updated only on a schedule of their choosing. There are legitimate reasons why large organizations insist on maintaining tight control of the software they run, but as a consequence, both Jive and its customers have higher operational costs. Also, improvements to the software are slower to trickle down to the end users of Jive's software. As of this writing, the current version is Jive 6, but many customers I talk to are running a 4.x or 5.x version.

Jive argues that it offers customers more freedom by offering both cloud and on-premises software options. At the same time, Jive is moving toward the cloud model. Although not all its customers will be convinced to switch, Jive is encouraging new ones (particularly midsize companies and teams within larger ones) to sign up for its cloud version. Jive has also begun to introduce new features in the cloud first, using the cloud as a proving ground for innovations that will later make it into the installed version of its software.

Still, many organizational leaders prefer on-premises installation of separate instances of their collaboration software on their own equipment or dedicated servers in web-hosting centers. Among other things, this allows them to upgrade on their own schedules, not at the whims of a cloud service provider. Cloud services are also commonly viewed as less secure, although there is an argument to be made that a cloud service can invest far more in information security than most organizations can themselves.

Regulatory requirements can render cloud computing a nonstarter, particularly in fields like healthcare and financial services. If you do business in a heavily regulated field, make sure that any social collaboration solution you choose complies with those regulations.

Even when an organization opts for on-premises social collaboration, employee expectations for the capabilities that business systems ought to offer are increasingly set by cloud services. When organizations fail to provide an adequate corporate solution, employees often resort to using unsanctioned consumer apps for their information sharing needs.

Making collaboration services available from anywhere

Employees increasingly expect collaboration services to follow them wherever they go and be available on whatever device they have handy, much like their Facebook and Gmail accounts. Wherever they go, access shouldn't require more than a username and password, plus an Internet connection. The unacceptable alternative (in most organizations) would be containing a social collaboration server within the corporate firewall and requiring users to access it with virtual private network (VPN) software.

Because cloud collaboration services aren't inside anyone's firewall, they have to be capable of protecting themselves. As a reward for going "naked" on the Internet, they can reach users at work, at home, or wherever they travel.

Web-based applications are available to anyone in the world with an Internet connection, but to be effective for global companies and business travelers, those services should be available from multiple data centers around the world. Having a copy of the software and related web assets available from a nearby server means higher performance because signals don't have to travel as far between you and the sever handling your request.

Just because a service provider uses the word "cloud" frequently in its marketing materials doesn't mean that it has this quality of geographic distribution. Even cloud products that run on top of Amazon Web Services may be available only from a single data center because they haven't paid for capacity from several of them.

Providing private cloud alternatives if public cloud is unacceptable

Cloud-crazy vendors who allow on-premises deployment often talk about a *private cloud* alternative to *public cloud* access to their software.

Private cloud is something of an oxymoron because it means that your software is running behind a firewall, or perhaps within a segment of a cloud provider's infrastructure that is walled off from the rest. Vendors may describe any software that can be hosted onsite as running in a private cloud. The more legitimate use of the term refers to an internal company software infrastructure that mimics some of the characteristics of the public cloud, often using virtualization software to make it easier to partition and clone instances of software and simplify the operating environment.

Whatever the terminology, organizations that implement social collaboration but choose to do so internally should seek to duplicate the advantages of cloud software, even as they hope to preserve more security and control.

One sensible compromise, offered by VMware's Socialcast division (among others), is an appliance-based model where the software runs on a virtualized application image that mirrors the functionality of the cloud version and gets regular software updates. This means the onsite software installation gets bug fixes and software improvements on approximately the same schedule as the cloud version, but all corporate data is contained within the corporate firewall.

Distinguishing between Cloud and Application Hosting

Cloud providers like Amazon Web Services provide storage and raw computing power on a metered basis. SaaS providers typically charge per user, per month on subscription contracts.

To understand the technology term *cloud,* you first have to understand how traditional applications are hosted. There are a few distinct types of application hosting:

- ✔ **Dedicated hosting:** The service provider hosts the application on a server (or set of servers) owned by the provider but reserved for the exclusive use of one customer.

- ✔ **Cloud:** You purchase a subscription entitling you to access the application rather than buying the software and installing it on your own equipment. All the IT details of keeping servers and databases running and performing well are off in the cloud — someone else's responsibility. This also means you as the customer don't control how the servers and databases that support the application are configured.

    Cloud services are typically *multitenant,* meaning that servers and databases are shared among multiple customers. This allows the service provider to use server resources more efficiently and keep its subscription price low.

✔ **Private cloud:** IT people use the term *private cloud* to refer to corporate data center resources and applications hosted in a cloud-like fashion, using virtualization technologies. Organizations pursuing a private cloud strategy aim to achieve some of the flexibility and cost advantages associated with cloud computing, without giving up corporate control.

Some cloud-based social collaboration services, including Socialcast and Socialtext, specifically market a private cloud version of their services: a virtualized image of their software that can be loaded into a private cloud environment. This means the data derived from collaboration activities is stored on servers controlled by the enterprise, which is important to some organizations. Meanwhile, because virtualization abstracts away some of the details of servers and operating systems, the cloud providers avoid some of the support headaches associated with traditional enterprise software.

This chapter is primarily about social collaboration in the public cloud. As far as I'm concerned, that's the real cloud, so I refer to it as just *the cloud* instead of the *public cloud.*

Other forms of application hosting and outsourcing are not cloud services in the same sense. For many years, Jive has provided managed application hosting services to some of its customers. The difference is that the software runs on dedicated servers, and the customer still decides when (or whether) to upgrade to a new version. The customer is still in control of how the application is configured but outsources the routine tasks of server maintenance. These customers continue to treat Jive as a traditional enterprise software product and have more freedom to customize it than they would get from a cloud provider.

Assessing the Advantages of the Cloud

Most traditional software vendors have adapted to some version of the cloud business model by now, offering customers a choice of software or SaaS. The advantage of choosing a product that is available in either mode is you can start in the cloud and later switch to an on-premises version of the software, and vice versa.

For all the concerns they may raise, cloud applications have distinct advantages over on-premises applications.

Reducing the burden on your IT department

The cloud shifts IT's role from maintenance to integration and innovation. With social collaboration in the cloud, IT personnel don't have to worry about racking and stacking servers or provisioning more storage as users share files. A cloud provider may also be able to provide storage and network resources more cost effectively than the internal IT organization can on its own.

Where do clouds come from?

By a loose definition, every web application may claim to be part of the cloud. The term comes from a convention in network architecture diagrams and web application, vendor marketing slides of using a cloud icon to represent the Internet. The cloud symbol pops up in other network graphics as well, essentially representing all the details and complexities omitted from a diagram. What this says in pictograms is essentially, "We know there is a lot of complicated stuff going on in this cloud, but someone else is handling that for us."

A diagram of a consumer e-commerce service may show the user on his browser at one end of the picture and some details about the web store's server architecture on the other, with the cloud between them. The following figure shows a traditional cloud diagram, where the cloud icon represents the Internet.

In normal operation, the merchant worries about the performance of the servers and how well the website loads in the user's browser, but not about all the mechanics of Internet routing, switching, and peering between telecommunications providers in between. That part just magically works or, at least, you don't worry about it until it breaks down.

Cloud computing is a way of packaging other computer services so they can be treated like Internet services, as utilities you subscribe to rather than own and manage yourself. In the form of cloud computing known as software as a service, whole applications including all their associated storage and database resources become part of the cloud, as shown in the following figure.

The expansion of the cloud concept to encompass computing services and applications means you can stop worrying about the details of how they work as well (if you so desire).

So what's left for IT to do? In some organizations, it may be an IT person who administers the service: not in the hands-on fashion of administering internal IT resources but through the cloud application's web-based administration console. Even if the administration function is designed to be self-service, IT personnel may be better equipped to know what check boxes to mark and what settings to tweak. Someone from IT or the web development team may also be in charge of whatever customization is allowed to the branding and appearance of the cloud service. I tell you more about IT's role in the "Addressing Concerns about Cloud Services" section.

Taking advantage of continuous improvements

Cloud software products get better day by day, with more major upgrades arriving several times a year. When a cloud product gets an upgrade, every user gets access to the new features at approximately the same time. If the software developers introduce a bug fix, the bug is fixed immediately for all customers. However, that's not how things work with enterprise software.

With the exception of bug fixes and patches made available for download, enterprise software products typically aren't updated more often than once per year. Then, after a major upgrade is released, it may be several months to a year — or more — before users see the version. First, the IT organization needs to decide to buy the upgrade and win corporate approval for the purchase. Then, there may be months of testing to ensure that any customizations applied to the software or the underlying database will continue to function following the upgrade.

Often, enterprise software installations lag behind, maybe for budgetary reasons or because customers don't want to go through the hassle of upgrading. It's not unusual to find customers running, say, 4.x versions of the software a year after the release of the 6.0 version.

Reaching out to telecommuters and traveling employees

Cloud applications can be particularly convenient for employees who work from home or while on the road, delivering the best web and mobile app experience to workers anywhere in the world. Some cloud applications can be accessed from multiple data centers around the world, reducing transmission latency for those traveling internationally.

Although a web application hosted in a corporate data center may be accessible from anywhere, it would be unlikely to match the performance optimizations that a cloud vendor can provide.

Automating account provisioning

Jive introduced the first real cloud version of its social collaboration product in mid-2012, partly to enable a streamlined 30-day free trial sales model that would allow it to reach small to midsize customers. Instead of having to manually provision trial accounts for new customers, now it allowed them to sign up online.

True cloud services can be purchased online and activated within a few minutes, usually requiring nothing more than a few clicks on a signup form. Payment is typically by credit card, but in the case of freemium and free trial offers, a card number may not be required up front.

Appreciating the Advantages of Cloud-Only Products

Many startup cloud software products are available only in the cloud. For the cloud service provider, focusing on one mode of delivery clearly simplifies things. The advantages of that choice also trickle down to customers.

Delivering continual innovation

Cloud-only vendors tend to move faster. They can operate more like web developers working on consumer services like Facebook, which sometimes displays unannounced new features to some fraction of its user base just to see how users react. Yammer has been known to experiment first on its nonpaying users. This also means Yammer can respond quickly to match popular new features that crop up on Facebook or in competing social collaboration tools.

Upgrades can be released on whatever schedule they are ready to go live. They may be packaged and released on something like a quarterly schedule, but that's more for marketing reasons than technical requirements.

Focusing on a single version of software

Pure cloud service providers have the advantage of not needing to worry about an installed base of customers who may require support on multiple versions of the software released in past years. They can run their software on exactly the hardware, operating system, database, and network configuration their engineers believe to be optimal.

In addition to simplifying operations within the cloud data center, this almost completely eliminates finger pointing between infrastructure hardware and software providers. If something is wrong with the application, it's the cloud provider's job to fix it. You just need to keep your users on a current web browser and keep their Internet connections working.

Upgrading difficulties become a thing of the past

Cloud application access also eliminates the traditional challenges of upgrading on-premises software, where the process may be significantly different depending on which version is currently installed, and what database, database version, OS and its version, and user customizations are in place. The process of porting content from the database structure of one version of on-premises software to the structure of the next may be a process that takes months of futzing around and testing the results on a staging server.

If a cloud application provider decides that the database structure must change to speed a critical query, it takes charge of porting any existing content to that new format. If the operator does its job right, the end user need never know anything changed.

Avoiding the Pitfalls of Free

At larger organizations, many of the stories about freemium social collaboration start with an ad hoc implementation of the technology, without the blessing of corporate IT. Yammer requires nothing more than a work e-mail address to initiate the creation of a social network associated with that e-mail domain. Subsequent users who sign up with an e-mail from that domain are assigned to the same collaboration network. Many other social software players have adopted exactly the same model.

What is absent from this scheme is any form of corporate administrative control, which is something IT administrators often find disturbing. Even though Yammer isn't invading the corporate network and pilfering information, IT sees it luring employees to collaborate and share company information on an unsanctioned service.

At least in past years, pre-Microsoft acquisition, some IT people who objected to this practice found it difficult to shut down employee accounts on Yammer. In the absence of a contract, Yammer treats those accounts as the assets of a bunch of individual users who happen to share an e-mail domain — that is, as personal rather than corporate property. Yammer's terms and conditions for free accounts state that they will be converted into corporate property as soon as the owner of the e-mail domain becomes a paying customer, which (of course) is the resolution Yammer is hoping for.

The way to shut down employee accounts without paying is to have your company lawyer send Yammer a stern letter referencing the Digital Millennium Copyright Act — the same tool movie studios use to get bootleg videos removed from YouTube — to argue the accounts should be deleted because they contain corporate intellectual property, posted to the service without permission.

Otherwise, the only provision Yammer provides for deactivating free accounts is a "challenge" mechanism that for example can be used to turn off the accounts of former employees. Any member of a free Yammer network can challenge any other member, at which point that person must respond to an e-mail prompt to reactivate the account. Assuming the company has removed the e-mail account of the former employee, that message will never be received.

All this proves is that free does not necessarily mean easy or simple. Other modes of free carry their own complications.

A 30-day free trial of Jive's cloud edition is meant to last just long enough that some pilot project team will be able to show practical results, leading to a more formal adoption of the product. One drawback is that 30 days may not be enough for a realistic assessment of the software (although Jive can point to its share of success stories). Also, if the trial generates productive activity but you decide not to sign with Jive, you may find yourself scrambling on Day 29 to download valuable content and conversations.

Embracing ad hoc efforts, where possible

Social collaboration doesn't always start as a centrally planned initiative, managed by the IT department, like a traditional software roll-out. Cloud services, particularly those offered on a freemium model, make it easy for any project team anywhere within the company to sign up and start collaborating right away, inviting co-workers as they go. Yammer is famous for enlisting hundreds of thousands of employees this way before an IT department knows it's happening, even when the use of outside cloud services may go against company policy.

So then what happens? What should happen? In some cases, there may be no choice but to shut down this activity. Perhaps for regulatory reasons, social collaboration in the cloud is unacceptable. Maybe IT blocks access to the cloud service's domain at the firewall and the demands that the service purge any company content from its servers. If that's really the way it has to be, so be it. Even if it's necessary to slap a few hands for violation of policy, though, give the rogue operation credit for trying to innovate.

In general, I recommend taking a serious look at embracing what network is already working. For every organization that violently rejects Yammer, a few will sign up to become paying customers, turning it into an official corporate solution. Many others will tolerate a cloud collaboration service that's either free or paid for departmental or project use — note that I said *tolerate it* — but not embrace it to be offered company-wide.

I don't mean this as a commercial for Yammer, which happens to be the most prominent example of a social collaboration tool that often takes root this way. Plenty of organizations I talk to have piloted multiple social collaboration solutions before picking one, and often Yammer is in the mix even if it was never an official pilot. Sometimes they decide Yammer is a good fit for their needs and an easy choice because it's already enjoying use. Other times, organizations decide that Yammer doesn't meet long-term needs and it goes by the wayside of another platform instead.

The same sorts of decisions may have to be made about other cloud services or collaboration applications built on an open source software product like Drupal, where that's not the corporate standard.

Before you decide to embrace the rogue solution or shut it down, do a little fact-finding. Is it really working? Are the employees participating in the collaboration network finding it to be a good fit for their needs? Or are they chafing at its limitations? If it doesn't meet your corporate requirements for security, administrative control, or integration, is there an upgrade path to a version that fills those gaps?

If the powers that be rule an ad hoc or unsanctioned collaboration community must be shut down, at least try to learn something from it first. What collaboration scenarios were most popular on the platform? What communities were active there, and what can you do to provide them with a soft landing on the official corporate platform for social collaboration? To what extent is it possible to port over content from one environment to the other, while preserving as much of the context as possible?

Unauthorized use of a social collaboration product

With cloud software, workers from anywhere in the company can procure applications without the need for IT support. This can be good because it enables innovation in circumstances where IT may be the bottleneck, or bad because it results in a loss of necessary control.

Your organization can prohibit such ad hoc purchases by policy and refuse to reimburse credit card charges for unauthorized services, but the providers have every incentive to tempt your employees into signing up on the spur of the moment. If employees are going outside corporate channels to buy access to applications

they believe they need to get their jobs done, maybe that's a clue to IT to do something differently.

And although unauthorized cloud access can cause headaches, the cloud is not necessarily the enemy of IT. Today, more IT organizations are accepting the cloud as a tool for stretching their own resources. Instead of preventing all access to cloud applications, IT and corporate procurement groups are trying to insert themselves into the buying process so they can address issues of security, integration, and contract terms.

Recognize the risk that whatever collaborative activity was flourishing may not survive being transplanted to a new environment. You can mitigate the risk by recognizing the value of the experiment and those who participated in it. Ask for their help making the new, officially sanctioned social collaboration platform a success. If you can get them on your side, broader success will be more likely.

Weighing Simplicity Versus Control

A key selling point for any cloud service is simplicity. The cloud provider's operations may be very complicated behind the scenes, and no doubt they are. You don't care. You just enter your password and go to work. No one on your payroll needs to worry about setting up or backing up servers to support these applications or fixing them when they break.

However, if you want the simplicity, you must compromise absolute control, including control of these items:

- ✔ **Limited choices:** Cloud operators are focused on achieving very high scale at low cost, and one way they accomplish that is by making their services as standardized as possible. For a cloud collaboration service, that typically means offering one version of the software (or at most, two or three editions), with only the configuration options offered through a web-based administration screen.

Can you change the background color and add your logo? Sure. Can you modify the source code of the software for the sake of integrating with a legacy app? No way. Can you dictate the database will be Oracle and the server processor will be from Intel? No, you're not supposed to care about any of that as long as it works.

✔ **Data storage:** Cloud computing also means storing business data outside the corporate network, which some companies find scary.

Big companies have been outsourcing data center operations for years, but the contractual arrangements and the control IT had over the configuration and management of systems is much different in a traditional outsourcing or managed service arrangement. Those outsourced data centers can be treated more like an extension of the corporate network.

Cloud startups tend to want to operate more like consumer services, such as Google or Facebook. Cloud divisions of traditional IT services businesses like IBM may be a little more accommodating, but they too must seek to simplify their operations as much as possible if they want to be price competitive with other cloud services.

Addressing Concerns about Cloud Services

Although the advantages of cloud services are real, that doesn't mean that the worries are all imaginary. After you get past the myths of how wonderful (or how scary) cloud computing is, you can start to focus on the reality.

For social collaboration, one of the things this means is deciding whether the cloud service can be trusted to host important business conversations, documents, and project planning tools. What would happen if a competitor got access to those resources? You don't want to find out. You should make sure the solution you choose provides at least the same level of security you would expect from e-mail, making it safe to share routine business discussions. If there are some sorts of information you do not want to trust to the cloud platform — for example, if contract negotiations are ruled out of bounds — you will have to address those issues with corporate policy.

You should also investigate how the cloud platform integrates with other applications, including on-premises applications, to make sure you will not be creating an island of collaboration isolated from the rest of your business.

Understanding key security practices

Application security deserves some extra scrutiny. There are several dimensions to the security of a web application:

- ✔ **Protection of data in transit:** This usually involves using the same encrypted version of the web's HTTP protocol used for consumer credit card transactions. Your browser displays a closed padlock icon when this is active, assuring that data you send to the web server cannot be intercepted — at least not easily.

- ✔ **Protection of data at rest:** Measures are taken to protect your data in whatever form it is stored in the cloud data center. For maximum security, data can be stored as well as transmitted in an encrypted format so that only an authorized user can decode it.

- ✔ **Authentication security for identifying authorized users:** This measure includes minimum standards for passwords and the security of password reset mechanisms that can be subject to abuse by hackers.

- ✔ **Data center security:** This includes building access control, limits on physical access to cloud servers, and process controls governing the behavior of server and storage administrators.

In the next section, I give you some advice for reviewing a service provider's security practices. If you're not completely comfortable at the end of your review of the cloud provider's security measures, you may approve the application for some routine business but rule sensitive topics out of bounds. For example, you may dictate that legal and personnel matters should be discussed through other channels but that social collaboration on sales and marketing topics is acceptable.

The need to restrict the types of activity allowed in the cloud also can indicate that your organization would be better off hosting its own collaboration software.

Trusting but verifying service provider security and reliability

During U.S. President Ronald Reagan's negotiations with Soviet President Mikhail Gorbachev, his approach to their arms control agreement was based on a Russian proverb: *Doveryai, no proveryai.* In English, that translates to *Trust, but verify.*

Some conservative corporate IT and information security managers have just about the same watchful attitude toward cloud operators. That is, if they're going to trust their data to the cloud, they want to see independent evidence that it will be safe there. How you approach this depends, to some extent, on the size, cloud, and attitude of your business.

- ✔ **Aggressive, paranoid standard bearers:** These firms want to peer through the cloud, get a tour of the operator's data center, and see an independent security audit of the facility's processes and procedures. Cloud providers are typically reluctant to provide this access, but they've been known to bend when courting large or high-profile "trophy" customers. Usually, only the largest customers can afford to invest the time and effort required for that kind of detailed review of a cloud operation, anyway.

  These are also the firms that push harder for Service Level Agreement contracts with guarantees of performance tied to penalties if the SLAs are not met.

- ✔ **The followers:** Many large and midsize firms watch what the larger, higher-profile ones are doing, figuring that any cloud operation they sign up with is probably trustworthy. They may also consider such benchmarks as a SAS 70 Type II audit of processes and controls for reassurance about the reliability of a provider.

- ✔ **Gut instinct believers:** For small businesses (and perhaps most businesses) the security and reliability of the application services available through a reputable cloud provider are likely to be better than what they can provide on their own. Cloud services are big targets for hackers, so they staff security professionals with the skills to prevent and detect security breaches. Cloud services are expected to operate 24 hours a day, 365 days a year, so they carefully optimize their software configurations and data center operations for maximum reliability, with contingency plans for what to do when something goes wrong.

When a cloud service fails or is breached, it's news, partly because it doesn't happen that often. As with the safety record of commercial airplanes versus passenger cars, cloud services are safer on average, but when they fail, they can fail spectacularly.

I'm generalizing here, which is dangerous, but I believe this assertion is true of the level of cloud service you can expect from Yammer, for example, operating with Microsoft backing.

Cloud application startups often buy data center and network capacity from Amazon, inheriting some of its cloud computing competence. However, that doesn't necessarily mean that their apps are as resilient as some of the rhetoric about the wonders of cloud computing would lead you to expect.

For example, Amazon suffered a rippling failure across the servers in its East Coast data center, and the social media marketing app HootSuite was offline for most of a day and recovered only by sacrificing some customer data that hadn't been backed up. Although Amazon operates multiple data centers around the world, HootSuite had not arranged for replication between them. And Some startups may not have even the technical backing of Amazon.

Any service that can provide instant activation over the web can represent itself as a cloud service even though it could be running on a rusty server under someone's desk. If you're going to try something brand new, there will be more *Trust, but verify* required.

Integrating existing resources

The most technically sophisticated aspects of working with cloud services are related to integration, particularly integration with on-premises resources such as a corporate directory server. Most cloud collaboration products, including those hosted in the cloud, offer some sort of integration or synchronization with Microsoft Active Directory (AD), which is the most widely used repository of network account information for corporate employees. Particularly in large organizations, it's important to have an automated way of activating new accounts on the collaboration network when employees join the organization and deactivating them when employees leave.

IT personnel may also play a role in integrating other applications with the collaboration network, or even creating custom applications that integrate with it in some way.

Complying with regulations

Industry regulation can complicate or even prohibit the use of social collaboration in the cloud. Consider the U.S. Health Insurance Portability and Accountability Act (HIPAA) and its provisions for patient privacy. Even though patient records per se probably wouldn't be stored in the collaboration system, any conversation between healthcare professionals about a patient's health can be considered patient data. That means for it to be stored anywhere outside of a healthcare facility, it would have to be encrypted, not just in transit but on the server hard drive or other storage system.

If a cloud collaboration service does not meet these requirements, that doesn't necessarily mean you can't use it at all, only that you can't use it for certain business functions or types of data. A hospital may use a cloud service in the marketing department, but not for use by physicians or nurses, at least not when discussing specific patients.

The European Union's Data Protection Directive also complicates the use of cloud services because it discourages the storage of personally identifying information outside of Europe. European firms tend to be particularly leery of storing data in the United States, worrying that it can be subject to access by law enforcement under the USA PATRIOT Act. If the cloud service has data center operators in Europe, European firms may be able to negotiate terms that their data will be stored only there.

Achieving integration across a firewall

By definition, cloud collaboration services operate outside corporate firewalls. When the data or documents employees most want to collaborate on remain inside a firewall, that presents a potential problem. If a copy of the data is placed on the cloud service and the data happens to be sensitive, you have a security breach. Alternatively, if a collaborator posts a link to the location of that resource inside the corporate network, home office and traveling workers can't access it unless they log in via virtual private networking (VPN) software. Not impossible, but awkward.

Some of the more interesting scenarios for using social collaboration in conjunction with other business applications also become more complicated if the collaboration service is in the cloud but the target applications are on the private network.

A cloud enthusiast's answer may be to move more and more applications to the cloud until traversing the firewall becomes a nonissue. Another strategy is to use an integration appliance, such as Dell Boomi, designed specifically to bridge cloud and on-premises applications.

Negotiating a Better Contract

Cloud application providers prefer to do business on a click-through contract model borrowed from consumer websites. When you sign up for an account and mark the check box saying that you agree to the terms and conditions, that's the beginning and the end of the contract.

In general, cloud providers offer their services on a *take it or leave it* basis, and most small-to-midsize businesses will accept the standard terms, perhaps with a minor amendment. Often, it's that or walk away.

However, negotiations are sometimes possible. A survey for the Cloud Industry Forum of 450 senior information technology and business decision makers in enterprises, small- and medium-sized businesses, and public sector organizations, published in early 2011 found that 52 percent of the organizations making use of cloud services had negotiated the terms of these services, and 45 percent stated they had no opportunity to negotiate.

According to a *Stanford Technology Law Review* article, based on research by the Queen Mary University of London's Cloud Legal Project, the top six issues cloud customers tried to negotiate were:

1. Exclusion or limitation of liability and remedies, particularly regarding data integrity and disaster recovery.

2. Service levels, including availability.

3. Security and privacy, particularly regulatory issues under the European Union Data Protection Directive.

4. Avoiding lock-in and security contract termination rights, including the return of data after termination.

5. Limiting providers' ability to change service features unilaterally.

6. Protecting intellectual property rights.

The #1 concern on this list is also the one cloud providers were least willing to compromise on, saying they cannot accept liability for outages or data loss. According to the authors, "providers state liability is non-negotiable, and 'everyone else accepts it.' Even large users had difficulty getting providers to accept any monetary liability, with one global user stating that generally it 'had to lump it,' and another saying, 'they won't move.' Refusal to accept any liability was cited as a 'deal breaker' by several users."

European users can sometimes secure an agreement that their data will be stored within the region although some users complain that verifying the physical location of cloud data is all but impossible.

Negotiation is a power struggle, where the relative size and clout of the participants determine how willing each side is to move. Unless you think you can get the upper hand, it may not be worth the effort.

Chapter 11

Standards for Social Networking and Integration

*T*here is a lot to love about the idea that an organization should have one integrated social platform for all its communication and collaboration needs. At the same time, one software product, or software vendor, or cloud service, probably cannot fulfill every business need, now and forever.

So, using multiple products implies the need for standards — or at least commonly accepted specifications, data formats, and protocols — for plugging applications into each other and sharing context. Otherwise, you will tend to wind up with not one collaboration network but dozens of them. In this chapter, I help you think through the difficulties of dealing with shifting standards, enumerate the different types of standards, and consider the viability of one in particular, OpenSocial.

Surviving Shifting Standards

The social software industry is still in the process of figuring out the best way to do social application integration. There are standard data formats, standard authentication security methods, and standard mechanisms for embedding one application inside another. The challenge with these standards is there are so many to choose from.

And because social collaboration overlaps with the public social web, which is rapidly changing and morphing to accomplish other trends (such as the rise of mobile apps), setting standards that will last is extremely challenging. The very nature of standards-setting organizations has also changed under the influence of open source software, which emphasizes the creation of working software over stacks of specifications. Meanwhile, de facto standards including those from public social platforms like Facebook are often as influential as any defined by a formal committee.

Standards organizations like the Internet Engineering Task force (the custodian of the most fundamental Internet protocols) are often in the position of formalizing the definition of technologies that are already being treated like standards by agreement among major Internet companies. In the process, they try to improve the quality of these technologies — for example, of the OAuth social authentication protocol discussed in this chapter.

As a buyer and manager of social collaboration platforms, you will have to bet on which vendors seem to be making the right choices and forming the right partnerships. You also have to judge how important social application integration is to your organization now and in the near future. For example, is close integration with another web application essential, or is it enough for users to be able to click a link that takes them to it?

Bottom line: Do you insist on compliance with certain standards, or can you afford to relax and let these things sort themselves out?

Insisting on standards

Dion Hinchcliffe, a management and technology consultant for the Dachis Group and co-author of *Social Business by Design: Transformative Social Media Strategies for the Connected Company* (John Wiley & Sons, Inc.) believes that large organizations ought to be more proactive in insisting on standards, as they did in previous decades with base technologies for networking, databases, and data exchange between applications.

"The runaway successes of ISA/PCI, TCP/IP, SQL, and XML, to name just a few standards that ultimately changed computing history, showed the way, as well as the promise, of coming together as an industry around a common way of doing things on a level playing field," he writes in one of his columns for *InformationWeek.* "By contrast, the social media world has had only a few such breakout successes around open standards. Many initiatives have come and gone over the years, with only OAuth and a few others (such as Activity Streams) achieving widespread acceptance."

Although some enterprise architects see the potential for standards in this space, "there's simply more focus right now in most organizations on just getting basic social networks in place. In other words, on-boarding a company's IT systems into the activity streams of their workers often becomes phase two or three in a social business implementation," Hinchcliffe adds.

Coping with immature technologies

No social collaboration platform exhibits the maturity that we expect from, say, a relational database management system (RDBMS). For that matter, the level of standardization between RDBMS products shouldn't be exaggerated. The general pattern of using linked tables of related data to organize a database became commonplace in business applications decades ago. But SQL, the Structured Query Language used to add, retrieve, and manipulate relational database data, is a standard with many vendor-specific variations.

The social authorization standard OAuth (explained in more detail here) is probably the most widely accepted of all social application integration standards, but implementations in software products and cloud services vary in the extensions that they implement.

The current OAuth 2.0 specification is more "official" than some of the others mentioned here, having been defined through a standards track process of the Internet Engineering Task Force (IETF), the body behind basic Internet standards like TCP/IP and HTTP.

Yet the section on Interoperability in the OAuth 2.0 specification begins with a disclaimer:

> OAuth 2.0 provides a rich authorization framework with well-defined security properties. However, as a rich and highly extensible framework with many optional components, on its own, this specification is likely to produce a wide range of non-interoperable implementations.

> In addition, this specification leaves a few required components partially or fully undefined (e.g., client registration, authorization server capabilities, endpoint discovery). Without these components, clients must be manually and specifically configured against a specific authorization server and resource server in order to interoperate.

In other words, adhering to the specification may be a good starting point, but when the developers of two applications want to integrate with each other, they still have to agree on a specific approach to applying OAuth. Nailing down those details is to be the subject of future work by the specification's authors.

Recognizing de facto standards

A *de facto* standard is one that exists in practice, because it is commonly treated as a standard regardless of what any committee may say.

The Facebook platform for developers is not a standard the way OAuth is (although it actually incorporates OAuth). Instead, the platform — also known as Facebook's Open Graph — is simply the way Facebook does things and defines some of the things developers will have to do, too, if they want to give their apps access to the social network's more than 1 billion active users.

Because Facebook has done so much to influence expectations about what a social network should be, enterprise social networking players, including Yammer and VMware's Socialcast unit, have chosen to model their application integration frameworks more on Facebook than on standards more influenced by enterprise architects, such as OpenSocial.

The Open Graph Protocol is a component of the Facebook platform that looks a little more like an open source or web standards project, with its specifications available on a freestanding website (http://ogp.me). However, if you want to participate in discussions about the future of the specification, you have to do so in a Facebook Group rather than an IETF mailing list.

The Open Graph Protocol defines a series of metadata specifications for web pages and applications defining how they should be displayed on Facebook. Other social software can parse the same data to achieve a Facebook-like look.

The web has long been influenced by de facto standards, defined by practice and common usage, as opposed to de jure standards set by committee.

Adobe created the PDF file format in 1993 without participation from any standards body, but because the associated Adobe Reader was freely available, PDFs became a standard for printable web documents and e-books. Eventually it became so pervasive that in 2005, PDF/A got the blessing of the International Standards Organization as a de jure standard.

HTML started out as a de facto standard, as did many browser-specific extensions of HTML that eventually became standardized. However, for many years, creating web applications that would display and function properly in multiple browsers was extremely painful. Only recently did web standards advocates make their voices heard loudly enough to get the browser makers to play nice.

The same could prove to be true of social networking standards.

Leveraging Common Social Web Standards

The road to standards nirvana may be rocky, but it's not impossible. Social applications can take advantage of all the web and web services technologies that have evolved over the last couple of decades.

The following are all basic web development technologies that aren't specific to social collaboration but are important elements of social application development and integration:

✔ **REST:** Representational State Transfer (REST) is not so much a standard as it is a style of interaction between web-based applications, using a short list of standard HTTP request methods — GET, POST, PUT, and DELETE — to interact with any remote resource. The virtue of this is *loose coupling,* as opposed to the kind of integration that requires applications to have intimate knowledge of each other. That makes REST a good match for building and integrating web and cloud applications.

✔ **JavaScript:** This rich scripting language for manipulating data and the display of data in the browser has evolved over time to include methods for asynchronously sending and retrieving data in the background, without requiring the user to download a new web page.

✔ **XML and JSON:** These data exchange formats were derived from HTML and JavaScript, respectively. XML (eXtensible Markup Language) is a method of encoding data wrapped in HTML–like tags that specify meaning and context, rather than formatting. JSON (JavaScript Object Notation) is a method of serializing all the data associated with a JavaScript object into a text format that can be transmitted over the network. When a browser-based application written in JavaScript downloads data in JSON format, serialized objects can be reconstituted instantly without the parsing that would be required for the same data transmitted in XML.

These things can be used together. A web application may include an interactive JavaScript application that runs in the user's browser, uses REST-style communication with a server-side web application, downloads data in JSON format, and uses that data to update what the user sees onscreen. This would be one way to build a web-based interactive chat application, for example.

In addition, there are several web technologies that are particularly relevant to social networks — OAuth, Activity Stream, HTML iframes, JavaScript APIs, and Open Graph — and I cover them in the following sections.

Authorizing social app access with OAuth

If you ever accessed a Facebook application that asked you to review a list of permissions that the application is requesting and then click OK, you have seen OAuth in action.

OAuth outlines a method for giving one application access to another, with the user's permission. In particular, the user is giving access to something private, such as an e-mail address, affinities reflected in a social profile (things Liked, groups joined), or a collection of photos.

Say you want to provide a printing company access to your photos on Facebook or another photo-sharing site to print a custom calendar with your kid's pictures.

The process goes like this:

1. Authorization is requested.

   The client application requests access to a protected resource. In my example, the client application is the printing service, and the protected resource is the photos on Facebook.

2. The authorization grant is returned to the client for approval.

   The user (you) grants access. This process is mediated by the social networking platform, which you presumably trust, in the form of a user interface that makes clear what rights you are granting. If you say no, the process stops.

3. The authorization grant is relayed to the authorization server.

   The client application presents the authorization grant as proof that it should be provided with an *access token,* which is a key that it will be able to use to access the protected resource.

4. The access token is returned to the client.

   The social networking server in charge of protecting your identity verifies that the digital credential presented as proof of authorization is legitimate and then returns an access token.

5. The access token is sent to the resource server.

   The server in charge of the protected resource (your photos) receives an access token (the key) along with a specific access request.

6. The resource is returned to the client application.

   First, the resource server validates the access key. If it checks out, the print shop app gets access to your photos.

After going through the process once, the client application can continue to use the key you have given it to unlock the server containing your protected resource. By granting access, you're saying that you trust this application to act on your behalf and not against your interests.

Here's another simple example: If you give an online magazine access to your social profile so it can show you more of the articles that you tend to like, it will be able to continue to access the most current version of your profile on subsequent visits.

Access tokens can be set to expire and can be revoked, however. When you remove an application from your profile, you're telling the social platform that access token should no longer be honored.

Much debate remains as to whether OAuth strikes the right balance between security and ease of use. When representatives of enterprise IT organizations and their vendors got involved in defining OAuth 2.0, some web purists complained that the specification was becoming unnecessarily complex. On the other hand, OAuth 2.0 was designed to be easier to implement than the previous version, and some security advocates worried it may become too easy to hack in the process.

OAuth may not be perfect, but it has been widely adopted as a way of sharing profile data and other protected resources between applications.

Standardizing feeds with ActivityStrea.ms

Just as the RSS and Atom data formats make it possible to syndicate and aggregate blog posts and news stories, the Activity Streams format is intended to enable the syndication and aggregation of social posts, comments, and related data.

Although the term "activity stream" is also used much more generically to refer to the user interface style of social news feeds, I'm specifically referring here to an open web specification (http://activitystrea.ms). In conversation, software developers and architects sometimes pronounce the "dot-ms" part to make the distinction clear (like saying "Amazon.com" to make it clear you mean the online retailer, not the river).

Unlike a feed of headlines, an Activity Streams feed is meant to be much richer, with room to specify that one item was in reply to another, or to include references to embedded applications that should be displayed within the stream. The core specification includes a base schema plus two alternative data format specifications: one based on JSON and the other on Atom.

The most common use I have seen so far is in specialized collaboration applications that integrate with a broader social platform such as Jive, IBM Connections, or Atlassian Confluence. The embedded app can provide its own social commenting function but also provide a feed that appears in the parent platform's activity stream (by which, in this case, I mean the social news feed).

Embedding apps in HTML iframes

The easiest way of embedding one web application inside another, without needing to do much to wire them together, is with an HTML iframe. This is a way of inserting an entire application into a new context. You may use an iframe to embed a business application such as expense approval into a social platform, or, alternatively, to embed social commenting functionality into an expense record.

Before exploring more complicated scenarios, I explain how an iframe works on an ordinary HTML web page. Embedding an iframe in a web page is just about as easy as embedding an image.

Just look at the similarity between an image tag

```
<img src="http://mysite.com/myimage.jpg" height="600" width="600">
```

and an iframe tag

```
<iframe src="http://mysite.com/myapp.php" height="600" width="600">
```

Either one gives you a 600 x 600 pixel region in the middle of the page filled by content from the specified source web address. In the first example, the embedded content is an image, but in the second example, the iframe can contain a complete web application with its own styling and scripts.

If you stop here, you have a convenient way of displaying embedded content. However, the embedded application knows nothing about the context in which it's running. And that's where JavaScript APIs come in.

Setting social context with JavaScript APIs

To function like an integrated part of the social network, an embedded application needs to know who is accessing it and in what context.

An application embedded in an iframe is said to be running within a container, where the container is the master application containing the iframe pointing to the embedded app. For a Facebook app, the container would be Facebook. For an app from the Jive Apps Market, the container would be your organization's instance of Jive.

The embedded app needs to talk to the container to access the user's social profile. This is usually accomplished through JavaScript APIs (application programming interfaces) that request resources from the container, which in turn kicks off the OAuth workflow.

Charting Facebook's Open Graph

While the Facebook platform is limited to Facebook, enterprise social network players such as Yammer have modeled their own approaches to embedding and connecting applications on Facebook's approach. For example, Yammer defined its own version of Open Graph for functions like using an embedded app for document management, provided by an external cloud service, and publishing "stories" about those interactions to the Yammer stream.

The Facebook platform is constantly evolving. As of this writing, it includes the elements discussed here and more:

- **The Open Graph Protocol:** A metadata standard for documenting how you would like a web resource to be displayed on Facebook. For example, if a product page on your website includes the correct Open Graph tagging, when a Facebook user shares a link to that page it will be displayed with the product image, title, and other data you specified. You can include a reference to a video demonstrating the use of your product, allowing Facebook to display it in an inline video player.

- **A set of APIs:** A documented series of mechanisms for requesting services from the platform, particularly on behalf of the user. This includes the Facebook implementation of OAuth and protocols for registering Likes and other actions.

- **The Facebook JavaScript library:** A standard starting point for developers to access Facebook platform services and display standard widgets.

- **Facebook plug-ins:** Simplified access to common Facebook widgets, such as the Like button or a Facebook comments feed, using code snippets that can be copied and pasted into any HTML page.

- **App embedding with iframes:** Using the tool available at `https://developers.facebook.com/apps`, any web developer can register a Facebook app or Facebook *tab* (an app associated with a Facebook page) by giving it a name and filling out the form provided. After you plug in the web addresses of the external program that will render the user interface, Facebook displays that resource within an iframe. It's then up to the developer to use JavaScript and OAuth to get the user's social context and do something interesting with it. For example, a music app may provide a way to share favorite songs with friends, or a news reading app (like the Washington Post Social Reader) may make it easy to share articles with friends.

The Facebook platform supports both application embedding within Facebook and the ability for external websites and applications to embed Facebook functionality.

Yammer and Socialcast mimic the Facebook style of application integration, but with an emphasis on business content and applications rather than social entertainment apps.

OpenSocial: Providing an Enterprise Standard for App Embedding

OpenSocial is "the industry's leading and most mature standards-based component model for cloud based social apps," according to the website of the OpenSocial Foundation (http://opensocial.org). While support for OpenSocial isn't universal (Yammer is a notable holdout), it has the backing of Jive, IBM, Atlassian, and others.

This is the enterprise-friendly version of something like the Facebook platform, providing a framework for embedding social applications inside each other and allowing them to communicate with each other. OpenSocial aims to make it easier for developers to make social software applications work together, or to bring business application functionality into a social context. OpenSocial can be used to embed application user interface widgets into the activity stream, a sidebar, or a separate tab of the collaboration software's user interface. The goal is to let users perform a greater variety of tasks without leaving the social collaboration platform.

With the release of OpenSocial 2.0 in August 2011, enterprise computing interests like IBM and Jive Software revived what was originally intended to be a social computing standard for public websites. OpenSocial strives to incorporate other popular web standards, such as OAuth and Activity Streams, while adding its own framework for how those standards should be combined and how a social container should behave. To keep the specification from becoming too abstract, OpenSocial is supported by a parallel open source software effort: namely, the Apache Shindig project (http://shindig.apache.org).

OpenSocial's winding path to social collaboration

The original version of OpenSocial goes back to 2007, when it was defined by Google, MySpace, and a number of other early social networks. Google's old iGoogle portal used Google Gadgets based on OpenSocial, and the gadgets mechanism found itself in some other websites and applications, including enterprise social products. Meanwhile, MySpace struggled, and Google itself seemed to lose interest. However, the developers of social collaboration platforms recognized that OpenSocial addressed many of the basics they needed for better social application integration, such as a standards for profiles, relationships, and activities within a social network.

Compared with some other concepts for web application integration, such as Java portlets, OpenSocial also has the advantage of being relatively light-weight. Applications don't have to be written in the same language or run on the same operating system. A PHP application can plug itself into a Java-based container just by serving up the right HTML and JavaScript code.

OpenSocial has also been enhanced to support embedded experiences, which allow users to access applications right from within the social stream. IBM sponsored the creation of an OpenSocial MIME type as part of the embedded experiences for the standard, making it possible to also embed OpenSocial apps in e-mail messages.

MIME — Multipurpose Internet Mail Extensions — is the protocol used by both e-mail clients and web browsers to render embedded multimedia content and file attachments for e-mail.

The most recent version of the Notes mail client takes advantage of this capability when used in combination with the IBM Connections enterprise social network.

An example of a business application delivered as an embedded experience is a vacation approval request that arrives in the activity stream of an employee's manager. Rather than clicking a link and being redirected to another web application, the manager can immediately approve or reject the request by using an embedded widget displayed within the stream or within a sidebar. When the request is approved, the employee gets confirmation in his own social stream and can reply with a quick Thank You!

As implemented on the Jive Software platform, adding an application widget to a stream is as easy as typing an exclamation point. Just like how most social platforms display a pop-up list of potential matches when you type @ followed by the first few characters of the name or username of a person you want to reference, Jive does the same thing when you type ! followed by the name of an application.

As a Jive user creating a discussion post or document, I can use this technique with a sample app that helps me give recognition to another employee. As soon as I type the exclamation point, I get the prompt shown in Figure 11-1 with the available options.

After I select the app I want to use, a compact rendition of its user interface is overlaid on the blog editor screen, as shown in Figure 11-2.

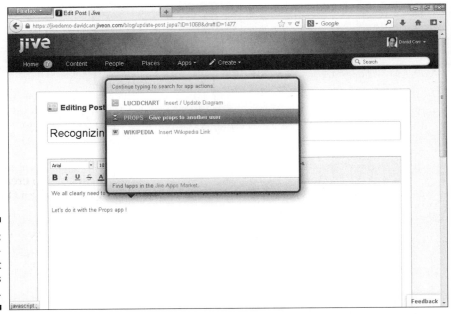

Figure 11-1:
Jive's excla-
mation point
access
to apps.

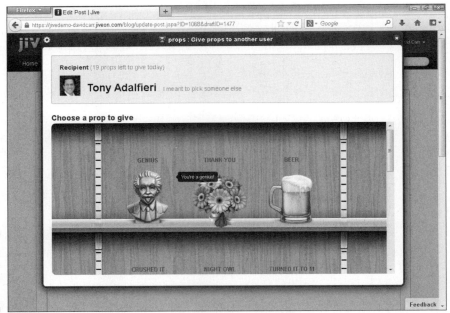

Figure 11-2:
An embed-
ded app
in Jive.

In this case, I chose the Props app, which allows me to choose a virtual trophy to award to another employee. Working with the embedded app, I can add a message about why my colleague is so wonderful. The output of the app gets embedded in my blog post, where I can write about his contributions, but the Props item also gets posted separately to the company activity stream and added to this employee's profile.

Using the same approach, I can access a flowchart or other diagram created in Lucidchart, or create a new one, and insert it into my document. The Jive Apps Market features a variety of embeddable apps for applications like task management and customer relationship management. IBM is promoting similar apps partnerships. SugarCRM co-founder and CTO Clint Oram recently joined the OpenSocial board to represent the interests of app creators. In some scenarios, the SugarCRM platform also can function as an OpenSocial container.

Atlassian, maker of the Confluence social software platform and JIRA issue-tracking tool, also has a representative on the board. Other social software vendors support OpenSocial, but with varying degrees of enthusiasm.

Calculating the Odds for the Future of Social Software Standards

OpenSocial shows great potential as an application integration framework for social collaboration. However, I keep watching and waiting for the day when it catches fire in the software market. Some of the smaller vendors support OpenSocial just to get access to a channel like the Jive Apps Market, but it's not clear that they can win a lot of business that way.

Meanwhile, Yammer's view is that the best Web 2.0 applications provide rich user experiences that don't fit neatly into an iframe. The Yammer software architects argue it's better to provide integration that reaches out from Yammer to connect with those other websites and applications and embeds inside them, while allowing them to pump updates into the Yammer news feed.

The biggest sign that OpenSocial may matter in the long run is that some enterprise buyers are starting to add it to their lists of requirements. For example, Ford Motor Company has some success stories to tell about its use of Yammer, but Ford IT architect Ed Krebs told me he has his doubts about it as a long-term solution. As a member of an advanced technologies group at Ford, he has been running experiments on Shindig and sees the potential of the technology that Yammer is snubbing. He is also working with a W3C

(World Wide Web Consortium) business community group on social software and sees OpenSocial as more aligned with that standards-setting process.

Here are a few things to look at when weighting these factors:

- ✔ Are you concerned with embedding applications in your collaboration network? Or do you see it as a tool for communication and collaborative work that stands alone?

- ✔ Do you see the potential for the integration requirement to increase as the collaboration network becomes more widely used?

- ✔ Do you have legacy enterprise applications that could be revitalized by being wrapped in a social container? That's something that can favor the OpenSocial approach.

- ✔ Do you make significant use of applications that support either of these approaches, or some other web application framework?

Part IV
Managing Social Collaboration

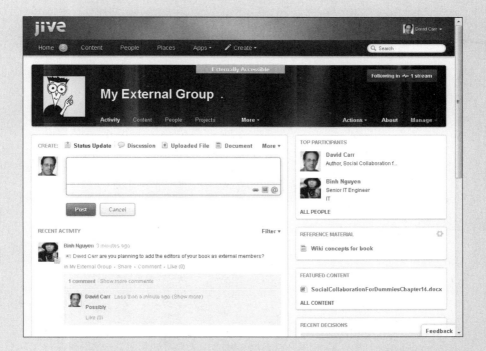

In this part . . .

- ✔ Get off to a good start and sustain a social collaboration initiative.

- ✔ Understand community management and why it's essential to the long-term health of any online community.

- ✔ Find out how to selectively invite external collaborators into your private community.

Chapter 12

Succeeding with Social Collaboration

*P*icking the right social collaboration platform is just the beginning. You may think that people who use Facebook in their personal lives would immediately embrace social collaboration for work, but employees often need a little help understanding how this relates to work. Even though the knee-jerk reaction of some executives is to worry about inappropriate use of an internal social network, the bigger problem is often lack of use.

More importantly, you want social collaboration to be productive. Connecting people from across the company is good. Getting them working together is better. Translating collaboration into new products, more sales, agile organizations, and lower costs is the goal.

Organizing Social Collaboration

Top-level community managers establish the overall framework but may delegate some of the training, support, and coaching activities to sub-community managers, help desk personnel, and others who play supporting roles in the health of the social collaboration network.

Putting someone (or some team) in charge of community management

The surest way to fail with social collaboration is to treat it purely as an IT implementation project. Yes, you need to pay attention to how the software (or cloud service) will be deployed and all the technical details of how the collaboration network will be configured and maintained. Just don't stop there. Failure is more likely to come from inadequate attention to the human network than the Ethernet network. That is why social collaboration success is so dependent on community management.

Some elements of success come from executive leadership — in terms of vision — yet vision goes only so far. Successful communities invariably have someone or some team leading at a more practical, detailed level on a daily basis.

A community is any group of people united by a common interest or purpose. In social collaboration, the entire company is a community that is (or ought to be) united around the purpose of making the company's success. A social collaboration network can also encourage the formation of more focused communities, represented as collaboration groups. These may reflect existing organizational structures, such as departments, but they can also pull together groups of employees who may otherwise not get a chance to connect, such as engineers who share a specific expertise but work in different offices.

Success for an online community depends on both management of technology and management of the social dynamics of the group. A community manager may have to double as technical system administrator, particularly in smaller organizations. Larger companies may have a community strategist overseeing the entire social collaboration network, plus a system administrator for the more technical work and a team of community managers for specific collaboration groups.

The guidelines that follow are for whoever is in charge of the community management team (even if it's a team of one).

Some work to be done by community leaders includes

- ✔ **Set strategy and priorities for the online community.** Deciding where and how to start is important. So is adjusting tactics, depending on what works. If you thought sales would be quickest to adopt the platform, but research and development proves more enthusiastic, maybe you should focus on showing results in R&D first and come back to sales later with some success stories to tell.

✔ **Manage technology.**

- *Yours:* Regardless of whether your collaboration network runs on servers within your corporate network or in a dedicated hosting or offsite data center environment, someone will need to administer servers and databases. Whether you're personally responsible for systems administration or delegate it to someone in IT, you will have to make choices about how the software is configured and when to upgrade.

- *The cloud:* If you take advantage of a cloud service, you have a different set of challenges related to keeping the external service synchronized with your internal network.

Either way, someone needs to continually evaluate whether the server or server options your organization has chosen are performing adequately and whether add-on software and services are worth the money.

✔ **Troubleshoot.** A social collaboration platform requires someone who can add or remove user accounts, reset passwords, recover deleted content, and figure out why things aren't working the way they're supposed to. You probably want to provide automated mechanisms to address the most common issues, such as resetting passwords. When those mechanisms fail, though, you need a troubleshooter.

✔ **Organize.** It can make sense to let communities be self-organizing, meaning that they can be created by any group of people who come together around a common purpose, without having to go through a group approval process. You can give them a sense of ownership by letting them take charge and providing them with the tools and advice they will need to be successful. Having said that, the short-term advantages of letting communities self-organize can be offset by long-range consequences, such as proliferation of redundant groups and documents. Community leaders watch for signs of disorder and compensate by urging overlapping groups to combine, highlighting authoritative content, and pruning away the dead wood. I tell you more about managing groups in Chapter 13.

✔ **Delegate authority and oversee community spaces.** Within the overall community for your organization, you want to have subcommunities or groups (the terminology varies) for projects, departments, and groups of employees with common interests or expertise. You make your collaboration network more manageable when you put someone in charge of each pocket of activity, delegating some administrative authority.

✔ **Monitor and measure community activity.** Always be aware whether overall community activity is rising or falling as well as which content, communities, individuals, and social applications are generating the most activity. Beyond the raw server log metrics, the community management team needs to be watching for the most productive activities. Figure 12-1 shows a Jive administrator's report for profile completion,

✔ **Set an example.** By using the collaboration network effectively, community leaders lead by example. By modeling productive behaviors — say, recognizing positive contributions by others and making good introductions — community leaders' actions suggest things that all members can do to make the community perform better.

✔ **Moderate conversations and enforce the acceptable use policy.** Considered as a system administration task, a person with moderation rights has the power to edit, reclassify, or delete content that others have posted. I tell you about acceptable use policies later in the "Setting and communicating acceptable use policies" section and more about moderating communities in Chapter 13.

Naming group community managers

I recommend that every group have an owner: namely, someone who takes responsibility for its success and for basic community management duties. The owner can either run the community or delegate the responsibility. Group-level community management is typically a part-time or spare-time responsibility. Even dedicating a fraction of the right employee's time and attention can make a big difference, though, allowing the core community management team to stretch its resources.

If a group is important enough — for example, being used for a strategic project — the corporate community management team may also delegate resources to making sure things go well.

Social networks and exponential growth

The power of networking is often explained in terms of Metcalfe's Law, after Ethernet pioneer Robert Metcalfe, which states that the value of a network is proportional to the square of the number of connected users or devices. Originally laid down as an organizing principle for telecommunications and digital networks, it can be said to apply by extension to social networks: that is, those with the most users become exponentially more powerful.

The problem with the analogy is that people aren't just nodes to be activated by attaching a cable and flipping a switch. On a social network, what really makes the difference isn't the number of users but the number of *active* users. The people with an account on a collaboration network but never log in are no help. The people who use the network every week, every day, or every hour are the ones more likely to see the benefits both in terms of regular work and spontaneous online encounters. It's one of those "the harder I work, the luckier I get" scenarios.

Your challenge is to line up enough of those people that the collaboration network catches fire.

Developing a Strategy for Success

Good results come from good beginnings. Although any initiative can get off to a good start and then stumble, anything you can do to show practical applications and quick wins for social collaboration increases your chances for long-term success. Each social collaboration implementation is different, but I can (and do) outline some general steps to take toward long-term social collaboration success.

Positioning your team for a quick win

Early success may involve an element of luck, but as Benjamin Franklin put it, "Diligence is the mother of good luck." In other words, your strategy maximizes the odds of good luck, and your planning allows you to recognize it and exploit it when it comes along. Here are some tactics to consider:

- ✔ Diligently think through what are most likely to be the most productive uses of social collaboration and start there.

- ✔ Diligently train and support your first users of the social collaboration service so they see the potential and take advantage when it can make a difference.

- ✔ Diligently watch for evidence of success and celebrate it loudly when it happens, regardless of whether it occurs where you expected it to.

Develop a series of scenarios for how social collaboration will pay off for your firm, even if they are largely fictitious in the beginning. Imagine how you would like employees to interact, predict how they are likely to interact, and (once you launch your network) monitor how they actually interact. Here are some ways to identify a productive social collaboration scenario:

- ✔ Find an opportunity to align your project with the things management cares most about, such as revenue generation and creating new products.

- ✔ Identify communications breakdowns between team members or departments that ought to be working together more smoothly, and develop a plan for using social collaboration to improve communications.

- ✔ Talk to the leaders who show the most willingness to try new technologies and change business processes and get them involved with the social collaboration system in a productive way.

In other words, determine where you can you find the best combination of low risk and big potential payoff.

A successful social collaboration initiative

Shortly after the professional services firm KPMG Australia began working with the tibbr social collaboration tool from Tibco, the initiative's advocates could point to a big client engagement KPMG won by virtue of working collaboratively. With the tool in place, KPMG could pool the knowledge and connections of many associates to assemble a better proposal and do it more quickly than would have been possible otherwise.

Suddenly, what may have seemed an academic exercise in creating a more collaborative organization had a direct connection to revenue for the firm. Company leaders paid attention, and the story began to spread globally across KPMG. This international network of tax, accounting, and business consulting firms operate under the laws of many different companies but share some centralized services. The story of how social collaboration had succeeded in Australia eventually inspired the global knowledge management team to adopt the cloud version of tibbr and offer access to the service to all KPMG firms, worldwide.

These priority applications can help you identify fruitful pilot projects. I discuss pilot projects in the context of product selection in Chapter 9, but a pilot is also a way of testing ways to use social collaboration productively. Even past the technical pilot phase, large organizations often don't make a social collaboration platform available to every employee, everywhere in the company, all at once. One impediment is an organization's limited capacity for training and technical support, which can be more easily metered out location by location or division by division.

While taking things in phases may be a practical necessity, beware of a slow, tentative approach. There is little point in fielding a social collaboration environment that only includes a small fraction of the potential collaborators.

The quicker you can show business results, based on actual experience within the company, the more likely social collaboration will win broader acceptance and adoption.

Going boldly forward

Grammarians maintain that the intro to the old Star Trek TV series should have been "to go boldly where no man has gone before" rather than "to boldly go," even though the latter sounds better to my ear. At any rate, the point was for the crew of the Enterprise to be bold. If the promise had been to *initiate a pilot project and then reevaluate the possibility of a slow, staged warp drive rollout,* imagine what worlds would have gone undiscovered.

I encourage you to boldly go forward with social collaboration because tentative initiatives often flop. Here are some steps you can take to get started:

- **First, check for technical problems.** For example, if you loaded in profile data from a human resources database, check that it displays properly. If you've integrated other applications into the social platform, are those integrations working as advertised?

- **Prepare for guests.** In addition to giving the social collaboration network a thorough technical shakedown cruise, you probably want to stock it with resources for your planned applications.

  For example, if one of your goals is to replace an old intranet page for your human resources department, the collaboration space for that department should be stocked with documents about vacation and benefits policies before you open the doors. Better yet, have a few conversation starter discussion threads already started.

- **Implement the program in phases if appropriate.** After you have a plan, move beyond the tentative stage of pilot projects as swiftly as practical. For very large organizations, a phased implementation may still be necessary. Even if you make social collaboration technically available to everyone within the organization all at once, you may still have to go department by department, business unit by business unit, or country by country spreading the word and offering training on effective use of the social tools.

- **Inspire participation.** You have to get past what experts in this field call the "empty bar" problem: that is, nobody wants to hang out somewhere that no one else is hanging out. You have to have social activity to generate social activity.

  As you work your way across the organization, start collecting stories about how collaborative processes are making a difference in helping employees get their work done better and faster. Build a list of advocates, from among the early adopters, who will vouch for the value of social collaboration to those who come later.

- **Demonstrate how colleagues can use the tool productively.** As soon as possible, start establishing clusters of employees with a real business need to connect and collaborate. They can help you make the business case for the use of the tools you're introducing. Sooner rather than later, you should be connecting people in different offices, if not different countries, who share challenges and interests. At the same time, provide those who already work closely together with new tools that will make them more productive, such as the ability to access and update the same work documents from home or while traveling that they would use in the office.

  Providing the tools is less important than showing colleagues how to use them productively; this is the critical *What's in it for me?* factor that convinces people to try something new.

> ✔ **Recognize colleagues for participation.** As individuals and teams begin to use the social collaboration network productively, thank them, celebrate and showcase their successes, and ask them to tell others about the value they are finding in the platform.

Seeking Strong Sponsorship

Most technology initiatives benefit from executive sponsorship, but social collaboration benefits most of all. Chapter 15 addresses social collaboration from the perspective of the CEO or executive leader. Here, I address strategies for the community strategist trying to win support from the top of the organization, either for an initial implementation or to expand the scope of a social collaboration network.

Social collaboration is as much of an organizational initiative as a technological one. Providing the tools will pay off only if employees are motivated to connect and collaborate in new ways — and believe me they will be rewarded.

The messages they hear and the behavior they see from the company leaders will set the tone. If social collaboration is promoted as a tool for being innovative and transparent, feedback from the CEO or other top officer who welcomes constructive criticism will go a long way toward validating that strategy as genuine.

CEO sponsorship is ideal. LeasePlan (an international vehicle fleet operator, and a big customer for IBM Connections) promotes its LinkedPeople social network with a video featuring CEO Vahid Daemi as well as ordinary employees talking about the value of collaboration and connectedness.

Some CEOs take an interest in social collaboration from the outset, perhaps seeing it as a tool to build a stronger corporate culture and pull together acquired companies into unified businesses. However, most CEOs think more in terms of strategy and the business results they want to achieve than they do about technology.

At Mercer (a global management consulting firm that helps other companies design benefits plans and employee programs), the mandate handed down in early 2012 from president and CEO Julio A. Portalatin was for "employee engagement and innovation within the organization and better ways to foster innovation," according to CIO Harry Van Drunen.

As a result of that business mandate, Van Drunen was able to revive a planned SharePoint upgrade — which had been shelved for budgetary reasons — and layer on social collaboration from NewsGator. The business case was to accelerate engagement and innovation by connecting people and ideas.

Since then, Portalatin has become probably the most active user of the platform's social capabilities, blogging about strategy and inviting employees to comment back, Van Drunen says. "He's embracing the opportunity."

Making the Case for Broader Use

A pilot project or an initial implementation of limited scope can help make the case for bigger things to come. Mine that example for both statistics on activity and adoption and anecdotes about productive use of social collaboration. Identify advocates of the social collaboration platform who will give testimonials or perhaps even offer to coach other communities on successful use of the platform.

Your business case for broader use will be more powerful if

- ✔ You can make a connection with revenue or some other financial metric. The trick is it's often difficult to prove the same results could not have been achieved in the absence of social collaboration. But numbers still tend to catch the attention of top management.

- ✔ Social collaboration addresses some known, persistent problem, such as communications breakdowns between marketing and sales.

- ✔ Your example shows the potential for shortening an important process, such as producing sales proposals. Because time is money, management may be able to make the translation to a monetary value for collaboration even if you do not attempt to make that calculation.

Few things are as powerful for establishing social collaboration as a standard within the organization as having the CEO and corporate leadership start to use it as a favored mode of communication, particularly if they not only blog but invite and respond to feedback on their posts. The executive blog can take the place of broadcast e-mails to all employees.

In small organizations, the company owner or leader may also participate in day-to-day discussions and brainstorming sessions on the social platform. In larger companies, the CEO is likely to be too busy to do more than an occasional cameo appearance. However, even occasional participation — for example, taking the time to comment *Great job!* on news of a significant sales win — will be significant to the person who gets that feedback as well as a sign to all that participation in the social network can be a way to win recognition for achievement.

When the global financial firm State Street Corporation organized an "innovation rally" a few months after the launch of its State Street Collaborate internal social network, the participation of State Street chairman, president and CEO Jay Hooley was important to the success of that online brainstorming project. The rally attracted 12,000 posts, which were later filtered to a dozen ideas for new products or operational changes with real potential business value. State Street then established collaboration groups for each of the most promising ideas aimed at bringing them to fruition.

Meanwhile, the burst of activity around the rally helped familiarize employees with the workings of the social collaboration platform and boosted its credibility as a business tool. For subsequent innovation campaigns, State Street graduated to using innovation management software (NewsGator's ideation module) to take some of the labor out of sorting through a large number of idea submissions.

Getting Employees Up to Speed

Sure, a social collaboration platform is supposed to make professional networking, content sharing, and collaboration easy — just as most software is sold as being "easy." Some users will find it easy and intuitive, while others won't. Make sure to provide everyone with the information they need so that they won't be horribly confused. Even those who pick up the basics naturally (such as using a Facebook-esque status post) may not find their way to the more advanced features of the platform without guidance.

Beyond helping employees use the social collaboration software, your goal as a community manager is to help them use it productively:

- ✔ Provide training relevant to their work.

- ✔ Communicate the organization's goals for the collaboration network and some of the intended uses.

- ✔ Present your acceptable use policy.

- ✔ Help colleagues understand when it's best to use the social collaboration system instead of e-mail and vice versa.

Some of your initial communication will probably have to go out by e-mail, particularly in the early stages when few people are watching for alerts from the social network. However, to keep in the spirit of things, you may limit the e-mail to a link and a sentence or two of introduction, followed by a link to a social post providing more detail.

Offering training resources

Depending on the platform your company chooses, various forms of training may be available:

- ✓ **From vendors:** Every social collaboration vendor offers some level of training in the use of the software, whether through on-demand video playback or screen capture sessions or live training sessions, in person or online.

- ✓ **Traditional classroom training:** A more formal setting may make sense for administrators and community managers who would benefit from getting some face time with the instructor and a chance to ask lots of questions.

- ✓ **Online instruction:** This more practical mode of delivery can reach across a large organization. Synchronous online events give employees an opportunity to ask questions live, via text chat or a call-in line, and on-demand playback of a webcast makes the class into a long-term training asset for people who missed the live training and also for new employees who join the company.

- ✓ **Help and tips:** The social collaboration platform can itself be a tool for training because it provides a medium for sharing tips and getting questions answered, allowing users who have mastered the basics to find out the rest for themselves. Meanwhile, the software vendors are working to make their user interfaces self-documenting so that the explanation of how or why to use a feature is presented in context.

Vendors and the training companies they partner with can provide live instructors and pre-recorded video to cover all the basics of the platform. To make the instruction more specific to your company, ask the instructor to tailor the material to your requirements or provide time for a community manager or project manager to say a few words at the beginning or the end of the class, or interspersed throughout. If you're working with pre-recorded video, consider mashing it up with clips from your own people about your own intentions and applications for social collaboration.

Jane Hart, a speaker, writer, and consultant from the Centre for Learning and Performance Technologies in the U.K., lists a half dozen ways instruction on social collaboration can be delivered, including games and simulations that allow employees to experiment with social collaboration in a mock-up environment stocked with virtual co-workers. She also talks about the value of "learning in the flow of work," defined as "natural continuous, informal, and social learning."

Figure 12-2 shows what Jive's document collaboration user interface looks like when accessed in Getting Started mode, which includes annotations that explain what should go in the title and the body of the document, how to associate the document with a specific community, and how to tag it so it will be easier for others to find.

Figure 12-2:
An anno-
tated
Getting
Started
screen
in Jive.

Focusing on the essentials

Don't assume that every employee asked to use your collaboration network is familiar with social networks. For those who have steered clear of Facebook, Twitter, and even stodgy old LinkedIn, explaining that a feature works "just like on Facebook" clarifies nothing. For those who see social networking as a waste of time, such appeals also undercut the case for using social collaboration as a practical business tool.

Instead, focus on these items:

- ✔ Business scenarios for networking with co-workers
- ✔ Sharing documents
- ✔ Getting questions answered

The active social network users will recognize the familiar user interface elements where they occur and benefit from that understanding. Meanwhile, those for whom social networking is still alien will have a better chance of catching on if you can refrain from assuming they know things that they don't.

Setting and communicating acceptable use policies

At any rate, tutoring employees on the software features is only half the battle. Help employees appreciate what social networking means in the context of work — not just generically, but within your organization specifically.

Provide colleagues with corporate guidelines for how the collaboration network should and should not be used. Make sure that all employees have access to the document. Often this can be adapted from acceptable use policies already in place for e-mail and other online systems.

An acceptable use policy may include (but isn't limited to) the following:

✓ **Definitions of prohibited and strongly discouraged behavior:**
Acceptable use policies typically spell out types of communication and online behavior that are prohibited, as well as some that are strongly discouraged.

You may spell out, for example, whether sharing jokes and other non-work communications is allowed, prohibited, or strongly discouraged. It would also clarify the finer points of the policy. For instance, sharing a silly but nonoffensive joke may earn an employee a mild rebuke but would be unlikely to be a firing offense. And even though sharing jokes may be acceptable in some organizations, sharing racist or sexually demeaning jokes would certainly not be acceptable in any medium for corporate communication.

✓ **Instructions for handling sensitive and confidential information:**
Other policies may restrict the types of business information that can be discussed on the social platform for regulatory reasons or because of concerns about security and confidentiality. For example, a hospital may bar physicians from posting patient records or discussing the conditions of patients on its collaboration network. Of course, all businesses want to keep Social Security numbers and other personally identifying information about customers from being shared in this way.

Many organizations will already have an acceptable use policy for e-mail and other network applications that can be extended and adapted to cover what is and is not allowed on a collaboration network. If not, establish one so that everyone understands the expectations and limits. You can get some hints from studying IBM's Social Computing Guidelines, which focus on the use of public blogs and social media and also cover many do's and don'ts that apply to any social network:

`www.ibm.com/blogs/zz/en/guidelines.html`

Acceptable use and corporate culture

In the social collaboration platform at some organizations, sharing the occasional joke or a link to the review of a movie you liked may be acceptable — a way of showing a little personality at work, akin to casual conversation about sports and entertainment topics at the proverbial office water cooler. Another company may reprimand employees for sharing anything other than work-related content. Certainly, any organization investing in social collaboration as a productivity tool is going to want the majority of the communications carried on the network to have a definite business purpose.

Personally, I think allowing a certain amount of levity on the collaboration makes sense as a way of lightening things up and generating interest, just as including a little humor in a serious speech helps keep the audience awake.

In addition to governing what can be posted, the policy should cover the appropriate use of content and resources shared on the internal network. That means keeping private communications and content private. Unfortunately, it does happen that the CEO's blog on company strategy, posted in the spirit of internal transparency, gets copied and pasted into a message to someone in the press or shared with a competitor. This is not so different from the phenomenon of the internal e-mail that somehow winds up as the centerpiece of a story in *The Wall Street Journal.*

When a breach of confidentiality occurs, you may be able to trace it to its source. On the chance you can, however, having a policy in place that prohibits such actions can be the basis for disciplinary action against the culprit.

Just as Facebook and Twitter make users sign off on a long list of terms and conditions when establishing an account, you can make employees give the same kind of click-through assent to the rules when they activate their internal social network accounts. Just as in those public social networks, though, you can bet that most people won't actually study the rules before they click OK. Thus, the most important elements of the policy will need to be reinforced with training or other communications.

You can require that participants sign an agreement before you grant them access to the social collaboration platform or even prompt them to give a click-through acknowledgement of the rules when they set up a profile. Unfortunately, just as consumers agree to long lists of terms and conditions associated with web services without understanding half of what they are agreeing to, you cannot be sure employees will read and comprehend the rules just because they are written down. That means the rules also need to be communicated through training and reinforced periodically through corporate communications.

Providing guidance on which communication tool to use

Evangelists of social collaboration often boast of its potential to cut down the volume of e-mail and eliminate confusing Reply to All e-mail threads and mailing list discussions. However, unless you plan to take away employee access to e-mail (rarely practical), employees need guidance when to use each mode of communication. For many, the tendency is to fall back on e-mail as the familiar option, whatever its shortcomings. You have to work harder to explain the situations where social collaboration works better.

For example, social communication makes sense when

- ✔ **You don't know who has the answer to your question.** When you have a question but don't know who to ask, you increase your chances of getting an answer when you throw the question out to the company or to a community within the company that has the right expertise. In that case, a single social post may replace a more disorganized process of hunting around the organization for the right person to ask.

- ✔ **You want to start a discussion.** Particularly if the discussion includes more than two, you can avoid the confusion of tangled e-mail threads and quoted messages by using the appropriate social collaboration tools.

- ✔ **You're engaging in an inherently collaborative activity.** For instance, if you're exchanging drafts of a document with one or more co-workers who will make additions and edits, rather than e-mailing file attachments back and forth, you can avoid confusion by collaborating on an online document.

In contrast, e-mail makes sense when

- ✔ **The conversation requires privacy.** Fall back on e-mail when you need to send a private message to one or two people.

- ✔ **The message recipient isn't in the network.** You must communicate with someone outside the organization without access to your company social network.

- ✔ **You're contacting someone who rarely uses social collaboration.** You must communicate with co-workers who are not regular users of the collaboration network.

    Of course, you want to be whittling down that last group of collaborators. Particularly in the beginning, though, you'll likely find some holdouts.

At UBM, the events and publishing company where I work, the CEO and some of the other executives regularly send e-mail messages that consist solely of a link to a blog post. They show their commitment to the employee social network by posting their messages to the organization as blogs, but they also follow up with an e-mail, so no one misses the message. In most cases, they can just as easily include the e-mail in the body of the message (although I've seen exceptions where the CEO's blog included multimedia elements, such as video). However, by sending only the link, they give people a reason to log on to the collaboration network if they want to be informed about what's going on within the company.

Putting Social Collaboration in the Flow of Work

Social collaboration should make it easier to get work done, not harder, eliminating steps in business processes, rather than making more work to do. This can be easier said than done. Employees who see work communications being split between e-mail and social collaboration may ask, quite reasonably, whether they have not in effect been given a second inbox to check.

One answer to that is to cut down on the volume of internal e-mail, so that the e-mail inbox becomes the one that must be checked only occasionally. That takes time, but meanwhile you can aim to put social collaboration *in the flow of work.* That phrase has gained more currency as the vendors of social collaboration software and services try to position their products as tools for getting work done, not merely for hosting discussion groups. What it really means is that social collaboration should be built in to work processes so that it becomes a natural part of getting them done better and faster. You can build social collaboration into work processes by encouraging colleagues to avoid sending duplicate messages on multiple platforms when possible, use project- and task-management tools, and simplify processes.

Avoiding duplicate communications

Efficiency comes from eliminating duplication of effort, wherever possible. Eliminating duplicate communications is important for social collaboration to take hold. If you send the same message by e-mail and on the corporate social network and have to keep track of responses through each channel, you're defeating the purpose.

Some overlap between e-mail and social collaboration is probably inevitable, at least as a transitional compromise between these modes of communication. Social collaboration tools typically include an option for users to receive e-mail notifications when someone interacts with their profile or mentions them in a post, or when there is a post related to a person or a topic that they follow. With some intelligent filtering, e-mail notifications can be useful. What's not so useful is to get every message twice.

Embedding project and task management

Social task management, which I discuss in Chapter 6, is one way of making social collaboration integral to work. Rather than sending someone an e-mail to assign a task, a manager can create a task that will be transmitted through the social network and tracked against the specified deadline. The person responsible for that task can then post updates on his progress with a series of comments on the task and check it off as done. When tasks are grouped together into projects, the project manager can see at a glance which are complete, or incomplete, or running behind schedule.

Seeking opportunities to simplify processes with social workflow

A similar opportunity is to weave workflow into the social environment so that a process requiring hand-offs between several members of a team before it's complete makes its way smoothly across the organization. If business process management technology is thrown into the mix, the workflow may include a mix of manual processes, automated processes, and steps requiring human judgment.

When social collaboration is part of the workflow, notifications come to each participant in the social stream, and activity feed stories can be auto-published as each step in a process is completed.

Recognizing Participation and Performance

One of the best ways to encourage the use of social collaboration is to celebrate the role of those who make the greatest contributions to it. Perhaps more importantly, the network is a great place to recognize contributions to the goals of the company (within which social collaboration is only a means to an end).

Show your people you like them

Which do you think would motivate an employee more? A ten-page, single spaced performance review delivered once per year, or a stream of daily affirmations that the person is doing a good job, along with periodic reminders of what he or she can be doing better. My bet is on the ongoing recognition over the formal performance review, which is probably going to consist mostly of corporate boilerplate and bureaucratic language, anyway.

Most people like to know that their contributions are noticed and appreciated. With a social collaboration tool, you have essentially two methods for acknowledging a colleague's contribution:

- **Like:** Click Like in response to a post. If one of the behaviors you are trying to encourage is the use of social collaboration itself, then making generous use of a Like button is as good a way as anything. Think of a Like as a digital pat on the back.

- **Comment:** If you have time, comment on an employee's status post or blog entry, saying more about what exactly you liked. Perhaps what you really liked is the substance of the post — the news of the sales win, or the new idea expressed — but in the process, you're also implicitly liking their active presence on the social network.

There are a lot of ways of providing this ongoing feedback through a social network, including some more structured ones like the use of Saleforce.com's Work.com tool.

Engaging participants with gamification

With the family of techniques referred to as _gamification,_ the goal is to engage the same kind of competitive passion in work processes that people bring to playing games. Here are two popular gamification methods:

- **Leaderboards:** A technique adapted from customer and technical support forums encourages peer-to-peer assistance by awarding points for activity on the social network and ranking the top contributors on a leaderboard, as if they were the people who had scored highest on a video game. Metrics can include things like volume of posts and comments, number of Likes, and number of followers, massaged into some overall formula for participation. Figure 12-3 shows a simple example of a top participants ranking in a Jive workspace.

    You may be able to configure the scale and the rankings to match the scale and language of your organization. My profile on UBM's company social network currently says I've achieved the modest rank of "yellow belt" (as if social collaboration were a martial art) and need to rack up another 1,112 points to achieve orange belt rank. Jive provided me with a demo account on the cloud version of its service where I'm more generously ranked as an "expert" (4 out of 5 bars on a different scale), perhaps because the other users I'm competing with are all virtual (dummy accounts, so to speak).

Figure 12-3:
Highlighting
the most
active par-
ticipants in a
community.

> ✔ **Badges:** A related approach is to award badges to users for different types of activity, or allow users to award badges to each other.

With gamification, you're getting co-workers to compete over how well they can collaborate. There is a paradox in there somewhere, given that collaboration is a *cooperative* activity. But if it works, who cares whether it's logical?

Highlighting corporate performance and network participation

Giving feedback to the individual employee is a good start, but remember to look for opportunities to use your social platform to make stars of employees who deliver exceptional performance. That is where you go beyond drive-by recognition in the social stream and build a blog post around how wonderful this person is.

This is a mechanism for recognizing corporate performance but also success stories about the use of the social platform itself.

However, when sharing a social collaboration success story, there is one thing to always keep paramount: The technology should never be the star. The employee who makes creative use of the collaboration network is the star. Social collaboration is worthless without people, and it's the people who deserve recognition, not the software.

Chapter 13

Managing Successful Collaboration Communities

. . . .

In This Chapter

▶ Keeping a social community healthy

▶ Forming a community management team

▶ Focusing collaboration in groups and project workspaces

. . . .

*O*nline collaboration becomes social only when you add community, which extends the scale of interaction between one project or one team, making it more widespread and ongoing. You can assign project team members to check into a collaboration workspace, and they will comply if their job depends on it. People come back to a community of their own accord because they find it valuable and want to be part of something larger.

Community isn't really a matter of technology. Tools can make a difference by providing an environment for communities to form and sustain themselves, but what matters a lot more is how those tools are used and how effectively communities are managed. In this chapter, I help you understand how you can manage a successful, healthy social collaboration community. When social collaboration fails, it most often fails because communities fail to form in the first place or because they fall into disuse and disorder.

Healthy collaboration communities have the right combination of spontaneous, free-form participation and enough organization to make it easy for members to find both content and people who are relevant to their interests and their work.

Keeping a Social Community Healthy

As a community manager, you know that productive collaboration communities don't just happen, spontaneously, with the activation of a software tool. Even those collaboration communities that get off to a great start don't remain healthy without proper care and feeding. Communities are subject to *entropy,* the tendency of the universe to devolve into disorder. What you're trying to avoid is the collaboration network that, in theory, seemed so promising as a way of organizing work and putting information in context becomes a rat's nest of overlapping discussion and project groups, duplicate versions of documents, and activities that waste time rather than making everyone more productive.

Avoiding these traps requires active community management and system administration. At the same time, the role of community management has to be one of coaching and nurturing communities. Communities do not form by management edict, or in response to a memo.

"You can't force community," writes Deborah Ng in *Community Management For Dummies.* "You can't put members in the same virtual room and expect magic to happen. Instead, you have to get the party started and keep it going." If you read her book (which I would recommend even if we didn't share a publisher), you will learn a lot about how communities form and function. However, her book is primarily focused on externally accessible online communities, such as the customer support communities many firms operate so their customers can share tips and answer each other's questions. In this section, I tell you what you can learn from those external communities, and I give you some guidelines for how you can keep an internal community healthy and productive.

Much of the material that follows on the types of people you encounter in an online community is adapted from *Community Management For Dummies,* with my own tweaks to make it more relevant to the work environment.

Learning from external communities

For the sake of maintaining focus within a broad subject area, this book primarily focuses on internal collaboration networks limited to employees and perhaps trusted freelancers and contractors. In Chapter 14, I cover scenarios where it makes sense to include selected external users, such as partners or customers, in a subcommunity within your collaboration network. This can be a useful way of engaging in projects that stretch beyond the bounds of your organization without giving those people access to internal strategic discussions.

Managing public social communities — such as those communities that companies provide for customer service and peer-to-peer sharing of tips among their customers — is a different kind of challenge and mostly outside the scope of this book. However, there are good reasons for internal community managers to study the dynamics of truly public social communities here.

✔ **Participation is voluntary.** The users of a public social community participate because they find the community interesting and useful. The community manager has no leverage to compel participation.

An internal corporate social network manager actually can compel a certain degree of usage — for example, by making essential employee information available only on the collaboration network. Still, active (rather than grudging) participation remains within the control of the individual, who will actively participate only if the community is interesting and useful.

✔ **Public communities are an open book.** Getting a peek at another organization's internal collaboration network can be challenging. If you want to see a lot of community managers at work, study public examples, such as:

- *Home Depot* (http://community.homedepot.com)
- *SAP Community Network* (http://scn.sap.com)
- *Jive Community* (http://community.jivesoftware.com)
- *IBM DeveloperWorks* (www.ibm.com/developerworks)

✔ **Public communities set expectations for private ones.** Watch public communities at work for clues to patterns (good and bad) that will also play out within your collaboration network.

Analyzing the community population

One of the roles of any community manager is to jump in as moderator, when necessary, deleting posts that are profane, offensive, or otherwise in violation of community rules. They must also deal with what are known in the trade as *trolls:* namely, those people who are aggressively provocative and disruptive, sucking energy out of the community rather than putting energy into it.

Internal community managers play the moderator role, too, but as long as the enterprise social network sets a reasonable standard of professionalism, trolls are rare. Although conservative organizations may fear inappropriate behavior, employees are no more likely to post long rants about management's incompetence than they are to stand on a chair in the cafeteria and shout the same message. Sure, you can imagine some unbalanced individual announcing her resignation that way. The more common scenario would be someone inadvertently giving offense or violating community rules.

What are the common elements of all communities, public or private? First, consider motivation. People voluntarily share in an online community for a few reasons:

✔ **They want to belong.** We are social animals and want to feel part of something larger. Sometimes the co-workers we have the most natural affiliation with are not sitting in the same office (or, in the age of tele-commuting, we may be alone in the office).

✔ **They know things that other people don't.** They want to give answers, enlighten, and maybe show off a little.

✔ **They are returning the favor.** The community has been helpful to them, and they want to pay it back.

✔ **They have tips or shortcuts to share.** They have found a better way to do something at work and hate to see others wasting time doing it the hard way.

✔ **They enjoy recognition.** When they share something useful, and other people click "Like," they feel good and know they are getting noticed.

✔ **They are scoring points.** By giving to the community, they are banking good will, which will make it easier for them to ask for help in the future.

✔ **They are establishing trust and credibility.** By dispensing a steady stream of useful tips and pointers, they know they are building credibility that will pay off when they have an important message to spread.

People will share information others may find useful out of the purest generosity, but they may also want to show how smart they are or burnish their professional brands. They want to build trust and credibility within the organization so they will have more influence and be able to get trust when they need it. They are looking to make connections that may pay off later in a promotion, a transfer, or a recommendation for a new job.

Not everyone participates at the same level. Here are a few of the common types you will encounter. The labels have been adapted from *Online Community Management For Dummies,* but the descriptions are mine.

✔ **The Lurker:** You rarely hear from lurkers. They are there in the background, watching, reading, and consuming content but rarely contributing. As I discuss later, community managers should appreciate passive participation over non-participation. If the lurker finds value in the community, even without actively contributing, that is a good thing. Still, a community that consisted only of lurkers would not work.

✔ **The Newbie:** Newbies are new members of the community. They may be new employees or employees who only recently created an account. They are still figuring out the software and may not understand the ground rules. Their level of participation ranges from tentative to over-eager. They need help from the community manager and the community at large finding their bearings and becoming long-term productive members.

✔ **The Regular:** Everyone knows The Regular as a familiar face in the online community. The Regular may win credibility as a known quantity, just by being so active. If nothing else, The Regular knows how to navigate the online community and can help guide others through it.

✔ **The Leader:** The Leader is a knowledgeable, established community member who is either self-appointed or appointed by the community into a leadership role. When The Leader speaks up, people listen.

The Leader may also hold some ranking position offline within the organization. Not always, though. Sometimes the online community provides employees with an opportunity to demonstrate leadership skills they have not displayed in other contexts — in which case, their online leadership may translate into greater offline success.

✔ **The Expert:** The Expert knows everything about everything — or claims to. You want people with legitimate expertise to participate in the community but will also have to contend with some know-it-alls.

Of these, the common label "lurker" is somewhat controversial with social collaboration strategists who take exception to its pejorative connotations. Although *lurker* is standard industry vocabulary for someone who sponges off the activity of others without contributing, perhaps we ought to show a little more appreciation for the relatively passive participants in a community because they tend to be the majority. That is, most users of a community will search, browse, and read what others are saying, rarely contributing a thought of their own. A few will comment, at least occasionally, on what others post, and an even smaller number will blog, start discussions, and generally post original thoughts.

Should you try to coax people toward higher levels of participation? Absolutely. Yet given that part of the point of social collaboration is to create a richer knowledge resource for the community, shouldn't you appreciate when people take advantage of that resource? One person who made this point to me is Tracy Maurer, a community manager and strategist at UBM, the publisher of *InformationWeek* and organizer of events including the E2 Conference series. The negative view of lurkers "where the idea was all they do is come in and watch — they don't contribute anything — I wouldn't say that's a fair assessment," she says. Throughout our lives, we learn new skills by observing how others do them before we try them ourselves, she points out. In other words, there is wisdom in listening and learning before you speak up. Part of the value of a social collaboration platform is to make it easier to publish information, she says, "and if you don't have readers, what the heck good is it?"

There are also some negative personality types to watch for:

- ✔ **The Malcontent:** Complains about everything from the collaboration platform to management and never has anything positive to say.

- ✔ **The Heckler:** Questions or comments sarcastically about everything, not so much to disagree as to show her own superiority or to make others look bad.

- ✔ **The Rabble Rouser:** Determined to incite the community to riot, rather than discuss disagreements in a respectful manner.

- ✔ **The Troll:** The anonymity of the Internet gives the troll the keyboard courage to be cruel to other members.

Compared with anonymous public social forums, the worst of these patterns are much rarer in a social collaboration network where obnoxious behavior or disrespectful talk about management can be a career-ending move. There may be some heckling and some rabble rousing going on, but it will have to be couched in the form of sarcasm or passive aggressive behavior to sneak under the radar.

Here are some suggestions for dealing with negativity on the social collaboration system:

- ✔ **Steer colleagues toward more positive expression.** Even cloaked, negative sentiment about the company and its goals tends to reflect poorly on the person expressing it. If you help the malcontents and hecklers understand how they are making themselves look, that may be enough to make them stop. Or, if there are legitimate concerns mixed in with their complaints, you can try to redirect them toward constructive criticism that seeks solutions. Worth a try.

- ✔ **Acknowledge complaints and do your best to resolve the issues or offer workarounds.** Will you have some malcontents and hecklers where the collaboration environment itself is concerned? Count on it. You should be prepared for their complaints about what the platform can't do or doesn't do the way they would expect it to. You may never win them over, but do the best you can to prevent them from putting so much focus on the platform's shortcomings that they distract other community members from discovering its practical uses.

If you can, address their legitimate complaints or feature requests with the vendor or by reconfiguring the collaboration network. Just understand that a habitual malcontent will not be satisfied no matter what you change.

Models of social community quality

The Community Maturity Model shown in Figure 13-1 was developed by Rachel Happe and Jim Storer, the co-founders of The Community Roundtable

(CR), an organization devoted to research and gathering best practices about community management and strategy.

Turning social community management from a casual effort to an organizational discipline that spans many teams and groups "is actually pretty difficult and disruptive because it requires cultural, leadership, strategy, workflow, and operational changes," Happe writes in a blog post on the model. "However, it is critical if organizations don't want to have their social efforts isolated from everything else, which doesn't work very well anyway." Her idea for avoiding this disruption was to develop a common framework and taxonomy for the elements of successful social communities, providing a common vocabulary for strategy discussions as well as training and certification.

The competencies laid out in the model are

1. Strategy

2. Leadership

3. Culture

4. Community Management

5. Content & Programming

6. Policy & Governance

7. Tools

8. Measurement

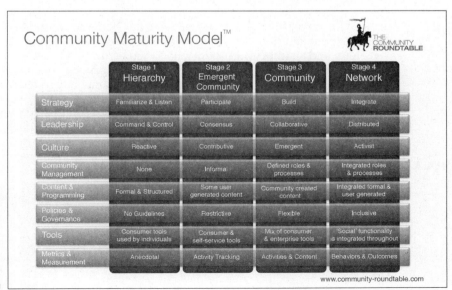

Figure 13-1:
The Community Maturity Model.

The value of active community management

The Community Roundtable is a membership organization in which community strategists, managers, and administrators — as well as executives seeking broader social business goals — gather to exchange tips and best practices. Learn more at `www.community roundtable.com`. One of the main benefits of participation is exposure to organizations that have developed some of the most mature community management practices.

In its "2013 State of Community Management" report, the CR reports that its members shatter the "90-9-1" rule that predicts that within any community

✔ 90 percent of members will be purely passive lurkers.

✔ 9 percent are contributors who edit or comment on other people's content.

✔ Only one 1 percent are content creators who create blogs or documents and start conversations.

On average, roundtable members reported a 55-30-15 breakdown (30% contributors, 15% creators), and the best performers saw something more like a 17-57-26 pattern, with more content creators than lurkers and well over half the community actively contributing.

That's the difference active community management makes.

At each stage of development (Hierarchy, Emergent Community, Community, and Network), the organization graduates to a more mature stage of each of these competencies. While the stages will play out a little differently in every organization, the Community Maturity Model attempts to show the patterns and connections among these competencies. For example, a truly integrated strategy is interdependent with achieving distributed leadership that spans multiple communities, integrated roles and processes for community management, and an integrated suite of social collaboration tools. Trying to implement a truly integrated strategy with a hodgepodge of consumer-grade tools would not really work, nor would the best most integrated tool suite make up for a reactive, command-and-control culture where community members are reluctant to participate because they don't know whether they will be rewarded or punished.

The digital strategist Oscar Berg pictures the relationship between social and collaboration activities as a pyramid (shown in Figure 13-2), where the broad base of more community-oriented social collaboration provides the foundation for more intensive team collaboration around specific projects and work processes.

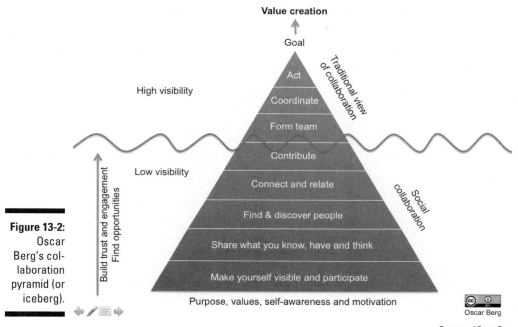

Value creation

Goal

Act

Coordinate

Form team

High visibility

Traditional view of collaboration

Contribute

Connect and relate

Low visibility

Social collaboration

Find & discover people

Share what you know, have and think

Build trust and engagement
Find opportunities

Make yourself visible and participate

Purpose, values, self-awareness and motivation

Oscar Berg

Figure 13-2:
Oscar
Berg's col-
laboration
pyramid (or
iceberg).

"The majority of the value-creation activities in an enterprise are hidden. They happen below the surface," Berg writes in his blog at www.thecontent economy.com. "What we see when we think of collaboration in the traditional sense (structured team-based collaboration) is the tip of the iceberg — teams who are coordinating their actions to achieve some goal. We don't see — and thus don't recognize — all the activities which have enabled the team to form and which help them throughout their journey."

In other words, if you really want employees to collaborate effectively to create and deliver new products, you need to pay equal attention to the social community underpinnings as to the more formal team collaboration and project management. Berg exalts the value of "ongoing community build- ing that makes people trust each other and commit themselves to a shared purpose."

These models provide inspiration for what an organization can aim to achieve with social collaboration. Now, how are you going to make it happen?

Moderating conversations

Responsibility for moderating online community content and conversations is typically divided among platform administrators, community managers, and the owners of specific groups or collaboration spaces. Moderation is considered a system administration task, and a person with moderation rights has the power to edit, reclassify, or delete content that others have posted. That is primarily what I'm talking about here although you can also think in terms of the role the moderator of a panel discussion plays, which is more about keeping the conversation going.

As I mention earlier, the need to delete offensive posts ought to be the least of your worries, yet you obviously want the power to prevent or correct bad behavior when necessary.

Some of the things you want to be able to delete are

- ✔ Profane, vulgar, or pornographic posts or images
- ✔ Personal attacks on other community members
- ✔ Sensitive private or confidential information shared too widely or in a space with inadequate security controls
- ✔ Inaccurate content about company leaders, policies, or procedures (may be better to correct than delete)

The power to delete inappropriate content is important and necessary, but preventing it from being posted in the first place is far better.

When it does come up, the decision to delete content deserves careful thought. There are extreme cases where it is obviously the right decision. Examples would include pornography or other blatantly offensive content, as well as confidential information posted in a public space.

On the other hand, suppose that someone posts a comment suggesting (inaccurately) that the CEO is about to resign. Other employees pile into the conversation asking whether it's true and speculating about what it would mean to the organization if it were. By the time this comes to the community manager's attention, the message thread has grown to dozens of posts. You have the administrative power to delete the whole conversation, but should you? Probably not, given that shutting down the conversation is more likely to encourage conspiracy theories about how you're keeping the truth hidden than it is to stop the speculation.

Instead, a more appropriate response would be to intervene by

- ✔ Reminding participants of the company's acceptable use policies, which you will have designed to discourage this kind of loose talk

✔ Posting a factual rebuttal of the misinformation being disseminated

✔ Encouraging the CEO to post his own response ("I'm glad to learn you don't want to lose me, but . . ."), gently chiding community members who have been misbehaving

✔ Limiting further responses to the thread to prevent it from going off track again

✔ Deleting the most egregious comments, or the most objectionable material within them, if necessary

  Rather than vanishing this content down an Orwellian "memory hole," you can leave behind an explanation of what was deleted and what policy it violated.

✔ Pinning the post containing the organization's official response to the discussion at the top of the list or otherwise highlighting it

Interventions of this sort ought to be extremely rare, but it's better to plan for them than to have to improvise.

Coaching community members for success

Where internal community managers want to be spending more of their time is encouraging positive behaviors. They want employees to use the collaboration network more actively and more productively, while doing their best to eliminate or minimize any frustrations with the social software environment.

Employees need to know that the community manager is on their side, enforcing rules where necessary but more interested in making all members of the collaboration network as successful as they can possibly be.

Here are some approaches:

✔ **Training how to use the social collaboration network:** Use in-person training, live webcasts, video tutorials, and company-specific documentation, as well as provide pointers to tutorial content from the vendor or other sources. Offer (re)training when you have major upgrades. All new employees should also get training as part of their company orientation.

✔ **Answering questions:** When community members ask questions about the best way to accomplish a task on the collaboration network, community managers provide answers or options.

✔ **Making suggestions:** When community members waste energy doing something the hard way, the community manager can suggest an easier path, introducing members to a new tool or software feature or introducing them to a person who can help solve the problem.

✔ **Sharing success stories:** The community manager studies what the most successful users of the collaboration network are doing right and shares clues with all the rest. If, for example, the sales organization within one business unit is able to cut its proposal preparation time in half and win more deals, you want that success to be replicated in other business units.

✔ **Mobilizing ambassadors or champions:** Successful collaboration network users can be its most effective advocates, regardless of whether they hold any official community management title or authority. Seek out the people who are enthusiastic about telling their stories and sharing tips and encourage them to do more of it. Then treat them like gold.

✔ **Encouraging productive outcomes:** A good community manager knows when to suggest that a speculative discussion should be turned into a research project to gather more facts and data. Or, if a debate over some issue is going in circles, maybe members should vote on one or more proposed resolutions rather than continuing to chase their tails. Or when an idea for a product or a process change coalesces, the community manager helps with the transition from fruitful brainstorming session to active project.

✔ **Listening to feedback:** When community members complain that the social tools don't function as they should or lack important features, community managers consider those remarks seriously. Sometimes they can suggest alternative approaches, or features of the collaboration network that a frustrated user was not aware of. Other times, they will acknowledge the gap in functionality and investigate whether it can be fixed with a customization, a plug-in, or by pushing the social software vendor to include the missing feature in a future release.

Build confidence with social interaction

UBM's Tracy Maurer says one of her favorite painless training methods is "allowing people to be social." Although I've heard just the opposite from traditionally conservative organizations (such as banks and insurance companies, which often tell employees the system is to be used for work conversations only), at UBM, it's okay to start the occasional discussion about kids or pets or movies.

"First, it gives people a way to learn the system that is less intimidating. I'm not as worried about grammar and mistakes if we're talking about our kids, or what I made for a recent dinner party. Second, it is a way for people who work remotely from one another to network," Maurer says. This is not so different from hallway conversations or lunch room chatter, except that it is shared more broadly, allowing people to get to know colleagues who may work in another state or another country. "If I'm less extroverted, I don't necessarily have to initiate the conversation, but can learn about others based on reading their conversations," she adds.

Like a company party or a team building event, socializing online brings employees together in a way that purely transactional interactions do not.

Structuring Collaboration with Groups

Social networking opens up possibilities for ad hoc, spontaneous collaboration, but it also benefits from a little structure. By mapping out your online world, you provide signposts to guide employees toward their most likely collaborators.

Groups or subcommunities are often structured around

- Departments or other organizational structures
- Functions, such as customer support
- Products or product families
- Project teams
- Common roles or disciplines of the participants
- Communities of practice, specifically geared toward promoting excellence in a process or discipline
- New employees
- Support of the collaboration network itself, particularly for new users
- Groups for off-topic or non–work-related discussions (if allowed at all), meant to build camaraderie, if not productivity

I use the term *groups* here generically. A group on Jive is roughly parallel to a community on IBM Connections. Jive also has *spaces,* which are sort of super-groups with some additional content management tools, including the ability to contain other spaces, or *subspaces.* Spaces are often used to represent formal organizational units, such as the human resources department, welcoming visitors with a carefully designed home page including links to important documents, with the activity stream as one widget on the page rather than the central experience.

Yammer has groups for internal discussions but also lets you define multiple *networks,* with one of the distinctions being that Yammer networks can include external users who have access to that one space but not the rest of the company social network.

Jive, IBM Connections, Podio, and a number of other environments also provide project workspaces as a group type, with task and project management features in addition to discussion and content sharing tools.

Bottom line: These are all subcommunities within the broader community of an enterprise social network. The terminology and the range of group types will vary between platforms, but in every instance, groups exist to focus the activities of the members of your collaboration network. The community manager helps social collaboration participants understand how to interact in these groups to accomplish their business goals.

In the beginning, you want just enough group structure to suggest the possibility of the platform but not so much that users will become lost. As the platform develops, you will want to assert enough control over group proliferation that you don't wind up with an impenetrable maze.

Controlling the proliferation of groups

One way to encourage more and more productive collaboration is to allow more of it to happen, allowing colleagues to organize their work the way that makes sense to them rather than imposing central planning on all online activities. Typically, participants create new social collaboration groups in one of two ways:

- ✔ **On demand:** When collaboration groups can be formed on demand, employees can start getting work done together immediately.

- ✔ **With administrator approval:** The alternative to on-demand group creation is to make employees submit a request to create a group or workspace and wait for a system administrator, community manager, or other gatekeeper to act on that request.

Setting the ground rules for group creation is a strategic choice. Allowing people to create their own groups seems more true to the spirit of social media (after all, you don't need anyone's permission to create a Facebook group, now do you?), but if you don't control the process up front, you may have to clean up the results retroactively.

The dilemma here is not dissimilar to the mess people can make when you make it easier for them to create and share content. I discuss the issues of document sprawl in Chapter 7, and the Jive Community members I turned to for advice tended to cite the issues of content and community proliferation as interrelated management challenges. Especially in a large company, it can be easy to wind up with thousands of groups being formed, many of them overlapping, redundant, or inactive.

When groups proliferate out of control, it becomes more difficult for employees searching or browsing the network to find the right place to ask a question or connect with a subject matter expert. On the other hand, imposing heavy-handed administrative controls can choke off opportunities for collaboration, engagement, and innovation. Successful community strategists don't all agree on the right approach, but here are some suggestions for reaching middle ground:

- ✔ **Start with on-demand group creation.** Allow self-service community creation in the early days of the collaboration network, when promoting adoption and engagement are paramount. Tighten up the process later, if necessary.

- ✔ **Provide an efficient group approval process.** Require advance approval but make the approval process as quick and easy as possible.

- ✔ **Impose tighter controls for certain types of groups or take them off the menu.** For example, some Jive communities restrict the creation of secret groups, which on that platform are invitation-only groups whose content does not show up in search results. Such groups may be warranted for secret projects like negotiating a merger. On the other hand, secret groups can more easily proliferate out of control because they're invisible.

- ✔ **Encourage open collaboration.** Enterprise community managers should discourage group founders from defaulting to the use of private or secret groups without good reason. Hiding information, or requiring advance permission to join a group, puts roadblocks in the way of collaboration. Most groups benefit more from openness.

- ✔ **Assign ownership of each group.** Make sure that every group has an owner responsible for basic community management duties within that space. If the group owner leaves the company or stops actively managing the group, make sure someone else is appointed or else shut it down.

- ✔ **Create a group for group owners and administrators.** Share best practices on community management and maintaining a high level of engagement.

- ✔ **Suggest that groups with similar purposes merge.** Where you see redundant groups, introduce the owners to each other and encourage them to join forces. You may not want to force the issue. Perhaps they will see important differences in their purpose or organization that aren't obvious to you. On the other hand, if they simply weren't aware of each other's efforts, they may be delighted by the opportunity to team up.

- ✔ **Monitor activity within groups.** Set a minimum threshold, such as six months or a year. If there has been no significant group activity within that period, consider it a candidate to be archived or merged with another similar group. Notify the group owner and members first to see whether anyone steps forward to revive it.

The range of tools available for controlling the creation and administration of groups is also an important factor in selecting a social collaboration platform. Even if you don't plan to require an approval workflow for the creation of groups, you want to have the tools to do so available if you change your mind later. Also, when trying to impose order retroactively, it's helpful if the platform provides tools for merging similar groups or automatically notifying the members of the one that will be closed that they are invited to join the other.

Most environments also support a range of options for group membership and privacy. Here are some common patterns.

- ✔ **Open:** Anyone can join, instantly.

- ✔ **Controlled membership:** Anyone can ask to join, but membership requires the approval of a group owner or administrator.

- ✔ **Invitation-only:** You must be invited to join. Depending on how this is set up, any member may be able to issue invitations or that power may be limited to a group owner or administrator.

- ✔ **Secret:** Not only are secret groups invitation-only, but they do not show up in search results or group directories.

These levels of access to membership can also be associated with access to content. Group membership is required to view or participate, but may not be required to view content. In some setups, users can *follow* a group (subscribe to its updates) without becoming a full member.

When membership is restricted for the purpose of providing space for private conversations and information — for example, a collaboration group set up to work on a merger that most employees are not supposed to know about — content from that group should be inaccessible to nonmembers and should not show up in search results.

Make sure you understand the privacy, security, and permissions model of the environment and help group members understand what it really means. For example, if they post something in a private group, will that content still be displayed in search results? Will nonmembers be able to read that content (but not interact with it on the same level as a member), or will they not be able to access it at all? Can nonmembers browse group content, but not contribute? Or are they stopped at the door by a digital bouncer who won't let them in until their group membership is approved?

The hazard here is that group members will assume their participation is more private than it actually is. Because they had to get approval to join the group, they may think of what they post as being secret when actually it is visible to any lurker.

Reserving the company-wide activity stream for items of company-wide interest

One reason for focusing activity related to a department or a function within a group is to keep the company-wide activity stream from drowning in posts that are of interest to only a subset of community members. The company-wide feed ought to be reserved for items of company-wide interest.

The uses of the company-wide feed are one area where the scale of an organization makes a big difference. In a small business, it may be appropriate for everyone to know everyone else's business to the point where groups are barely necessary. For very large organizations, the company-wide feed of posts can be almost useless without filtering — almost as if you tried to drink in the full fire hose of conversations on Twitter. There are automated systems that process the full stream, but humans would find Twitter unusable if not for the ability to choose whose updates to follow.

Similarly, social collaboration networks let employees filter the total company activity stream to show just the activity of the people and groups they follow. Some platforms will automatically add supervisors, company leaders, and official news sources such as human resources to that list, but users can also make their own choices.

If you still find that important company announcements are being drowned out by too much irrelevant chatter on the company-wide feed, consider creating an official company news group that only authorized personnel can post to. Make subscribing to that group feed mandatory or strongly encouraged.

Segmenting discussions to cut down on noise

Segmenting discussions according to project, interest, department, or any other organizing principle also cuts down on the noise for the people within that group. It's like taking a few colleagues into a conference room and closing the door to get some work done, away from the hubbub of the rest of the office. If you're working on a project together, you can share all your planning documents within that space so all participants know where to find them.

When you focus social collaboration activity, you also gather together people who share that focus, making groups an excellent way of identifying people with common expertise or interests. The idea of finding people and expertise through content is fundamental to social collaboration, but identifying groups associated with that content or those authors can be even more powerful. Instead of posing your question or request or suggestion to one person, you can direct it to a whole group of people.

This works best when group content is accessible (open) and searchable even for nonmembers.

Encouraging open group access

As a general principle, group membership and the content within groups ought to be open unless there is a strong reason why privacy is needed. That is the expectation set by social networking, where you make your own decisions about whom to friend or follow, or what groups to join. You curate the connections that make sense, associating with people and entities you find interesting or want to interact with. Openness and transparency of information throughout the organization also serves the knowledge management goals of social collaboration. You want to put content and context to work making the whole organization smarter, and anything that makes it harder for people to access information or make connections is contrary to that goal.

When nonmembers can browse and search content, discussions, and activities, a group can be considered relatively open even if visitors have to ask permission to join and participate more actively. Given active management by a group owner or administrator who will act on those requests promptly, making users ask permission to join is more of a speed bump than a road block to access. If this option is available on your platform of choice, consider it a compromise to offer those whose first instinct is to keep group membership private.

Legitimate reasons for approving members individually may be to limit membership to people who have some professional qualification, such as a law degree or a Project Management Professional (PMP) certification, or who are actively involved in the project served by a project group. You can argue allowing posts from members who don't share that qualification or purpose would dilute the focus of the group. Maybe you can allow interested nonmembers to follow the group without being members (again, if that option is available).

Another exception to the principle of self-selection is where group membership is automatic or mandatory. For example, all employees of a given department may automatically be made members of a group for departmental collaboration. All new employees may be added to an employee orientation group, with the option of leaving the group once they feel themselves to be sufficiently oriented.

Supporting private groups, where appropriate

You can make openness the default and strongly encourage it in most cases, but in business, there are also many scenarios where privacy is necessary and required. Although private collaboration may be anti-social, your social platform would not be very useful as a business tool if it failed to support private groups, private documents, and private discussions. You wouldn't want to make the users of your network switch to some other collaboration platform or (gasp) revert to e-mail whenever they need to collaborate on some activity that not everyone in the company should be able to see.

The nomenclature, options, and degrees of privacy vary between platforms, but I use the term *private* to mean an invitation-only or approval to join required group within which content is not shared with nonmembers. For instance, on the Jive platform, the only information about a private group available to nonmembers is the name of the group. A secret group is similar except that even the name of the group is unlisted in search and the group directory, making it hard for nonmembers to even know it exists unless they get a request to join.

Some private group scenarios include

- ✔ A group restricted to senior executives who have to be confident in the privacy of their communications if they are to use the collaboration network for discussions of strategy, prior to announcing the strategy to the broader organization

- ✔ A collaboration group devoted to a secret project, such as a potential acquisition, where shared documents may include drafts of the purchase agreement

- ✔ The project group for a super-secret unannounced new product

- ✔ A management group devoted to the discussion of personnel matters

- ✔ Any group that works with documents containing personnel records, health records, or any other data for which access must be restricted on a need-to-know basis for regulatory reasons

- ✔ Any group that has a strong desire for privacy and doesn't buy your arguments in favor of openness. Ultimately, you don't want to presume to know their business better than they do.

Note that some of these scenarios may be ruled out of bounds for a social collaboration environment in the first place, depending on the type of information you deal with when doing business and any regulations that govern your industry. For example, an organization doing social collaboration on a cloud service like Yammer may rule that documents containing Social Security numbers and data covered by regulations on personal privacy should never be shared there, regardless of the privacy settings of the collaboration group. Make sure you know your organization's policies for handling sensitive information.

On the other hand, companies that have been comfortable in the past using SharePoint team spaces to organize a planned acquisition may find a private group on a collaboration network worthy of the same kind of trust.

If information needs to be kept truly secret, arguably it should never be written down in any way, particularly in any digital form that can easily be transmitted via e-mail or copied to a portable storage device. If you're plotting a tax-fraud scheme, organizing it in a private group on a collaboration network is probably not your best option. All this private information is still being stored within a company-owned information system, making it subject to legal discovery in a lawsuit or criminal investigation.

The content of private groups can also be accessible to system administrators either within your company or at the cloud data center or hosting facility that maintains your servers.

If you need to put a lot of faith in the privacy of your collaboration system, make sure you understand just how private its private groups are.

Chapter 14

Engaging External Collaborators

*S*tart to demonstrate success with internal social collaboration, and very soon there will come a day when some piece of collaborative work needs to extend outside the organization. Maybe your employees need to collaborate with their counterparts at a distribution partner, manufacturing partner, or ad agency on the launch of a new product. Maybe you want to run an online focus group discussion with a dozen of your most loyal customers, connecting them with your engineering and product development groups to brainstorm about new products within a secure workspace.

This is different from operating a public social community, which is more the territory covered in *Community Management For Dummies* and *Social CRM For Dummies*. To create a public community, you may take essentially the same platform Jive provides for internal use and set it up on a public website and allow anyone to sign up by filling out a short registration form. Or you can set it up as an invitation-only/registration-approval-required community for business partners, which only the employees of certain companies are allowed to join.

But even organizations that use Jive internally typically run public communities on completely separate instances of the software. Ditto for IBM Connections and other social platforms that support both internal and external communities.

This chapter is about inviting selected *external* users into your *internal* social network, providing them with just enough access to engage in a specific collaboration activity.

Recognizing How External Collaboration Is Different

You may have external users whom you treat essentially the same as employees — say, freelancers, contractors, and consultants whom you trust enough to give full access to your internal social network. Sure, you may have them sign their lives away on a nondisclosure agreement (NDA) form before you give them passwords, but you consider them no more likely to breach your trust than your regular employees.

Don't give out accounts like candy, however. If you let too many external users roam the digital hallways of your business, eventually, you will regret it.

There are more cases where you want to invite external users in for a specific purpose, without giving them access to the CEO's blog and the latest sales projections. Even if you deem a few freelancers or contractors trustworthy enough to treat like employees, there will probably be dozens of others you would prefer to keep on a short leash. You have a need to collaborate with them, but you pulled them in to work on a specific project and have no particular way of knowing how trustworthy they are. Instead of giving each participant the equivalent of an employee account on the social network, you provide each external user with a login that allows that participant access to a specific collaboration group or workspace. When they sign in, they see only the content in the groups they have access to.

For the external user, this is more like being invited into a meeting in a corporate office where a security escort takes you directly to a specific conference room and escorts you wherever you go for the duration of your stay.

In business today, it's common for companies to be partners in one context and competitors in another. So you may want to collaborate intensively on the development of one product, while keeping your partner in the dark on another.

In a customer focus group scenario, you might invite consumers to give feedback to your products group on proposed products or your marketing group on concepts for advertising campaigns. This information is confidential, and you make them sign an NDA that provides you with some legal cover, but you have no deep reason to trust them. You definitely don't want them to have access to any information beyond what you specifically decided to share with them.

When you create a group with mixed internal and external users, make sure employees know what they can and can't share in that group. Generally, social collaboration platforms try to make the external context very obvious. Jive features a big orange Externally Accessible label at the top of every page for an external group (as shown in Figure 14-1), and documents associated with the group are similarly flagged. On Yammer, the whole color scheme changes when you move from an internal network to an external network. This, in essence, is the *Here, there be dragons* warning on the map of a collaboration network to make employees think twice about what they share there.

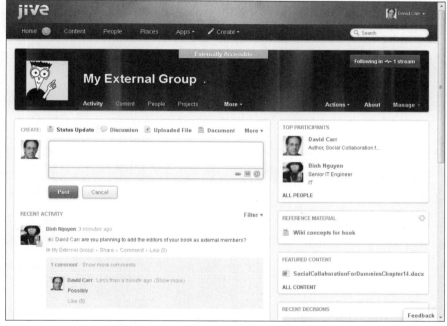

Figure 14-1:
External groups should be labeled so it is clear that content will be accessible to outsiders.

And you may want to think twice about which employees have the judgment necessary to make those calls. Perhaps for that reason, Jive dictates that externally accessible groups must also be configured as private or secret, meaning that employees can join them only if explicitly invited by the group administrator. That also means content within those groups is invisible to nonmembers, including employees.

Yammer supports a similar model but also a more informal one in which all employees can join without an invite: a check box option. Yammer external networks can also be configured, optionally, so any member can invite other members to join, just by providing an e-mail address. Figure 14-2 shows external network creation in Yammer. As of this writing, Yammer was also working on a way of allowing external sharing of individual conversations or documents without the overhead of creating an external network. This reflects Yammer's traditional emphasis on flexibility and agility over tight administrative control.

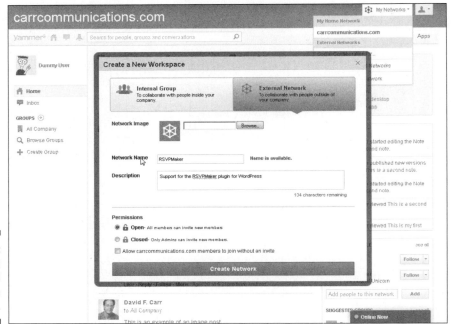

Figure 14-2:
Creating an external network in Yammer.

Setting Ground Rules for External Sharing

The group owner should make plain to all participants who the external users are and whether the composition of the group is fixed or changeable. For instance, a private group created for the collaboration between the finance department and its auditors may exist specifically for sharing all sorts of documents and details related to the company's finances, whereas sharing that data with any other group of external users would be completely inappropriate.

External networks require clear ground rules to prevent misunderstandings about what should and should not be shared with external participants.

The same acceptable use policy for corporate systems that covers what sort of information employees should not e-mail to an external collaborator or post on an external website can be a starting point. Given the many types of participants who may be engaged through an external collaboration group, each group should also spell out its own rules. For consistency, consider defining a few model policies for different classes of external users, which can be tweaked as necessary for different business scenarios.

Suppose you create an external group for collaboration with a business partner on joint development of a new product. Of necessity, group members would be free to discuss all sorts of confidential matters related to the development of that specific product, but not outside of that scope. For example, if you also have a business relationship with that partner's competitors, it would be inappropriate to share confidential information about that other company.

Other examples of information that would be out of bounds for discussion in an external group would include:

- ✒ Financials for a public company that have not been publicly released or other information that can materially affect the stock price
- ✒ References to internal strategy discussions or content quoted from a CEO blog post intended for internal consumption only
- ✒ Jokes or cynical discussion about real or perceived dysfunction in company business practices

Providing for Proper Security

You want your collaboration network to be secure to begin with, but engaging external collaborators is bound to prompt a re-examination of the security characteristics of the platform.

When you invite members into the network but try to keep them inside a box, the next logical question is whether they can escape that box. If you were physically inviting them into your corporate office, the parallel question would be how easy it would be for them to sneak out of the conference room and give themselves an unscheduled tour of the research and development department. These people are inside your collaboration network, with only the logical security model of the software preventing them from accessing things you don't want them to access. What are the odds they could hack their way past those restrictions?

Information security specialists call this an *escalation of privileges attack,* in which users who start with limited privileges give themselves a promotion — in this case, from outsider to insider, or even to system administrator.

The relevant questions are

- ✒ How likely is it that they would try?
- ✒ If they were to try, how likely is it that they would succeed?
- ✒ If they were to succeed, how likely is it that they would be caught?

You can minimize the first risk by screening external users more carefully or inviting only people you already trust. The other two boil down to requiring an assessment of your confidence in the security competency of your software vendor or cloud operator. Even in the absence of a hack, a software bug or data center operations error can expose confidential information more widely than expected. Such problems have cropped up periodically with cloud collaboration applications like Google Drive and Dropbox. You wouldn't have chosen your collaboration network vendor in the first place if you didn't believe it took security seriously, so maybe you will be convinced that the probability is very low — but it's not zero.

As with most information security decisions in the web era, if the risk is worth taking, estimate the risk and do whatever you can to minimize it.

Engaging Customers

Inviting customers into an external group attached to your internal social network can be a way of forming intimate connections by providing them with exclusive access. This is not the way to provide mass market, self-service customer communities. However, if your business works with a relatively small number of large customers, creating an external network for your work with each of them can make perfect sense and be the only social customer service solution you need. Or, you may provide a publicly accessible community for your broad customer base but invite a select few into a deeper working relationship.

Make sure all employees involved understand to treat customers as honored guests, displaying their absolute best manners, while also understanding the limits on what information can be shared with them.

When you invite customers into an external group on your collaboration network, you are inviting them into a private space where none of your discussions are going to wind up in a Google search.

Uses of an external group for customers include

- ✒ **The group dedicated to your work with a single large customer:** Consulting firms and engineering organizations may use this structure to share project plans and respond to day-to-day issues.

✔ **The elite customer group:** These representatives from your biggest customers want to be able to ask questions in private and work directly with some of your top people. Support staff may still play a role, as may peer-to-peer interaction between customers, but at a more exclusive level.

✔ **The focus group:** These members are not necessarily elite, but you do want to make them feel special for helping you formulate product and marketing plans.

Bringing customers into an external group also changes the experience for the employees participating in those groups, who will be connecting and collaborating with customers in the same environment they use for internal collaboration. If the company operates a public social community, some employees may have been in the habit of putting in cameos there: for example, software engineers dropping by to answer questions that the technical support staff may not be able to address. Now, instead of signing into a separate social community for customers, they have customers coming to them.

Engaging Partners

Like customer communities, partner communities are often supported on a separate social collaboration platform from the one used internally, where both are in play. Partner communities are typically more private, with their membership restricted to firms that have an existing business relationship with your organization. An example would be a reseller network sponsored by an electronics manufacturer.

If you have thousands of partner relationships to manage, using a dedicated social platform for that purpose is probably the better choice.

Reasons for extending access to your internal collaboration network to partners include

✔ You don't have (and don't think you need) a separate platform for partner collaboration, but you do have certain partners you want to be able to work with more closely.

✔ You have a major project (or series of major projects) requiring intense collaboration between your engineering and marketing people and those of your partner.

✔ Some collaborative work requires more privacy than is afforded by your existing partner collaboration platform.

✔ You require access to collaboration tools that are present on your internal collaboration network but not your existing partner platform.

Part V

Playing Your Part in a Social Business

For tips on how to run an online executive town hall meeting, see www.dummies.com/extras/socialcollaboration.

In this part . . .

- ✔ Learn the role you play in the success of social collaboration, and the benefits you can expect from it, as a CEO or executive leader.

- ✔ Find out what integration issues you'll need to resolve when you implement a social collaboration system.

- ✔ Help colleagues increase productivity through social collaboration.

- ✔ Inspire your sales team to share information.

- ✔ Learn about the best ways to use a social collaboration system in your everyday tasks.

Chapter 15

The CEO and Executive Management Guide to Social Collaboration

Social collaboration can be used as a leadership tool to drive innovation as well as a tool to encourage more employees to act like leaders. In this chapter, I begin with an example of how one company launched a successful social collaboration system with support from the top of the organization, and then I present some ideas on how you might inspire innovation in your company with social collaboration tools. Later in the chapter, I tell you how CEOs typically use these tools, explain how you can benefit from tuning in to the social collaboration activity stream, and tell you what you can do to help your colleagues use these tools most effectively.

Is it a cure-all? Hardly. A tool is just a tool. A hammer and chisel are tools in every pair of hands, but only Michelangelo had the right touch to find King David in the rock. On the other hand, given a 3D printer and the right software, creating a scaled-down replica of the Statue of David wouldn't be so tough. Part of the challenge of leadership is to make the best use of all the tools you have available to you, technological and otherwise.

Without resorting to hype, I will argue that social collaboration is a significant organizational tool, worth some fraction of a CEO's attention. Many of the biggest technology investments of the past several decades have been poured into Enterprise Resource Planning (ERP) platforms and other transactional systems. In contrast, social collaboration platforms are *systems of engagement,* meaning that they are judged by how they connect people rather than how they manipulate numbers. Numbers are certainly important, but organizations run on the talents and decisions of their people.

At the same time, social collaboration is far less expensive and risky than implementing an ERP system, a project management challenge sometimes associated with IT disaster stories. What's required most is organizational commitment, not technological wizardry. When collaboration networks fail, they fail for lack of active and productive use.

Leading with Social Collaboration

Success with social collaboration doesn't necessarily require an endorsement from the very top of the organization, but when that happens, it can make a big difference.

When The Community Roundtable began publishing a series of reports on *The Social Executive* in early 2013, it started with a profile of UBM CEO David Levin. Levin leads an events and publishing company that has grown through more than 100 acquisitions between 2005 and 2012, and he has been a prominent executive sponsor of social collaboration as a method of knitting the organization together.

He is also my boss (several levels removed) because UBM is the publisher of *InformationWeek* and organizer of the E2 conference series. I probably would not have chosen to focus on him as the model leader (for fear of being seen as sucking up), but Community Roundtable co-founder and principal researcher Rachel Happe picked him as the perfect example of how executive leadership can make a huge difference in the success of social collaboration. You can find the full case study and other research on effective community management at http://community-roundtable.com.

UBM "is a company whose whole market had been completely disrupted by the Internet," Happe says, making it necessary to "evolve the organization in different ways than they ever did before." Originally known as United Business Media, UBM needed to innovate to stay ahead of the accelerating shift of publishing (and advertising dollars) from print to the web. With the events part of the business showing more vigor, Levin decided that the organizing principle of the business should be community, whether that was the community that comes together for a conference or the community of readers on a website.

If community were going to be so important externally, it needed to become more important internally. Levin wanted to create a collaborative organization that would break down artificial distinctions between events, publishing, and other divisions of the company. He wanted to get everyone working toward the same goals and sharing constructive criticism when products and processes were not working as they should.

The way he personally brought that about was by doing it himself.

As the Community Roundtable case study tells the story, UBM's first social collaboration experiment at the executive level was a wiki used to support an executive meeting in 2008. Participants found it an effective way to collaborate and endorsed leaving it active for general company use. However, "within a month it was a ghost town with little or no engagement."

In other words, just making the technology available was not enough. To be successful, social collaboration needed someone to take charge of making it successful. UBM Global Community Manager Ted Hopton became that person, transferring to a job in the human resources department where he would be responsible for advocating for use of the tool and driving the cultural change it was meant to achieve.

UBM also moved from that first experimental wiki to Jive Software's broad social business platform, which includes a variety of collaboration and community tools, including blogging. Internally, this social platform is known as The Hub. Immediately after the soft launch of the new platform, on a Saturday morning, Hopton was surprised to get an e-mail from Levin asking for some coaching on the mechanics of how to create a blog post with Jive.

"I knew David was passionate about it, but I didn't expect him on a Saturday morning to be posting to his blog," Hopton says. However, this started a regular series of "Dear UBM" blog posts, which replaced the company-wide e-mails Levin had been in the habit of distributing to employees about once per month.

And this shift was significant, as Happe's case study explains: "While no one would have considered a 'reply to all' on one of the CEO's e-mails, it did not take long before people began to comment on his blog posts, starting a conversation between the CEO and 6,000+ employees that was never possible in the past. As David got more comfortable with this dynamic, his posts became more casual — and unedited — powerfully modeling a behavior for the organization that in essence said, 'It is more important that you share and communicate than that you do so perfectly.'"

Also, because these messages no longer went out by e-mail, employees needed to log on to the internal social network if they wanted to keep up with what the CEO was thinking. Okay, slight exaggeration: As an employee, I can tell you that I get e-mail notifications whenever an announcement of great significance appears on his blog or the blog of another top executive. However, what arrives in the e-mail is just a link, not the whole message, and to follow the discussion it generates, you have to be on the blog.

Certainly, participation in social collaboration is only one way how UBM executives lead, but it is an important one.

Happe says Levin's motivation reflects what she sees from all the executive leaders she has found who have taken an active interest in social collaboration. "Almost every executive we talked to was trying to figure out the innovation equation," she says. "Most people in organizations don't view themselves as doing innovative work, but right now companies need innovators."

In other words, more employees need to discover their inner innovator. Often what's required is not necessarily revolutionary innovation but process innovation that any employee who sees the organization's inefficiencies can make suggestions about, Happe says.

Driving Innovation by Getting the Whole Organization Thinking

The executive sponsors of social collaboration are looking to drive innovations both large and small. The ideal may be the creation of a profitable new product, but companies today also need process innovation and constant, incremental improvement, Happe says. With social collaboration tools, you can drive innovation. Here are some suggestions:

- **Solicit ideas through contests.** In lean years, an organization may have to be innovative about "doing more with less." Some social collaboration success stories revolve around engaging employees in contests to come up with cost-saving ideas. Cutting your way to success can't be the only strategy, however, or the organization will wind up whittling itself away to nothing.

- **Host online brainstorming sessions.** One way to get the organization moving in the right direction is to encourage everyone to think about breakthrough possibilities and then build on each other's ideas.

- **Identify the best candidates.** Once you have gathered a critical mass of ideas, methodically whittle them down to the most promising ones.

Here's an example of how one company used input from online brainstorming sessions from various teams throughout the company to create a better product. The creation of UBM's Future Cities product (www.ubmfuture cities.com) began with the recognition that many divisions of the company were producing events and publications addressing different aspects of urban planning and urban life and ideas for how it may be improved. The concept of "smart cities" spans everything from architecture and building management to electrical systems, transportation, government, healthcare, and Internet use.

As reported in the Community Roundtable case study (www.slideshare. net/rhappe/the-social-executive-ubm-case-study), the product "generated revenue for UBM within three months and leveraged 10 percent of UBM's workforce to contribute in a variety of ways. Not only would that type of initiative not have happened before the existence of The Hub because of its cross disciplinary complexity, it sparked another similar effort that started to generate revenue within one month. This project — Big Data Republic — showed value in both enabling initial innovation and transferring lessons from that innovation quickly to another team."

These products also arrived with a more modern and social look and feel than the websites of some of UBM's older media properties, including *InformationWeek,* which started as a magazine and migrated to the web. The result is articles that are formatted as blog entries and that also invite active conversations with readers rather than passive consumption.

InformationWeek is migrating to a similar format, reflecting UBM's strategy of becoming a community-driven business rather than a traditional print publisher.

Managing innovation

Internal online brainstorming efforts are a variation on *crowdsourcing,* a technique some consumer product firms have used to engage Internet users in coming up with new ideas. For example, Ben & Jerry's has run contests inviting customers to come up with new ice cream flavors.

Applied internally, crowdsourcing for ideas is sometimes known by other names, such as "innovation management" or "ideation," but the basic idea is still to generate a lot of ideas in search of a few gems. By soliciting ideas in a format that invites the participation of the community, we can have other participants comment on an idea and help improve it, so that the final result is better than anything any one person may have come up with.

Instead of inviting anyone on the Internet to submit ideas, an internal campaign can be limited to employees to allow for private discussion of proprietary issues. Or you may include some select group of external users, such as close business partners.

Because the participants in this internal crowd know more about the business, they can recommend improvements to processes outsiders would never know existed. This can be a great way of generating cost-savings ideas. For example, the Canadian airline WestJet saved more than $10 million in the first three years of an internal crowdsourcing initiative that challenged employees to submit cost-cutting ideas.

While the potential group of participants in an internal innovation campaign will not be quite as large as in a public crowdsourcing campaign, it can still be very big, particularly within a multinational corporation.

A few months after State Street Corp. launched its enterprise social network, it held an "innovation rally" that attracted 12,000 posts on ideas to improve the business. Of course, it couldn't act on all those ideas, but that wasn't the point — the exercise got employees from across the business engaged with coming up with ideas to improve the business. The financial services firm then established collaboration groups for each of the most promising ideas to refine the best of them into concrete business plans.

Focusing innovation

At the E2 Conference in Boston in 2013, in a keynote stage interview with James McQuivey, vice president and principal analyst at Forrester Research and author of the book *Digital Disruption* (Amazon Publishing), my boss *InformationWeek* Editor-In-Chief Rob Preston asked about the potential for a "democracy of ideas" to produce the best innovation.

Launching a general call for innovation ideas "is not the way to go," McQuivey said flatly. That's true even if you use more specialized innovation management software more sophisticated than Jive ideas. "It's not that the tools aren't good, but they are more often misused," he says. Ideation tools can be helpful when used in combination with a focused strategy, but if the approach is open ended, "I guarantee you that will fail," he added.

The ideal is to challenge employees to come up with ideas targeted at a specific business problem, specifying as clearly as possible the goals and the criteria for choosing winning ideas. When the rules of the game are left unspecified, the employees whose ideas are not selected are more likely to be left with hurt feelings and suspicions of political intrigue, McQuivey said.

In a 2011 white paper produced for AIIM, an industry organization that promotes content management and collaboration technologies, Andrew McAfee made a similar point that most open innovation environments are not focused enough. "Most deployments allow participants to contribute ideas on any topic, instead of asking them to concentrate on specific opportunities and challenges facing the business. A main problem with unstructured environments is that people don't know what constitutes a good or valuable contribution, or why their idea was not acted on," he wrote.

Organizing ideas for improvement

To get real results with a social innovation initiative, you can't stop by tallying up all the ideas submitted and declaring victory. Ideas only produce value if you can translate them into action in some way, by creating a product or implementing a money-saving new process.

The bulk of the ideas generated in a brainstorming session, online or off, will be terrible, impractical ideas. A small number will have potential, and one or two, if you're lucky, will be dynamite.

You want to design a process for graduating the promising ideas to the next stage of consideration and leaving the duds behind. As McQuivey suggests, you want the criteria for selection to be as plain and obvious as possible, reinforcing the belief that the process is fair.

The process of graduating from one stage of consideration to the next can have several steps, making it possible to keep refining the pool of ideas. By making the process collaborative, we can keep the discussion going to add to and enhance ideas so the winners are even better at the end of the process than they were at the beginning.

Making a game of it

When trying to take advantage of mechanisms like voting on ideas that work best with mass participation, it helps to understand what motivates participation. In fact, if you want to succeed with this approach, you don't want to be above manipulating your people's desires and emotions. Idea management applications are some of the most aggressive and creative users of gamification techniques that aim to make software use as compelling as playing a game.

In addition to an employees' natural motivation to see the company do better, you can tap in to their sense of competition, desire for recognition, or interest in winning a prize. The most valued prizes aren't always monetary, or even big money payoffs where money is involved. A lunch with the CEO can be a prize. Or an Amazon.com gift card. At AT&T, the winners of one innovation contest win seed money from an internal venture fund and the chance to turn their ideas into reality — an ego boost and a career advancement all in one.

Rating the best ideas

The most obvious way of keeping score in this scheme is the ratings on ideas. Those who get the most votes will rise to the top. Maybe some will even be motivated to campaign for votes, asking friends to help them raise their ranking. Cheating? Not necessarily, given that someone with the political instincts to campaign for votes may also have the skills to get it implemented if it achieves the right recognition. You can also limit the potential for gaming the system by adding objective criteria for recognizing the winners in each round.

The idea authors are not the only people whose participation should be recognized. Everyone who votes or comments should also be earning points because they are the ones doing the work of organizing and improving the submissions.

In addition to rewarding participation, look for ways of recognizing higher-quality contributions, such as comments on an idea that wind up improving the idea itself. Offer recognition to the most discerning and helpful community members.

Some systems include the notion of an online status or reputation ranking, which can be made visible with the use of badges, which are icons connoting status displayed like a badge of honor next to an employee's profile picture.

Showcasing leaders, recognizing winners

Organizing the innovation management process into multiple stages allows you to build suspense, which is a natural pattern for creating engagement in games and storytelling.

At the end of the process, you will announce your winning ideas, but don't wait until then to create buzz about the results. Showcase your semi-finalists — recognizing both the ideas and the people who submitted them — and ask members of your community to take another look at the ideas as they have been refined through the process.

When you pick the ultimate winners, make an even bigger deal out of them. In addition to recognizing their contributions, you want to motivate others to compete next time.

Blogging and Sharing for Leaders

How much time should a CEO or other executive leader plan to spend personally posting and sharing on a collaboration network? A few minutes a day would be a terrific start, just enough to make her presence felt and check in on what's going on. In smaller organizations, where the company leader is personally supervising projects at a detailed level, that person may need to be active on the network throughout the day.

According to Happe, the most popular format for executive participation is the blog post rather than the status post. Regardless of whether the network uses this terminology or makes a sharp distinction between post types, what this means is that executives tend to share their thoughts in the form of longer, somewhat more formal messages. These may be produced, at least some of the time, with some help from the company's internal communications team. However, it helps if the posts read like informal communication.

For company-wide announcements, composing a social post doesn't need to take any more time than an e-mail with the same content. Moreover, a blog entry puts more communication tools at a leader's disposal, such as embedded video and other multimedia.

When UBM CEO David Levin has a significant announcement to make on his firm's internal social network, The Hub, he publishes it as a post on his "Dear UBM" blog. However, he also participates in a more casual fashion with status updates and comments on what others have posted — often, very simple ones like, "Well done! thx David." Other times, it will be a simple check-in style note, like "Enjoying a spring day in New York . . . at work." On the day I took the screen shot shown in Figure 15-1, the folk singer Richie Havens had just passed away, and Levin posted a tribute, including a series of links to videos of Havens's performances.

The frequency of his updates ranges from several times per week to once every other week. It's not reasonable to expect a busy executive to be on the collaboration network constantly. For that matter, you don't want any employee spending all day posting and reading posts.

For a social network to be productive as a business tool, it needs to be used to get work done — not allowed to become a time drain.

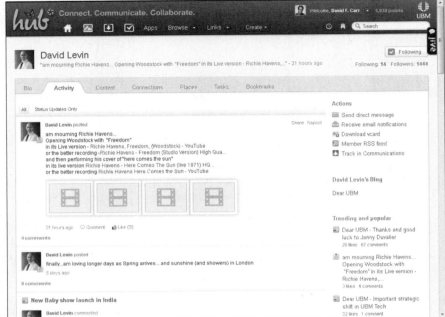

Figure 15-1:
UBM CEO
David
Levin's
activity on
The Hub.

Listening to the Social Network

Collaboration networks are designed to encourage conversation, so effective participation means listening to what others are saying as much as broadcasting your own messages. Marketers have come to value public social networks as ad hoc focus groups, providing insight into the opinions, sentiments, and behavior of consumers. Organizational leaders have a similar opportunity to gain insight into what employees are saying and doing and struggling with in the course of their work.

Despite the limits on time, many leaders find this valuable because they sometimes feel lonely at the top, surrounded by so many handlers that they feel they're getting only a watered-down account of what's going on in the company, Happe says.

Yet making time to scan through unfiltered conversations remains a challenge. "I don't think CEOs and people at that level do a lot of browsing," Happe says. More likely, they will have an executive assistant scan the activity stream and point out things that the boss ought to be aware of or comment on.

Because a discussion can grind to a halt or lose its spontaneity if the CEO jumps in to the middle of it, the more natural mode of online conversation for a company leader tends to revolve around comments on his own blog.

Still, when using a collaboration network, leaders can get the opinions of many more people, including those who are closer to front-line operations. "They get to scale themselves," Happe says. "Executives spend their entire days in meetings. Why? Because they want to talk to as many people as possible."

Understanding the Implications of Transparency

Transparency is generally a positive word in the language of management consultants and social business advocates. To be transparent, a business must strive to be more open and honest with its customers and employees. The enlightened leader is supposed to proclaim commitment to transparency and also welcome constructive criticism.

That's the theory. In organizations that buy in to the theory, social collaboration may be introduced at least partly as a means to achieve greater transparency. Or the implementation of social collaboration may be blocked specifically because some leaders fear it will introduce more transparency than they're willing to tolerate.

Executives are not the only ones skeptical of the argument for transparency. A June 2012 report by Jessica Stillman on the GigaOM blog was titled, "Employees skeptical of execs touting enterprise social, survey finds." Drawing on research by Deloitte, she writes:

> *Among the primary selling points of enterprise social tools is their ability to prick the executive bubble and allow business leaders to get at the perhaps less than beautiful truth about what's actually going on at lower levels of their organizations. By facilitating information sharing across organizational divides and hierarchical levels, this argument goes, social tools will help businesses forge a more cohesive and transparent culture.*
>
> *It's an argument to which employees apparently respond: Oh please! According to a surprising new survey from Deloitte, many executives have bought the party line on the effects of enterprise social media far more than frontline employees, who largely view social as more empty rhetoric out of the C-suite.*

In other words, employees believe their leaders are willing to talk about transparency but not necessarily to follow through on the promise.

Just don't use the rhetoric of full transparency if you're not really committed to it. Make the limits clear. Set the acceptable norms of behavior through policy and by modeling appropriate uses of the social platform. I tell you more about how to approach those tasks later in the chapter.

What's most important here is that leaders and employees alike understand the ground rules. Adopting social collaboration implies acceptance of a degree of transparency because the technology enables open discussion and commenting. If an employee gets fired, for instance, for sharing a critique of company strategy on the social network, no one in the organization will ever believe that frank and open discussion is welcome.

On the other hand, employing the social technology doesn't necessarily mean the organization will tolerate open dissent or disrespect toward its leaders. There is no rule saying that the CEO of a social business must walk around with a Kick Me sign on his back. The collaboration network need not turn into a bottomless comment box for employees to register complaints.

Encouraging Connections Across the Organization

One of the most common reasons for a CEO to support social collaboration is to form one cohesive organization from a loose collection of business units.

Simply implementing social collaboration software won't make this happen, at least not to its maximum potential. A memo or blog post from the CEO stating the goal of unifying the company through collaboration is a good start for setting direction, but this sort of message needs reinforced over time. At a large company, most of the work of forming, coaching, and aligning cross-functional groups will necessarily be delegated to community managers.

However, the CEO can set an example by bringing together people from different parts of the company to accomplish common goals, encouraging them to use the collaboration network in their planning. When those efforts are successful, celebrating the success of the collaborators can be a good way of showcasing the potential of the system. The point being, the people should always get more credit than the technology.

For example, UBM CEO David Levin wanted to see more collaboration between his event management and publishing groups and also between different locations. (The company is headquartered in London, but also has operations in San Francisco, New York, and around the world.)

By actively using the social collaboration network himself (as described above), he encouraged its use as a unifying force for the organization.

Former SuperValu CEO Craig Herkert endorsed Yammer for social collaboration because the company had grown through acquisitions and many of its other computer systems were fragmented. The collaboration network supported the formation of groups for store managers with common interests, such as operations in college towns or seashore locations, even though those managers were attached to different store brands and separate org charts.

When the multidivisional, multidisciplinary magic happens, the result can be new products, new efficiency, a greater sense of organizational unity and purpose — all sorts of wonderful things.

A CEO whose organization is taking advantage of social technologies in other ways — such as marketing, market research, and customer service — should consider the role that social collaboration plays in the broader picture of social business. After all, social business is a vision (and a hot marketing term for many vendors) of the unification of all sorts of social network interactions, both internal and external.

For example, when a customer complaint or question comes in through a company's Facebook page, it ought to be simple to hand off that issue through the company collaboration network. Let me rephrase that. It *ought* to be simple, but it typically isn't. If you take the time to identify these types of needs before implementing the social collaboration solution and work with your chief technology officer to find a solution that fits those needs, your social collaboration tool will be much more effective.

Today, systems for customer engagement outside the company tend to be managed with different technologies and by different people than the systems for collaboration inside the company. The evangelists of social business argue that ought to change — and that it eventually will.

Dion Hinchcliffe, a business strategist and enterprise architect for the Dachis Group (who has written for me at *InformationWeek),* believes that the few businesses who have put all the pieces together are indeed more productive. They are quicker to respond to opportunities and threats and better able to organize cross-functional activities. However, most social business initiatives operate at the departmental level, leading to "social silos of different tools, policies, and staff," he says. This fragmentation is partly the result of an immature software market and new business best practices that are still being defined. This leads organizations to place a variety of bets, rather than staking out an all-encompassing strategy.

Because of that, many companies wind up with separate productivity tools that help salespeople collaborate around sales, marketing people collaborate on campaigns, and customer service people collaborate around service and support, without making it easy for these groups to collaborate with each other. Often, insisting on a single-vendor solution that meets the requirements of all those groups isn't practical, and integration of the various systems may prove elusive.

As a company leader, you can encourage better organizational alignment between these groups, regardless of whether the technologies are fully integrated. One way to do it may be with cross-functional initiatives, coordinated through the company-wide collaboration platform and instigated by the CEO.

Chapter 16

The CIO Guide to Social Collaboration

In This Chapter

▶ Understanding how to integrate your social collaboration solution

▶ Evaluating the needs of users and the enterprise

▶ Planning for long-term success

▶ Charting your course for future integration

▶ Understanding the importance of social collaboration tools

*T*echnology leaders have the same interest in social collaboration as other executives: to help communicate, collaborate, and get the teams reporting to them functioning better. The emphasis in this chapter is on technology leadership strategies for using social collaboration, rather than the kind of tips on leading through social collaboration that I share in the preceding chapter. If you're a chief information officer (CIO) or chief technology officer (CTO), read Chapter 15 because it applies to you, too. This chapter addresses the additional responsibilities you have that other executives don't.

Regardless of whether the title is CIO, VP of IT, or some newfangled title like Chief Digital Officer, someone should be in charge of making sure the social collaboration platform is reliable, secure, and appropriately integrated with the rest of the organization's technical infrastructure.

Integrating Applications and Organizations with Social Collaboration

Community managers and management consultants who advocate for social collaboration are fond of saying that the technology is the easy part — and maybe that's just because it's not the part they're responsible for (I address their responsibilities in Part IV). Technology alone won't create a successful social platform, but failure to make the right technology choices will limit the chance of success. Suppose the collaboration network goes offline when employees need it the most — or through some glitch, displays confidential information? If something like that happens on your watch, it could be time to polish your resume.

In general, social collaboration isn't a high-risk proposition compared with many other technologies in your portfolio. And if it fails, it usually fails quietly with a whimper and not a bang. Success, on the other hand, requires thoughtful implementation and becomes more probable if the technology team has thought through the possibilities as well as the risks.

Issues to be addressed include

- ✓ **Security:** Decide how users will be authenticated and data will be protected. You also need to consider how far the platform can be trusted to prevent unauthorized access and what that implies for what information will or will not be entrusted to it.

- ✓ **Identity management:** Consider how the enterprise can provide a single, consistent employee online identity across social collaboration and other systems.

- ✓ **Knowledge management:** Think about how you can preserve the best content from social collaboration as organizational knowledge for the long term.

- ✓ **Architectural quality:** Focus on how you can maximize the lasting value of your social collaboration platform, rather than merely addressing tactical requirements.

The integration opportunity

One way of making social collaboration more useful is by integrating the collaboration platform with other applications. For example, you can add comment streams to records displayed in a CRM or supply chain system, allowing employees to add informal comments or easily share a link to a specific record with any other user on the social network — say, a "Hey, this is something you ought to look at" type of message that may be a heads-up on a problem or an opportunity.

At a basic level, a social post can link to any web resource available at a distinct web address. On Facebook and Google+, and in many social collaboration solutions, when you include a link to a file or video in a post, the software creates a preview of a document or a video. Creating an appropriate preview for a business application record is a little more complex because (understandably) you can't have the system display information that the user doesn't have the right to access.

Using the emerging web protocols for authentication and authorization between applications and social profiles, you can generate static previews of application content and also achieve deeper integration between applications and social streams. I discuss these possibilities in more detail in Chapter 12.

Regardless of whether you want to invest staff time in creating custom integrations, you ought to at least be aware of any integrations available, whether "out of the box" or through partnerships between vendors. If you choose Salesforce.com's Chatter, for example, you get integration with Salesforce CRM as part of the package. Cloud software vendors are aggressively partnering up and offering proprietary app stores full of integrations with other products.

You may discover that at this point — particularly in the beginning — you don't need to do anything particularly fancy. Just keep your options open for the long term.

The importance of making exceptions

Technical integration is only part of the story. Another reason for implementing social collaboration in an enterprise setting is organizational integration that helps employees work around gaps in business software and business processes. Loosely structured social collaboration can be a means of keeping the company moving when formal processes break down.

This is a form of *exception handling,* which is a way of making systems more resilient. Technologists may know that term from programming, where it is a technique for catching software glitches and handling them as gracefully as possible. In social collaboration, exception handling means giving people the tools to work around problems that standard company systems do not address.

Here's an example. Say, your official process is for the employee to fill out a form in the order management system and mark one of three check boxes. However, the worker runs into a situation that doesn't fit choice A, B, or C. Faced with situation D (and whoever designed this system never thought of choice D), the worker marks C as the closest match but can add a social comment about the real status of the order, tagging the person who is next in the workflow with an @mention, which means they will get an alert.

Grease the right wheels

Exception handling is one of the best arguments in favor of social collaboration, according to John Hagel III, who has investigated these issues as co-chairman of the Deloitte Center for the Edge.

Deloitte estimates that 60 to 70 percent of the time workers invest in their jobs is actually spent handling exceptions, which Hagel defines as "things that get thrown out of automated processes." These are all the examples of events that don't fit into the formal rules, policies, and processes, and they are time consuming because we usually can't resolve these issues on our own: We need to scramble to find other people who can help.

One of Hagel's favorite examples is from a consultation with the transit agency for a city that originally thought its most productive use of social technology would be to create a Facebook page for riders. Suspecting that other, more central processes beyond marketing would have a greater impact, the Deloitte consultants pressed for more detail about the organization's key metrics. They latched on to the cost of bus maintenance, which was driven by the amount of time buses spent out of service after breaking down.

"When we drilled down to the next level of front-line performance, we found that the problem was the parts that were supposed to be readily available weren't where they were supposed to be — a classic example of an exception condition," Hagel says.

I'm quoting from an interview published in MIT's Sloane Management Review, but I heard him tell the same story when he keynoted at the E2 conference. You can find the Sloane interview here:

```
http://sloanreview.mit.edu/
article/how-finding-exceptions-
can-jump-start-your-social-
initiative/
```

Hagel wouldn't tell me which city this happened in, only that social collaboration greased the right wheels to get buses back on the road. Just the ability to post parts needed and parts available at various locations — regardless of where the inventory system said they were supposed to be — made a significant difference. Hagel particularly gets a kick out of the fact that it was the "grizzled older guys out in the maintenance yard" who became the system's biggest advocates — after they saw it would help them get their jobs done, that is.

Balancing Requirements: User, Community, and Enterprise Needs

Technology leaders are used to balancing requirements. Security versus ease of access is a classic balance that comes into play when implementing social collaboration. Users want to be able to collaborate anywhere, anytime, from any device, using nothing more complicated than a password. And many users think that the system should recognize them from the last time they accessed it and log them in automatically, without the need for a password. On the opposite end, the security zealot on your staff wants to enforce 16-character passwords with a mix of letters, numbers, and symbols, which users should be forced to change every week. (Okay, I'm exaggerating a bit here, but the tension is there.) So, if your security measures are too Draconian, users won't use the system, and you may as well not have bothered to implement it. On the other hand, if security is too lax, managers and responsible employees may be uncomfortable discussing important issues on the social platform. Again, why bother if you wind up with a platform that is only good for trivia?

To successfully implement a social collaboration system, you need to consider various requirements and needs throughout the enterprise, some of which I outline here. Then determine what system may work best for your organization. You probably want a web-based application that runs outside the firewall, either in the cloud or your own public-facing server, so users can access it without going through a VPN. I can't tell you specifically how to balance these demands or predict the specific variations that will arise for your organization, but don't say I didn't warn you that they're coming.

Another complication is that different business units may favor different social collaboration platforms. For instance, the sales team wants Chatter, marketing has been happily piloting something Jive, and the employees of the startup you just acquired say they can't live without Podio. So how important is it, really, to get them all on one common platform? If you don't, you obviously lose the potential benefit of having one unified profile for every employee that shows all their social business activity. But does any single platform truly meet everyone's needs?

On top of that, packaged applications of all sorts are sprouting activity streams, with the vendors often treating them simply as a new user interface element to jazz up software. Activity streams have popped up in software products for business intelligence, recruiting, training, social media monitoring, and other applications. How acceptable is it for them to create their own islands of social activity? Or should you insist on feed and profile integration with your broader social collaboration network?

And here's another challenge. Perhaps your internal social collaboration gained momentum based on unsanctioned use of a freemium cloud product, meaning one like Yammer that makes a basic version of its cloud software available to use for free. Now that social collaboration is being turned into a program of record, the IT department recommends moving to an on-premises system based on Microsoft SharePoint. Should the technicians be allowed to force the issue? Is their justification compelling? Or will forcing active communities to migrate from one platform to another kill off something promising?

Something like this dilemma cropped up at the SuperValu grocery chain. The free version of Yammer had been adopted by one group within the company, but the cloud software would not have been the first choice of the IT staff. As CIO Wayne Shurts tells it, then-CEO Craig Herkert broke the tie by ruling in favor of keeping Yammer as the collaboration platform that was already proving itself through unofficial use. He wanted a tool to bring together otherwise fragmented operations within the business, which had growth through acquisitions, and he didn't want to wait for IT to find and implement its idea of the perfect technical solution.

Building Communities to Last

As a technology leader, part of your job is to think a few steps ahead. You don't want to be responsible for choosing and implementing a system that initially makes your users happy but soon collapses under its own weight. For instance, if you agree that a cloud-based option makes the most sense for your organization, you want to be reasonably confident in the quality of the technology and the stability of the business behind it. Conversely, if you opt for an on-premises collaboration server, will you wind up with buyer's regret when it falls behind the pace of innovation associated with cloud competitors? Or are there security and compliance concerns far more important than lagging behind on a few incremental features?

These issues are addressed in Part III, in the context of product selection, but the IT leadership team has a special responsibility for evaluating the operational implications of any given choice and questioning the assumptions that other members of the leadership team may make.

Beyond platform choice, the quality of ongoing systems administration and community management make a big difference. For example, if you require that each new discussion or project community get approval before it becomes active, make sure your staff can adequately handle that queue of requests. Or, if part of your organization's goal with social collaboration is accumulating organizational knowledge, community managers need to help users tag content appropriately for later retrieval.

Social collaboration advocates may boast about reaching beyond the limits of boring, old enterprise systems, but a CIO needs to think about boring, old information management principles like reliability, consistency, and security. Social data may be structured differently, but it's still corporate data — and that needs to be protected and organized to be useful in the long term.

Planning for Integration

If you're on the fence, or just decide to wait a bit before starting a social platform, leave open that possibility. You may even start to prepare for that day even though you're not ready yet. For example, you can start to gather the right metadata in document repositories for an anticipated integration with the social platform you choose.

Some organizations tend to want to address basic integration requirements sooner rather than later. At the top of the list is integration with Microsoft Active Directory or another network directory services tool. Your social platform of choice will almost certainly let you upload a batch of profiles exported from your corporate directory as a starting point, but that doesn't mean that it will do a good job of ongoing synchronization with the directory.

Another typical top-priority concern is to make the integration tight enough that departing employees have their access to the collaboration network cut off as soon as they're removed from the corporate directory. On the cheerier side, you want new employees to get their social collaboration accounts turned on the same day as their e-mail accounts.

Identity is also at the core of social collaboration, so making sure that identity data is consistent across all versions of a person's profile — social, HR systems, e-mail directories — is pretty important. For example, when someone changes a surname, that person shouldn't have to change it several different places in your online systems. And if your organization is going to operate multiple social collaboration systems — say, Chatter in sales, but NewsGator in other parts of the company — someone with a profile in both should be able to expect that basic elements like phone number and office location will be kept consistent between them.

Because activity streams are currently proliferating across multiple software systems (not just enterprise social networks), I also recommend thinking about a strategy for aggregating those streams where appropriate. Employees should able to see the activities of colleagues they are following regardless of whether their colleague posted a comment on a customer record, a sales dashboard, or to the social collaboration network directly. It's supposed to be the activity that matters, more than the software.

Embracing Innovation

If your organization positions social collaboration as a driving innovation, you can position yourself as an innovator by embracing it and doing your part to make it successful. Chapter 15 discusses social collaboration as a tool for encouraging innovation from the perspective of the CEO, but it is as much or more of an issue for the CIO.

"Social is the biggest tool in our toolbox around effecting change in our organization," says Chris Laping, CIO at Red Robin Gourmet Burgers, which has established Yammer accounts for store managers as well as its central administrative staff. In adopting Yammer, "part of the argument I made was 'I need this tool, my team needs this tool. I need a tool that will let me get out a message and get feedback immediately if assumptions aren't playing out right and we need to make modifications.'"

In my *InformationWeek* role, I picked Laping as our Social Business Leader of the Year for 2012 and interviewed him onstage at the E2 conference. I also spoke with store managers who had been around long enough to think of Red Robin as a company that ran on outdated software, and so the implementation of social collaboration came as a pleasant surprise to them.

Old patterns in which IT had all the sophisticated technology and metered employee access to it have been turned on their ear, Laping says. "Now, it's IT that's got the stupid stuff, where you've got 10 times the connectivity at home, plus access to mobile and YouTube." In other words, it's IT that needs to match or at least the approach the sophistication of consumer technologies, he says.

Information technology organizations themselves need to become more collaborative and social, says Frank Wander, the author of *Transforming IT Culture* (John Wiley & Sons, Inc.). Those qualities lead directly to more successful technology projects and fewer embarrassing failures, he says. While serving as CIO at Guardian Life, Wander advocated for the adoption of social collaboration, although the company's adoption of Yammer happened after he left to form the IT Excellence Institute. To his mind, the technology is the smallest part of "working social."

"I think the most important thing is obviously creating a culture where there is trust and collaboration," he says. "Without that, I don't think the tools are very important. With that, the tools become very important. They allow us to work together in a quicker and more meaningful way."

Chapter 17

The Workplace Leader's Guide to Social Collaboration

S ocial collaboration is an important tool for creating a more productive workplace and a more engaged workforce. By making people feel more connected to each other and the organization as a whole, a collaboration network can help motivate employees to work harder, contribute more actively, and seek to advance within the organization (rather than jump ship to a competitor).

A survey by APCO Worldwide and Gagen MacDonald (www.gagenmacdonald. com/ism/power-internal-social-media) found that employees in organizations with successful internal social networks are

- ✔ 39 percent more likely to recommend their company's products and services

- ✔ 60 percent more likely to give their company the benefit of the doubt in a crisis

- ✔ 67 percent more likely to purchase the company's stock

- ✔ 78 percent more likely to support government policies that their company supports

In short, these employees are more fully committed to the organization they work for. This chapter is for anyone — including human resources and corporate communications professionals, organizational development strategists, and managers — seeking to use social collaboration to create a better workplace or organizational culture.

Maybe it should go without saying, but adding social collaboration won't magically cure all the ills of an otherwise dysfunctional organization. The social element needs to be more than just a veneer: It needs to dovetail with broader policies and corporate behaviors that invite and reward employee engagement.

Using Social Collaboration to Create a Welcoming, Productive Workplace

Here are some of the ways that you can use social collaboration to help create a better workplace:

- **On-board new employees.** You can introduce new colleagues to a support network of co-workers and people who can answer questions. The activity stream is a great place to introduce new hires, and you may even introduce a new hire to groups that are relevant to the person's position and responsibilities, if that option is available.

- **Bring the corporate directory to life.** A social collaboration system includes social activity and shared content, not just basic phonebook info.

- **Extend learning opportunities.** In a social collaboration system, networked learning can extend beyond the boundaries of what's taught in formal corporate training. There may be no course that covers what an employee needs to learn but plenty of people willing to teach or coach the motivated learner. The network can also supplement more formal training, through social groups students participate in parallel with class work, which they retain access to after the class is over.

  At Hitachi Data Systems (HDS), Vice President of Learning and Collaboration Nick Howe, says of all the things employees need to learn to do their jobs, only a fraction lend themselves to being taught in a traditional corporate training course. Meanwhile, in a fast-changing technological business (HDS primarily sells computer storage), just-in-time learning is often a better match anyway.

- **Provide employees with ongoing feedback.** Performance review time isn't the only time that employees need feedback. In a social collaboration network, they can get ongoing coaching and recognition from peers as well as supervisors.

✔ **Engage employees.** Within the activity stream, within groups, or wherever is appropriate, you can actively involve employees in discussing the goals and future of the business or their part of it.

✔ **Identify the best collaborators.** Analyzing patterns of collaboration to understand which people and groups are working together most actively. A manager who pays attention to those patterns will know which teams to assign to projects requiring collaborative work.

✔ **Flattening the organization.** You can shorten the chain of command and streamline organizational communications by letting the CEO and other top leaders engage in two-way communication with employees at every level.

✔ **Help colleagues communicate beyond silos.** Encourage collaboration across business units and functions by making it easier (opening the door to productive uses that I discuss throughout this book).

✔ **Court "digital natives."** As new employees who have grown up with social media enter the workforce, while others have their expectations raised by consumer technologies, using social collaboration helps make work systems feel more competitive with those we enjoy at home. For example, a social collaboration network that works well on mobile devices will be attractive to an employee who has grown used to being able to do everything on a smartphone.

✔ **Unite the workforce.** Make employees feel more connected to each other and the organization, which tends to make them feel more engaged and happier in their work. A social collaboration network makes it possible to get the big picture of what is going on in the company, no matter how organizationally or geographically distant from the individual employee.

✔ **Establish or reinforce a productive, effective corporate culture.** You want your people working to act like part of the same team. With its emphasis on sharing and cooperative work, a social collaboration network can help.

Knowing Who Leads on Workplace Design

It's not always the head of human resources who takes the lead on workplace transformation. It can be, and maybe it should be, but often it isn't. Sometimes, HR is one of the obstacles — the rules-based bureaucracy that knows all the reasons to say "No." Or HR may be a supporting player in an initiative that starts elsewhere, with corporate communications, training, operations, or a culture change initiative directed from the CEO's office. HR leaders may see it as their job to make the workforce more productive, innovative, and engaged. Or they may be too bogged down in the practicalities of hiring and firing atop managing benefits.

Many organizations are embracing elements of "social HR" in the context of using public social media for human resources purposes, such as recruiting and backgrounding potential new hires on LinkedIn. They are not necessarily focusing on the internal applications of social technology, however.

Yvette Cameron, a Constellation Research Group analyst who covers the intersection of social technologies and HR, argues this is a mistake. Rather than leading on workforce innovation, too many HR leaders are involved as supporting players, if they are involved at all. Or, they may be active naysayers, giving too much weight to the risks related to regulatory compliance and too little to the potential benefits, she says.

"Sometimes, I think we wear the HR hat a little too tight," agrees Heathre Moler, a human resources executive who led the implementation of a social performance management application at her organization. The orthodox tasks of hiring, firing, and benefits management are necessities, meaning. "You have to do them, but not any better than the next guy," she says. "You need to reduce as much of the non-value-added work as you can."

At the same time, one of the mega-themes you hear from management consultants and business analysts about how the best organizations function concerns crafting of corporate culture. Jim Collins, the author of *Good to Great* (HarperBusiness) and other books about how great companies create and sustain values, emphasizes that culture is not a mission statement or a values statement but rather the alignment of an organization's core values with how it actually operates. In the article, "Aligning Action and Values," Collins explains. "For instance, many organizations say they respect and trust their people to do the right thing, but they undermine that statement by doing X, Y, and Z. The misalignments exist not because the statements are false: these companies believe what they say. The misalignments occur because years of ad hoc policies and practices have become institutionalized and have obscured the firm's underlying values."

Where such misalignments occur, who is responsible for correcting them? Who within your organization is responsible for making the organization itself more cohesive and productive? The CEO has ultimate responsibility for setting the right direction, but who is responsible for following through on it?

My employer, UBM, has a People and Culture department that includes human resources but has cultural change as part of its organizational mission. The challenge of creating one cohesive culture of many merged organizations was one of the motivations for our social collaboration initiative. Our Global

Community Manager Ted Hopton reports into that group, although he works closely with Collaboration Systems Manager Tracy Maurer, who works in IT. Naturally, the online collaboration initiative is only one element of the UBM strategy of aligning culture and action.

At SAS Institute, an analytics software company routinely ranked as one of the world's best places to work, social collaboration originated as an initiative of corporate communications, independent of HR. The introduction of Socialcast as an internal social network was "a good fit for what our culture already is," rather than an attempt to change it, says Becky Graebe, the senior internal communications manager who oversees the system. "It's a way for employees to do what they already do naturally, except we're connecting to a broader group of people."

If anything, the project has forced a culture change within the internal communications group itself, away from broadcasting information in the form of newsletters and toward enabling two-way communication with employees and networked communication among employees.

Choosing Social Workplace Applications

Workplace applications can be social without necessarily being part of a general-purpose social collaboration platform, such as Jive or Yammer. Like many other sorts of software, applications for corporate training, performance management, and employee recognition have been sprouting activity feeds and user profiles. What would be unfortunate is to support entirely separate feeds and profiles from those that exist in your company-wide collaboration platform — assuming you have one, that is. You have to decide whether that's important to you or whether the social functionality in the standalone application is really what's most important.

Many learning management systems now boast social features, where the idea is to augment online courses and on-demand, video training modules with peer-to-peer interaction between learners, which can continue after a course is done.

Hitachi Data Systems runs its HDS Academy program on learning management software from Saba Systems that includes a number of collaboration features, including video conferencing and social discussion streams. In fact, Saba has built out those features into its own social collaboration offerings, but Howe says by the time Saba had a complete social platform he had already committed to Jive.

Another category where there is overlap is social performance management software, which uses social networking and gamification techniques to track and motivate employee performance. Consider the case of Rypple, which began life as a startup with offices in Toronto and San Francisco focused on "re-inventing processes," such as employee goal setting, evaluation, and peer recognition. One of the reasons why Rypple had such a good Facebook-like user interface is that it won Facebook as a customer: The social media firm integrated the software with its own custom internal collaboration environment. Rypple was also identified with the trend toward gamification of workplace software, challenging employees to set ambitious goals, compete to achieve them, and win visible recognition in the form of badges.

Rypple can operate as a social collaboration environment onto itself, but it was really designed to replace the traditional annual review cycle of employee feedback with ongoing recognition and performance management. Rypple also worked on integration with other products, becoming one of the first participants in the Jive Apps Market with the Rypple Thanks app.

Acquired by Salesforce.com at the end of 2011, Rypple was eventually rebranded Work.com. Work.com can be used independently although Salesforce.com encourages using it in combination with Chatter. Figure 17-1 shows how Work.com data looks in the Chatter stream. Meanwhile, because the integration with Jive is unlikely to get much love going forward, Jive has introduced a simple employee recognition app of its own, called Props, into its apps market as a free alternative.

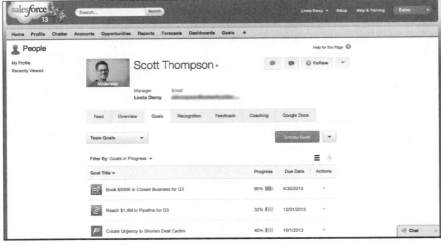

Figure 17-1: Work.com makes employee goals (and progress toward them) part of a social profile.

Courtesy of Salesforce.com

At the end of 2012, IBM moved to solidify its "smarter workforce" strategy with the acquisition of Kenexa, creator of a suite of apps for recruiting, on-boarding, learning, and compensation, as well as performance management. Expect to see Kenexa more tightly integrated with IBM Connections over time. SAP's social collaboration strategy is built around its acquisition of SuccessFactors, which is a suite of human capital management products that also includes recruiting, on-boarding, learning, and compensation. An accompanying social collaboration product, SuccessFactors JAM, became SAP JAM following the acquisition, reflecting a broader focus on social integration across all SAP business applications, with the SuccessFactors HR-related apps still in a favored position. Oracle has amassed its own family of HR and social technologies, as have other competitors.

Meanwhile, a handful of other social performance management players continue to compete as independent companies.

Social HR and workforce applications are more powerful when combined with a collaboration network that can also be used for other purposes. If you use a social application to bestow recognition on an employee for doing a good job, you want that recognition to be published widely. That way, the person's friends will see it in the activity stream, without necessarily logging in to the recognition app. If you connect with someone through a social performance management or learning application, you want to be able to click through to his profile on the collaboration network and find out more about him, beyond his interactions with that one application.

If HR and workforce technologies are providing the initial impetus for the use of social applications in your organization, give strong consideration to a collaboration platform that either comes from the same vendor or offers a robust integration.

However, if you're working within a large enterprise, you may not have the luxury of choosing a single, integrated stack of social collaboration and HR applications. The organization may have made several previous independent decisions to choose applications or whole suites of applications that it is committed to. In some cases, there may be one dominant vendor you deal with, such as Oracle or SAP, that also offers a social collaboration solution. If it fits your needs and you have the power to choose, that should probably be your choice.

On the other hand, the choice of the company-wide collaboration platform is just as likely to be dictated by the needs of IT and other constituencies for use in a broader array of business scenarios, and that may lead to a multivendor solution. Even then, you can investigate the options for technical integration. If there is an available software plug-in or prepackaged integration between these islands of social collaboration, try to work that into the budget. Creating your own custom integration may also be possible but more expensive.

You may just have to accept that perfect integration is impractical. If both your social applications and your core collaboration network offer a good experience, employees may value them without noticing the gap between them.

Recognizing Achievement

Whether you employ a structured employee performance app like Rypple or more informally recognize performance with comments in the activity stream, an internal social network provides a means of recognizing employees in front of their peers and encouraging more of the behaviors that drive corporate results.

Employees are already using social technologies at work, whether sanctioned or unsanctioned. "You've got to figure out how to leverage that to improve the performance of your employees and beat the competition," says Heathre Moler, the human resources executive I quoted earlier.

When she led the implementation of Rypple at ETS-Lindgren (a manufacturer of radio frequency and microwave shielding products), it wasn't part of any grander plan for social collaboration, but it was an important step toward changing some basic human resources processes, she says. Although she has since moved on to an HR role at another firm, she says, "I haven't let go of what I believe about the value of providing a more real-time tool for performance that includes having social, visible goals people can share and contribute to."

Now that Rypple has turned into Work.com, it may prove fortunate that ETS Lindgren is also a Salesforce.com customer. However, at the time she brought in Rypple, the sales team was just starting to experiment with Chatter and the two initiatives were unrelated. The first real experience the company got with internal social media was turning on the MySite feature of Microsoft SharePoint; that was the first collaboration environment in which every employee's participation linked back to a profile with a photo.

The real impetus for introducing social performance management was a conversation with ETS-Lindgren President Bruce Butler about the company's traditional performance review process, which was the subject of "a lot of belly aching from managers and employees alike" because no one saw the value in it, Moler says. "Employees would set goals at the beginning of year, but they probably didn't get looked at again until review time the following year. The only time we would have a discussion about the performance review was when someone wasn't doing well." As a result, the company wasn't "proactively rewarding good behavior" or helping employees calibrate their performances to line up with their goals, she says.

By introducing a continual, social feedback loop, the company introduced a much more dynamic process of tracking employee progress against both their personal goals and their operational goals for their roles within the company. The new process improved employee engagement with frequent feedback and informed a mentoring program the company instituted to coach employees toward better performance, Moler says.

Any social collaboration system will support the informal shout-out to someone who has done a good job. You can imagine that employees may be encouraged to publicly commit to their goals for the coming year with a status post as well. What social performance management applications add is the tracking to turn this from an ad hoc process to a structured one.

Because not every accomplishment that is important will be captured or have a badge associated with it, managers should be encouraged to post impromptu messages of praise and appreciation, too.

Synchronizing with HRIS

Regardless of whether your social collaboration environment is an extension of your human resources information system, it can benefit from Human Resource Information System (HRIS) data, particularly to enrich employee profiles. Because one of the goals of collaboration networks is to make it easier to locate expertise within the organization, the data about an employee's educational attainment or completion of corporate training courses logged in the HRIS system should also be reflected in the social profile.

Between the HRIS system and a corporate directory (such as Active Directory), it ought to be possible to pre-populate every profile with at least a starter set of data also including contact information. Even in the absence of a live connection with ongoing synchronization, sometimes IT will use a mass import of HR and directory data to get profiles started at the launch of the collaboration network. If there is a photo in the system — for example, a security badge photo — that can be added to the social profile as well. Naturally, you want to provide colleagues with the option of replacing that photo with a better one and making other corrections.

Just as often, employees are welcomed by a blank profile screen and prompted to fill in the blanks manually. Often, they won't be motivated to do a very thorough job of it, particularly if you're asking them to supply information they would expect the company to already know.

If at all possible, you want to present employees with a social software environment that already knows a lot about them and is ready to learn more.

Chapter 18

Social Collaboration for the Sales Team

Sales collaboration done right promises one of the greatest payoffs (if not *the* greatest) for social collaboration.

Sales is often associated with cutthroat competition, but in many industries sales teams are truly teams. Further, their teamwork is even more powerful if it extends outside the sales organization to include peers in marketing, product development, and other business functions. This is particularly true of business-to-business firms with complex products to sell. Social collaboration can be a tool for building cohesive teams and extending their reach.

Although many sales organizations have gotten a taste of social collaboration because of Salesforce.com's promotion of Chatter, often it's introduced so casually that it's never used effectively (more on that later in the chapter).

To get the most from any of these social platforms, sales leaders need to show how their teams can use social collaboration platforms for purposeful collaboration, not just casual networking.

Coordinating Sales Teams

The most successful users of social collaboration for sales have a focus on accelerating the most valuable types of collaboration, and it isn't limited to the sales organization alone. As a leader in a sales organization, here are some things to emphasize about the productive use of social collaboration:

✔ **Position social collaboration as a business tool.** Help your team understand that instead of using the tool for purely social purposes, they should be networking to exchange contacts and strategies for winning deals.

✔ **Encourage sharing.** Promote routine sharing of information about sales wins, opportunities, and objections to be overcome that go beyond the CRM record.

✔ **Reward teamwork.** Establish a collaborative culture, with incentives that recognize the work of the team, not just the person who closes the deal. Sales leaders can set an example by using the social activity stream to monitor the whole series of events that lead to success and recognizing contributions people make along the way.

✔ **Extend your reach.** Social collaboration reaches beyond the sales team into other divisions of the company. Success often comes to salespeople who know when to ask for help from people in other parts of the company who can answer a potential customer's question about future product plans or bend the rules about granting discounts. For maximum success, you want the use of the social collaboration network to extend throughout the company.

Figure 18-1 shows how sales team members can work together in Chatter to assemble the necessary information to win a deal.

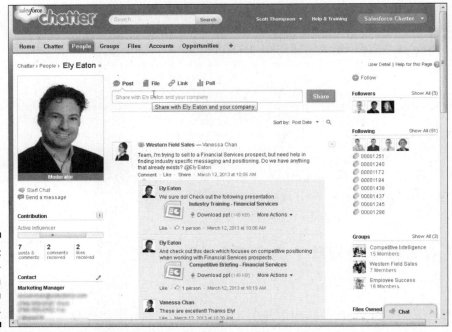

Figure 18-1: Collaborating on a proposal in Chatter.

Choosing the Right Tool

This chapter easily could focus entirely on Chatter, the social collaboration tool bundled with the popular suite of sales and marketing tools from Salesforce.com. Chatter makes it easy to start conversations about objects in the CRM system, such as customers and opportunities, and Chatter is commonly the social collaboration tool for sales even in organizations where other departments use a competing product. Microsoft bought Yammer, another cloud-based social collaboration tool, partly to integrate it with Microsoft Dynamics CRM as a competitor to Chatter.

Still, many organizations report making their sales organizations more efficient using another product, such as the Jive platform, that's not joined at the hip with a CRM system. Meanwhile, some Salesforce.com customers who have taken advantage of the ease with which they can enable Chatter have seen few benefits from it, namely because they never got beyond turning on the software. In organizations where the business value of social collaboration hasn't been established, Chatter adoption even within the sales team may be poor because representatives do not see how it can help them get their jobs done.

At OpenTable, social collaboration started in sales and spread to other departments. And that's one reason why Chatter became the social collaboration environment of choice. In other companies where a social collaboration platform such as Jive or IBM Connections has taken root, often the argument against Chatter is that it's intended only for sales. Chatter may wind up earning a place anyway, as a tool for collaboration within the sales team, while another platform supports cross-functional social collaboration. Too, because Salesforce.com has such a dominant market position in CRM, some of the other social collaboration platform vendors are also offering technical integration fixes for integrating Chatter feeds with their own.

Also, although Jive doesn't come from the same sales force automation roots as Salesforce.com, part of its corporate identity is as one of the leading social CRM companies because its software can be used to manage public customer communities as well as internal employee communities. That gives Jive a strong sales orientation, which particularly appeals to firms that use its content management tools to manage sales documents and market intelligence as well as social discussions about the sales process. Figure 18-2 shows a Jive workspace for a sales team, with content including a discussion thread, a congratulatory blog post about the best performers, and an assortment of proposal documents and templates.

Jim Buck, the senior community manager at F5 Networks, says sales is his number-one internal customer and was already using Chatter when he was hired even though adoption wasn't particularly high. Buck had experience with Jive, which he had used with a previous employer to build collaboration networks to connect the company with its channel sales partners, but F5 was a different organization asking him to solve a different set of problems.

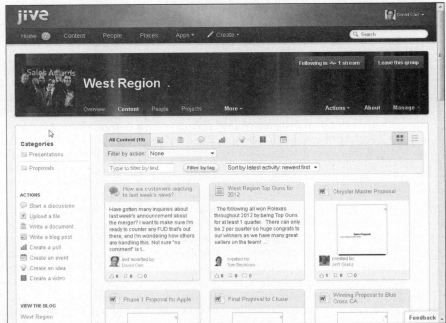

Figure 18-2:
A Jive work-
space for a
sales team.

"Jive was not a given when I came in," he says. "We asked several different companies to provide a request for proposal (RFP), but at the end of the day, Jive just had more things" than F5 needed for a complete solution. "Chatter had very low adoption and was really too sales oriented," he says. "We wanted to bring in more of the company, not just the sales organization."

One goal of the project was to create a more unified content management and collaboration environment, using Jive to replace multiple tools — for example, taking advantage of Jive's capability to manage video to replace a separate product that had been purchased for that purpose.

In addition, F5 wanted to help "expedite the on-boarding process through sales," meaning the process of getting new sales representatives to understand the company's products and be able to locate information about them (or people who could answer questions) more quickly. "It's all about getting them selling faster, with better productivity."

The only thing this proves about the tools is that there is not necessarily one right answer for every organization. How you use the software you choose is at least as important as which software you choose.

Cracking the Market for Sales Intelligence

Making social collaboration mandatory for the sales team is one sure way of getting adoption. This is one of Senior Vice President of Sales Mike Dodson's tactics that many other organizations would not want to attempt and may not be able to make stick, but it arguably helped enlist people from other constituencies (such as marketing and operations) who did not report to him. Employees of those departments may not have been compelled to use Chatter, but they did need to use it if they wanted to communicate with the field sales force that was communicating exclusively in that mode.

The most important lesson of the OpenTable example is that capturing the "real-life, realtime experiences from the field" paid off with a greater accumulation of sales intelligence for management, marketing, operations, and the field sales team itself. That's the same thing Buck aims to accomplish for F5 and a core element of every sales collaboration initiative.

"In most companies, there's a black market for sales intelligence," says Joe Galvin, a sales strategies and technologies analyst with Miller Heiman. "It's the informal knowledge network that exists within and among salespeople in every organization." The most successful salespeople know who to call to learn information not published in any official market analysis document or secure an extra discount not on any price list. Although these back-channel connections may make a few individuals look good, they subvert the goal of making the entire sales organization more effective, Galvin says. As new employees join, it can take them a long time to build up connections and crack the internal knowledge networks, he says. The question social collaboration poses, he says, is, "What would happen if we took that black market and made it a public market?"

Salespeople are more willing to collaborate than the stereotypes about cut-throat competitors may suggest, Galvin says. Sure, you'll see lone-wolf competition between salespeople, but these days you'll probably find far more environments where salespeople are highly interdependent, succeeding or failing as a team, he says. Business-to-business (B2B) sales is dominated by complex deals where producing a winning proposal requires input from many people, each of whom has a different expertise.

And that's certainly the story I've heard from consulting organizations, such as KPMG (finance and accounting) and CSC (systems integration). Social collaboration has taken root there as a means to gather input for a proposal from more people and do it faster than before, winning more deals as a result.

André Huizing, who leads the collaboration practice and technology consulting firm Avanade, says sales is a good place for social collaboration to start particularly for any B2B organization that must respond to large request for proposal documents. "An RFP is a project in and of itself, often involving a few weeks of work with people around the globe," he says.

"You have to lead by example," he adds. "No sales guy is going to use these tools if his boss doesn't."

Building a Culture of Collaboration

Successful social collaboration does require getting people to see the point. As OpenTable's Dodson discovered, many sales teams' first reaction to a collaboration environment that looks vaguely like Facebook is to use it as they would use Facebook: that is, for casual chitchat rather than for sharing meaningful business information. Senior company leaders may be dismissive of the value of the tool, particularly if they see it being used in a trivial way.

"You have to say very clearly, this is not about social chitchatting," says Bonnie Cheuk, a global knowledge and collaboration director at Citigroup who works primarily in support of improving sales productivity. "I think we should drop the word 'social' altogether because when you use that they have the perception that this is for my kid, this is Facebook."

She contrasts that with what happened when a member of the sales team shared the presentation deck it was using to pitch banking services to a national airline, which led to a lively and productive discussion with others who were also pitching business to airlines around the world. Being able to show how the collaboration network drives sales productivity is critical to encouraging more collaboration that leads to more sales productivity, she says. A story like that "allows a glimpse into what a social platform can do," she says.

I heard a very similar story from Roland Hulme, who manages both internal and external social media for Tyco. When a company representative was trying to win a major deal to install security equipment at a stadium in Mexico, the Yammer network let him connect with the select club of others around the globe who had also worked on stadium deals and knew exactly what they required.

"He got all this great info that helped him win the contract, whereas he wouldn't even have known who to call up in a business unit in Europe" with the information he needed, Hulme says.

Those productive connections are possible but not automatic. When Yammer was first made available within Tyco, its use was dominated by "water cooler conversations," Hulme says. "People were posting questions like, 'Which do you like better, coffee or tea?', which was our most popular thread for several months. Upper management was looking at it and saying, 'I can't believe this is such a waste of productive time.'" One way he changed that pattern was by gathering and publicizing examples of productive uses of the platform — not only for sales but in other disciplines like inventory control — and promoting expectations for professional behavior.

F5's Bruck says social collaboration can be a great way for sales leaders to set clear goals and objectives for their organizations. Too often, those goals are not well defined, and employees can't find them written down anywhere. As a result, employees are not always clear on whether they are delivering on what's most important to the boss.

Executives know what they want to achieve and are often passionate about expressing their goals although "very infrequently" in the context of a sales meeting. Social collaboration can be a way of "getting in front of the people looking to you for leadership" and doing it on an ongoing basis. "This is a way for them to set the tone for the company," he says.

Vala Afshar and Brad Martin of Enterasys describe the importance of getting their CEO Chris Crowell involved in using Chatter, in their book *In Search of Social Business Excellence* (Charles Pinot). Their firm, a networking equipment maker, uses Salesforce.com CRM to track all sales activities, giving Crowell ample opportunity to celebrate every time he sees a big or strategic win pop up on his dashboard.

"Chris's chats go to everybody — all 1,000 employees," they write. "In effect, he publicly promotes the salesperson for winning. At the same time, he reminds the other sales folks competing around the world that 'you too can win.' He is connecting the dots by connecting the people, because when Chris promotes our win of a university deal on the West Coast, an account executive on the East Coast fighting to win another university deal can now chat or collaborate with her colleague to find out how she won her new business."

Peer recognition is just as important, if not more so. If you can get your sales team engaged with contributing to and celebrating each other's success, that's where the magic happens.

Sharing to Win Sales

One of the big cultural shifts that needs to take place in many sales organizations is toward sharing information, rather than hoarding it as a source of power.

Citigroup's Cheuk says she sees that as one of the barriers to overcome in the banking world, where salespeople ask why they should share information that others can take and use to their own advantage. Yet when individuals share their observations of the market, the entire group gets a better picture of it. Meanwhile, market researchers can use that discussion as a source of intelligence and add their own data points. Rather than holding research for distribution in something like a monthly newsletter, "they can publish insights as they come in, getting them on the platform every hour, every minute, instead of waiting a whole week," she says.

Getting good analysis into the social stream also requires coaching employees on the value of open discussion — including the willingness to occasionally disagree with the boss about the best way to accomplish something — in search of a better answer.

"Those are not tech problems, those are cultural," Cheuk says. "You have to think through what kind of intervention would you introduce to take those barriers away? The technology will not do that."

Although most employees in her organization still use e-mail communication as the default, and "trying to wean them from their e-mail addiction" is a huge culture change challenge, she does see more sales leaders starting to blog. They don't even want to call it blogging (which "sounds too technical" to them), but they are sharing their thoughts using the Jive blogging tool. And within minutes of a post, there will be a flurry of comments, she says.

Put the jargon aside and focus on helping your people do what they are paid to do, Cheuk says. "The reason for having the tool is to help them get done what they need to get done, better and faster."

Capitalizing on Competition

The dynamics of social media can be a great way of encouraging healthy cooperation. Sure, collaboration is a wonderful thing, but salespeople are and ought to be competitive. After all, their job is to beat the competition, every day, and they (naturally) will compete with each other as well.

One common way of doing that is by incorporating elements of *gamification,* which is the use of the techniques game designers use to motivate and reward behavior, applied to business purposes. A simple example of this is the use of a *leaderboard,* which is a ranked list of names like you might see for the top golfers in a tournament or the high scores on a video game. This makes it easy to see who's ahead of whom in the rankings and what they need to do to catch up. By putting the leaderboard in a social context, you can show faces as well as names and encourage discussion about the rankings — even including some (hopefully good natured) trash talk about the competition.

The Chatter Leaderboard shown in Figure 18-3 ranks users by participation in the social collaboration environment itself (it's a free app from Salesforce. com's labs group), but more sophisticated gamification software will allow you to rank by all sorts of business metrics.

One way of spreading the credit is to have rankings on more than one metric: say, customer satisfaction and renewals rather than raw sales alone. Many gamification systems also incorporate the concept of awarding *badges,* which are icons displayed on a user's profile to recognize some achievement. You may have a badge you give to anyone who closes a $1-million sale, for example. Another tactic is to allow team members to award badges to each other as a form of peer-to-peer recognition for their contributions.

Figure 18-3:
A leader-
board for
the most
active
Chatter
users.

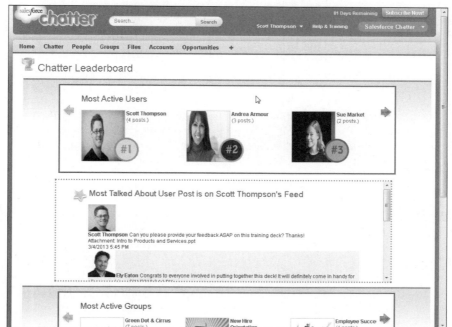

Then, when the badge is awarded, it is published to the social stream, allowing colleagues to offer their congratulations.

Give careful thought to the design of these game mechanics and what you are really rewarding. If part of what you are trying to promote is the performance of the team, you should reserve at least some of your recognition for teams rather than individuals. You can still take advantage of the social medium to make it easy to see who's on the best ranked teams and who the most valuable team members are.

Recognizing Achievement

Badges are cool and trendy and can be effective if used right, but a simple *Good job!* or *Way to go!* from the right person can be even more powerful. Sales professionals are famous for being motivated by commissions and other financial rewards, but like all people they also crave simple, human recognition that they're doing a good job.

For those chasing large business-to-business deals, big paydays come only every so often. Managers can help them stay focused by also recognizing smaller victories, such as securing an appointment for the sales team to make its pitch to someone who may be too many levels away from the ultimate decision maker but still closer than before. *Good job!* Then, when the big win does materialize, recognize the achievement of everyone who contributed to making it happen and share that recognition as broadly as possible. The bigger the win, the more appropriate it is for that recognition to come from someone senior in the company, if not the CEO.

OpenTable's Dodson says that securing "top-down buy-in" is a critical success factor, which is why he involves CEO Matthew Roberts in sending a congratulatory note to the sales team when it has a good month. "If he's on it, he's embracing it; it's going to happen across the executive team and across all the departments," Dodson says.

At every level, when you are generous about recognizing success, you will tend to have more of it.

Examining a Successful Implementation

OpenTable's Dodson says that his firm, a longtime Salesforce.com customer, had to recover from starting down a dead-end path with Chatter. Initially, the product was introduced as "Facebook for the enterprise," with little guidance on its proper business uses. As a result, Chatter was "more about fun and games, right down to the photos," in the beginning, he says. Employees were as likely to post photos of their dogs as they were to share anything work-related, he says. It wasn't until after a briefing with the Chatter product team that Dodson recognized the tools had a potential to be more than that.

"Once I made the decision this was something we had to get serious about, I decided we've got to take all the fun and games out of it," Dodson says. He also told his field sales team he didn't want to see any more e-mail from them. Their reports of their successes, frustrations, observations, and questions needed to be reported in Chatter where everyone could see them. With e-mail, people would tend to write to a small circle of people, which often doesn't include everyone who needs to know that information or may have an answer to a question.

Dodson particularly wanted to improve communication and collaboration among the members of his field sales team (most of whom work from home offices around the world) as well as between them and headquarters. These are the people who sell OpenTable's online reservation service to restaurants.

I happened to speak with Dodson on the day after Groupon (the discount deals website) announced its own Groupon Reserve service, based on an acquisition it had made the year before of a restaurant reservation startup called Savored. That is exactly the sort of the news that prompts a lot of questions from the field, meaning that the OpenTable marketing department needed to arm them with at least a few bullet points on competitive positioning. That information *could* have been distributed over e-mail, giving the sales force marketing's perspective. By doing it over Chatter instead, though, they also got the advantage of seeing each other's thoughts about this development, including intelligence about what the representatives had been hearing from restaurants that had been contacted by this new competitor.

"Rather than being in a panic mode for 24 hours as we tried to disseminate the information, everyone could see 'my peers see this as a non-issue for the following reasons' — that's how we get information out to the field very fast," Dodson says. The marketing organization also winds up being better aligned with the true needs of field sales.

One of the keys to success with Chatter has been getting it used by people outside sales, in functions such as marketing, operations, and engineering, Dodson says. Otherwise, sales representatives wouldn't be able to get answers to their questions for marketing, operations, or engineering through Chatter. Particularly with large customers, the OpenTable sales process can include addressing technical issues of software integration, which is why engineering needs to be in the mix.

If you make your sales team alternate between a social tool and e-mail depending on what they're asking and whom they're asking, "it's never going to happen," Dodson says.

Employees sometimes complain that social collaboration effectively gives them a second inbox they need to check (in addition to e-mail), but the OpenTable field sales team doesn't have that excuse. "Any communication with the sales team has to happen via Chatter, so there is one inbox for them," Dodson says.

He did admit that his own communications habits are more mixed, partly because he has to be in communication with people in other business functions whose habits don't revolve around Chatter. Also, even though Chatter supports private conversations, he says he was never comfortable with it as the right tool for communicating with senior sales managers about unsettled issues of strategy or compensation. "If we're having a conversation we want everyone to understand and reference, that's when Chatter is where we go," he says.

Social collaboration can also be overdone to the point where it pushes out one-to-one contact and leaves salespeople feeling alienated, Dodson says. A good leader needs to know when to take his hands off the keyboard and pick up the phone or meet with someone in person. On balance, though, the effect is overwhelmingly positive.

"For me as a sales leader and my direct leadership team, the real advantage is this gives us more insight, more of a window into what's happening in realtime in multiple markets in the field," Dodson said.

Chapter 19

Social Collaboration for the Worker Bee

Social collaboration can be helped immensely by strong leadership from senior executives, but its success ultimately depends upon the contributions of a lot of people. This chapter is for every member of a social collaboration network, regardless of rank, who wants to maximize the benefits of the technology and be a productive member of the online community.

If you're a manager at any level, you can use social collaboration to organize and motivate your team. Or, if you're a worker bee with great ambitions, you can exploit the collaboration network to show your leadership potential. No matter who you are, you can make the network more powerful by participating in it — and in this chapter I tell you how to do that wisely.

Using Social Collaboration for Everyday Tasks

What really makes a difference in the context of work is that you use the collaboration network to get work done, celebrate accomplishments, and help the organization learn to perform better. Use the platform productively, and you will stand out as someone who knows how to get things done. In this section, I outline the basics of using the social collaboration platform to get stuff done, and I also help you evaluate when it's appropriate to use social collaboration in place of e-mail.

Working out loud

One of the best ways of raising your profile and getting more out of a collaboration network is by routinely narrating your work or at least the important parts of it that your co-workers need to know. Give a brief description of what you're working on in your status posts. Share your problems and your questions as they arise, and you have a better chance of getting solutions and answers from your network. This is often referred to as "working out loud" (see the upcoming sidebar).

The ideal approach is to give a glimpse of your work in progress, rather than make an announcement only when you accomplish something. This does go against entrenched work instincts, but narrating your work in process opens up opportunities for collaboration. Figure 19-1 shows how that works for a traveling executive who lets others know she is on her way to Boston and as a result lines up additional productive meetings for her visit.

Figure 19-1: The "working out loud" strategy.

> **Celeste Martin** 7 minutes ago
>
> I will be traveling to Boston next week, Wednesday 7/6 to Friday. Boston-based folks, give a yell if you would like to meet up or have clients you would like me to meet with while I'm in town. ✉ Tripp Grosman will you be around? I know I owe you a beer for your work on that MIT deal.
>
> in **Celeste Martin**'s status updates · Share · Comment · Like (0) · Repost

In addition to letting colleagues know what you're up to, working out loud includes the following practices:

- ✔ **Asking questions:** When workers have a question, a common (and entrenched) time-consuming strategy is to start small, asking co-workers or people you know. Too often, those people don't have answers. With a robust social collaboration system in place, though, you can save time by posting your question as a status update in the company activity stream or by posting the question in a relevant group.

- ✔ **Giving feedback:** Similarly, when you have the insight or "the answer," you ought to share it proudly (often, not the case). If you see a question in the social collaboration network and know the answer, answer it. Be as helpful to everyone else and as constructive in your criticism as you possibly can be. Spend some time Liking and commenting on posts, participating in discussions, answering questions, and so on.

If all you do is push your own content and wait for it to be praised or post your questions and expect answers, you're not acting like a member of the community — and you won't be treated like one.

✔ **Pacing your involvement:** Naturally, you will need to budget your time so you aren't spending so much time on social collaboration that you neglect other duties. If you can carve out a few minutes every day, you will establish yourself as a regular presence in the community. You can always spend more time when you find a productive reason to do so.

✔ **Sharing generously:** A big part of the work out loud concept is integrating social collaboration into daily work, creating more documents as shared documents rather than isolated desktop documents and more communications as social posts rather than e-mail. (I tell you more about document sharing in Chapter 7.) If you can make participation routine, then participation in the collaboration network ought to feel less like extra work. Do it more consistently, and you ought to start seeing your work stretch farther.

As you build your network and your reputation, you gain the ability to help others spread their message or get their questions answered. Use that power generously. If you don't know the answer to a question, but you know someone who would, make sure he sees it. (I tell you how to use tagging and @mentions in Chapter 4.)

The internal social network can also be a good place to share links to content from the external world. If you read a good article on management or marketing strategy or developments in your industry, post the link with a few comments about what it means for your organization. Not every thought you share on the collaboration network has to be original. Your colleagues will appreciate you if you bring them relevant news and analysis that they may have missed otherwise.

✔ **Recognizing others:** Internal social networks are routinely used to announce promotions or congratulate a sales team on a strong quarter, but social recognition doesn't have to stop there. Anyone can thank anyone else for doing a good job. Thank your peers, your subordinates, and your superiors (without being a toady) whenever they do a little something extra to solve a problem or help you complete a project. When you get credit, spread the credit around.

Some companies have instituted peer recognition systems featuring badges employees can award to each other. That's great, but a simple message works, too. Don't be a phony about it, but when you feel grateful, let it show.

Everybody likes a pat on the back, and the cycle of mutual affirmation makes the online workplace a friendlier place.

More on working out loud

The notion of "working out loud" was popularized by Bryce Williams of Eli Lilly & Co. and John Stepper of Deutsche Bank, and you can read more about it on their respective blogs:

✔ http://thebryceswrite.wordpress.com/tag/work_out_loud

✔ http://johnstepper.com/tag/working-out-loud

Their idea is to celebrate the value of regularly sharing notes about your work, including progress, setbacks, observations, and plans. Why? Because you never know when someone in your network may be able to answer your question, solve your problem, or help you seize an opportunity. You never know, and you never *will* know what they can do for you, if you don't let them know what you are working on.

Standard disclaimer: The blogs I cited are personal blogs, not necessarily a reflection of their employers' views. However, both men have been charged with promoting the productive use of social collaboration within their firms.

Understanding when to ditch e-mail

If you can provide easy-to-access information to everyone in your organization who may need it, you're doing everyone a favor. Many people say they can't possibly use social communication for the majority of their work because e-mail habits are too deeply rooted in their organizations. But when you're answering a question from a colleague, think twice about whether the person asking the question is the only one who would be interested in the answer.

If you find yourself writing a detailed e-mail reply packed with lots of information, chances are that you're creating organizational knowledge that will wind up stranded in one person's inbox — but shouldn't.

Solution: Put your reply in a blog post, wiki document, or post to a discussion group on the collaboration network. E-mail back a link to that resource, inviting your colleague to add his thoughts in a space where others can also comment and build on your ideas.

Bryce Williams, the Eli Lilly community strategist and "working out loud" believer, gives the example of getting an e-mail request for examples of his firm's collaborative platform in sales and marketing. He hesitated at first to reply with a link to a post on the internal network, but he did it anyway. Within hours, a colleague in Europe edited the page to add other examples he had missed. Within a few months, it grew from a list of 9 resources to a list of

30. When a similar question came up as part of a conference call with another group of employees, he was able to refer them to that document, getting more mileage out of his previous work.

> *"Don't think that every example has to go viral with thousands of hits to be a successful outcome of working out loud,"* he writes. *"As soon as that wiki page went from one view to two views I had increased the return I got and that my company got from that initial interaction...for what amounted to the same effort on my part."*

The only caveat he adds is to be careful not to shift conversations from e-mail to social collaboration where there is a risk of disclosing information your correspondent may deem sensitive. When in doubt, ask permission to share your answer more openly, rather than with an e-mail reply.

Of course, Williams is an IT professional who has staked part of his professional reputation on social business, so he has a selfish interest in making this strategy work. But this strategy can work equally well for someone in HR: say, answering a recurring question about benefits with a link to a shared document.

Think about your own work life and the questions you find yourself answering over and over. If you're in a situation like this and e-mailing back just a link feels too terse or rude, another strategy is to give a short version of the answer in the body of the e-mail, followed by a link to a document providing more details.

I have to say persuading others to change their habits is at least half the battle. I recently started what I hoped would be a productive online discussion on our collaboration network but was foiled when one of the other participants copied and pasted the message into a multirecipient e-mail. Thereafter, the conversation continued half on our social collaboration platform and half in e-mail, with different participants tuned in to each fork. Worst of both worlds!

Practicing Proper Etiquette

Who you connect with and how you interact with them will be governed by organizational culture and rules of etiquette, often unwritten. As an individual, you need to understand what's "normal" and acceptable within your organization.

In this section, I remind you how to mind your manners and also give you some tips for navigating tricky situations.

Keeping Discussion Productive and Professional

By all means, share good news and congratulatory notes on the collaboration network. What about the not-so-good news? An endless stream of happy talk seems fake after a while, particularly when everyone knows the organization faces serious challenges.

The collaboration network can be a place to share your thoughts about what's not working right, particularly if you can do it with some tact. There are many times in business when raising a concern privately is best, particularly if there is a personal dimension to the discussion like the need to identify an individual who isn't doing a good job. Raising an issue broadly makes more sense when the issue is one of collective responsibility, like a communications breakdown between departments that needs to be rectified, or when the best person to address the issue has yet to be determined.

If processes are breaking down or customers aren't getting the service they deserve, raising those issues can be a way to show you care about making the business better. You may even say that it's your duty.

Still, before you speak up, take the temperature of your organization — how open is it to self-criticism?

- ✔ **Present yourself as a problem solver.** Assuming you decide to be brave, you certainly want to be polite and professional. When you share a message publicly, you must make it clear that you are seeking solutions, not just griping.

  "Transparency" is a popular word among social business advocates, but executives sometimes worry that introducing social collaboration means opening up a can of worms by giving employees a forum in which to complain and vent. You don't want to be the person who brings all their worst fears to life. On the other hand, if the organization is at all serious about using social collaboration to solve problems, it has to be willing to acknowledge that problems exist within the organization. I discuss the importance of executives understanding the implications of transparency in Chapter 15.

- ✔ **Find a connection to company goals.** If possible, tie your issue to concerns that have been raised publicly by the leaders of your organization, showing how *your* concern links to achieving *their* goals.

- ✔ **Be respectful.** Never blame, insult, or demean any other individual. This has nothing to do with whether people should be held accountable if they have indeed caused problems; a social network isn't the right place to sort out those issues.

✔ **Invite colleagues to communicate.** On the other hand, the network can be the perfect place to sort out teamwork and communications problems. Most business processes succeed or fail based on the quality of the teamwork, not the good or bad qualities of a single player. For instance, if a customer who works with two divisions of your business is unhappy because of poor coordination between them, networking the right people together to address the sources of friction and save that customer from defecting would be a huge win.

Don't just complain. Raise the problems you believe must be solved and then help solve them.

Building Your Professional Brand

In Chapter 5, I cover some of the routine activities associated with making and nurturing connections. I also draw a comparison with LinkedIn, which is best known as the social platform for building connections to help land your next job. Participation on a corporate collaboration network is a way of building your professional brand within your current employment.

How do you make yourself stand out on a collaboration network?

Many of the things that apply on a public social network factor in:

✔ You contribute regular, interesting posts.

✔ Others Like and share your content.

✔ You like and share content from other people.

✔ Your photo and profile project a positive image.

✔ You build a strong network of connections and followers.

One of the people who stands out on my employer's Jive-based collaboration network, The Hub, is Steven Carlisle, an assistant marketing manager who has earned an outsize online reputation through his work habits. Because The Hub's managers have been experimenting with *gamification techniques* (using game-like virtual rewards to engage users), his reputation actually has a score attached to it. On the ranking of internal social network users, our professional community managers are at the top of the list (as well they should be). As of mid-2013, CEO David Levin is #7, and Carlisle is #10. In other words, he is a lot closer to the top of the organization online than offline — and that visibility should help him get ahead overall.

Confession: By that same ranking, I'm #388, with 5,800 points, compared with 35,900 for Carlisle. He racks up points every time he logs in and posts his status, but it counts for more every time someone else Likes or shares his content.

One reason for his high score is that whenever he initiates a project, he creates a project group and uses it to assign tasks that will build toward getting something accomplished.

A recipe for social collaboration success

My colleague Steven Carlisle offers some insight into what makes his social collaboration efforts so successful. Here are some excerpts from an internal blog post he prepared on his winning ways (reprinted by permission):

I do not see myself having a routine for using The Hub. Instead, I sort of incorporate it into my daily schedule. I also do different tasks depending on the day. So instead of a daily Hub routine, I am going to tell you how I use The Hub in general.

There are some activities that I do (well, try to do) daily to keep in touch with things happening around UBM. These are basically what most people do each day. They are

- ✔ Log in.
- ✔ Check my Inbox.
- ✔ Check the Connections Stream.
- ✔ Check other custom Activity Streams. For example, I have an Email Marketing Stream that has the group Email Marketing and UBM Canon Email and Web Analytics in the stream.
- ✔ Post any Status Update.

Other than the basics listed above, there are a lot of ways to use The Hub; you can be an active user and participate, or you can be a lurker. I like to participate in The Hub as I feel it helps me do my job better and hopefully helps me learn more about different topics. Some of the additional uses of the Hub include: adding documents, commenting, blogging, etc. at different times during the day and week. Here are some examples:

1. When I attend a webinar, I write a blog about the takeaways so I can share what I learned with my colleagues.
2. When researching a topic on the web, I use the Jive Anywhere browser add-in to post the page on The Hub.
3. I direct message people through The Hub instead of e-mail depending on the topic. Similarly, I share things I find on The Hub with the Share feature.
4. I post current projects on The Hub to share with the organization as a history: for example, The Scoop [an internal newsletter].
5. I read different blogs related to tags I like to watch: for example, Email_Marketing.
6. I tag documents, blogs, etc. (as allowed) when I think the item should be tagged a certain way. Tagging helps people find your content through search.
7. I participate in polls as needed.
8. I rate, like, and comment on blogs, documents, etc.
9. I join *and* participate in groups.

As you can see, there are many ways to participate in The Hub. As one big diverse company, The Hub helps bring us closer together.

Part VI
The Part of Tens

Enjoy an additional social collaboration Part of Tens chapter, "Ten Cloud Collaboration Services You Can Try for Free," online at www.dummies.com/extras/social collaboration.

In this part . . .

- ✔ Learn social collaboration success factors to emulate.
- ✔ Get a heads up on pitfalls to avoid.
- ✔ Figure out how to achieve a payoff that will impress the boss.

Chapter 20

Ten Common Themes in Social Collaboration Success Stories

. . . .

*W*hen social collaboration is successful, it makes the organization adopting it more successful. The payoffs come in the form of innovation, efficiency, camaraderie, and engagement.

What distinguishes the successes from the flops? I try to answer that in this chapter, based on common themes in social business success stories I've encountered during the research for this book, as well as my work for *InformationWeek* and the Social Business Leaders program at the E2 conference.

Not every success story exhibits every one of these characteristics, but most could cite several of them.

Executive Sponsorship Makes a Difference

I discuss the CEO's perspective in Chapter 15. Not every initiative is fortunate enough to have a CEO who starts blogging and commenting and promoting the social collaboration network as soon as it goes live, as UBM's David Levin did. He seized on the introduction of the platform as a way to encourage better communication and more cohesion within a diverse, multinational company.

More often, the most passionate social collaboration advocates are several levels removed from the top of the company, whipping together a pilot project on a shoestring and trying to demonstrate enough value that senior executives will pay attention.

Seek executive sponsorship at whatever level you can find it. Inspiring a department head to participate on the network and encouraging his people to participate will give you the opportunity to show what social collaboration can do on that level, which can in turn be an argument for broader use and a more official endorsement from leadership.

Some executives, particularly older ones, may give their consent without becoming active participants on the network themselves. Thank them for giving the okay, but keep working to recruit them as at least occasional participants. At a minimum, educate them on how a collaboration network works and what to expect from it.

Executive *tolerance* is just as important as participation. If you tell people the goal is an open and transparent organization and then have company leaders punish those who speak their mind, the online conversation will come to a halt. That doesn't mean the organization and its leaders ought to tolerate extreme disrespect or rudeness or clear violations of the acceptable use policy for the collaboration network. If the online behavior is extreme enough, the community will expect it to be dealt with appropriately. But if a statement could possibly be considered constructive criticism, it probably should be.

Community managers may have to manage up the organization, coaching executives on what to expect and the most productive ways to respond to criticism.

Familiarity Is Just a Starting Point

Successful organizations don't assume that employees will figure out how to use the collaboration network productively, just because it looks something like Facebook. Consumerization is your friend, but it gets users only so far. Make sure to provide the necessary guidance, training, and encouragement so that employees are successful in using your social collaboration tools productively.

Because it exists to help organizations get work done, social collaboration is as different from a consumer social network as it is similar. That means documentation, training, and coaching are required. The good news is that after users pick up the basics, the platform itself can become the vehicle for sharing ideas about how to use it better.

One way to deliver rewards along the way is to use *gamification,* a user interaction strategy that applies some of the techniques that motivate game players. Techniques adapted from games can be used to motivate and reinforce other sorts of behaviors, such as the effective use of specific software. A simple way to do that is to award stars or rankings based on a user's level of participation. New users on the network can even be assigned "missions" related to fleshing out their profile or posting their first status.

I discuss gamification product selection criteria in Chapter 8 and the use of gamification in Chapter 12.

Don't Hamstring Use

At the same time when companies must win over employees who resist social networking, they also need to tap in to the knowledge and energy of those who have been using Facebook and Twitter for years. If they find that their supposedly forward-thinking organization has turned social networking into a bureaucratic chore, they will not be impressed. Don't focus so much on preventing misuse of the social collaboration network that you prevent productive use.

Restaurant chain Red Robin made a conscious decision to implement its Yammer collaboration network without a lot of rules around how to use it, other than basic acceptable use policies. Restaurant workers adapted pretty readily to social media interaction because Yammer looked and functioned a lot like Facebook, says CIO Chris Laping. Social collaboration "gets out of the hierarchy and works the network," Laping says. "To me, it's the essence of fast companies and next-generation companies."

When Red Robin introduced its Tavern Burger product line, store manager feedback on Yammer proved to be an important part of refining the product and its delivery. Customers "talked to the servers, the servers talked to the managers and the managers got on Yammer," Laping says.

Using those store manager discussions on the enterprise social network (internally branded as Yummer), Red Robin was able to refine the recipes and the operational processes in the restaurants in about four weeks — a process Laping estimates would have taken 6 to 18 months in the past. Without it, operations leaders would have been "scratching their heads" wondering why the product wasn't performing as expected, he says.

Build on What Works

Social collaboration advocates should pay attention to what works, and then do more of that.

For instance, when social collaboration starts at a grassroots level, give strong consideration to building on its technology of choice, even if it would not have been the first choice of enterprise IT. In some cases, that won't be possible because the rogue product is truly awful, missing critical enterprise features. In that case, shut it down, but try to give the people involved a soft landing on your new, official platform.

Build on successful teams and processes as much as technology.

TD Bank started with a simple experiment, using simple tools: not a full collaboration system, but software that let employees comment on newsletter articles posted to the company intranet. The response showed people would take the time to share their ideas about improving the business. For example, an article asking about bank workers' biggest frustrations prompted one teller to suggest that a paper-based enrollment process could be handled much more efficiently online. Hundreds of other employees quickly voiced agreement and added ideas about how it should be done.

"The idea had come up before, but until social [networking] amplified it, it was not a priority," says Wendy Arnott, TD Bank's VP of social media and digital communications. That small success led to bigger plans for social collaboration, based on the IBM Connections platform.

"Once you get to having communities of thousands of people, it becomes a self-fulfilling prophesy — people want to join so they can see what is going on," says Mark Torr, the administrator of a technology practice interest group on The Hub, an internal social network at SAS Institute that is based on Socialcast. That group currently has more than 2,000 members who participate in discussions on technology marketing.

Torr said it's true that although an enterprise social network adds yet another channel for business communication on top of e-mail, at the same time it potentially cuts down on some e-mail. "It's just like when they invented e-mail, the phone didn't stop ringing," he said. "On the other hand, on social networks people don't tend to write quite as verbosely, so you get to the point a lot quicker."

Get Off to a Good Start

There are many ways to get started with social collaboration:

- ✔ Embrace a grassroots effort and start to expand it, now with the organization's blessing.

✔ Launch a pilot project for one particular department or function, making the collaboration platform available to only those employees.

✔ Launch the collaboration network to everyone at once, making a big splash, company-wide.

✔ Launch the collaboration network to everyone at once, but target a particular department or function for training and support. If adoption spreads to other groups, that begin using it on their own initiative, terrific.

Any one of these can be successful, but the targeted approaches tend to work better. Pick a department or a function that you think has a good chance of success with social collaboration and try to generate some proof points that will convince others to come onboard.

Show Relevance

Gloria Burke, director of knowledge and collaboration strategy and governance at Unisys, wishes she had started earlier to tailor training to different types of jobs. Focused training works, as does encouraging employees to share lessons about how social tools work or don't in a particular job.

"Nothing drives the adoption of something new more than a colleague telling you it works for them," Burke says.

Unisys's social business initiative has succeeded partly because of a top-down push from executives who recognize its importance, Burke says, and because of the groundwork laid by prior knowledge management initiatives over the past decade. The IT services company uses NewsGator's Social Sites for SharePoint as its company-wide enterprise social networking platform. Sales and marketing teams use Salesforce Chatter collaboration software, but they also have access to NewsGator when they need to reach the broader organization.

What's most important is helping people in sales roles achieve the goal of "market agility," says Burke. One example is using a mobile device to post a customer's question to colleagues during a client meeting. Using a search of employee social profiles can find an expert in order to "get the answer before they even leave the office," says Burke. "That's impressive to the client." In a case like that, the tool of choice would be NewsGator because it reaches more people, across different areas of expertise.

Conquering Time and Space

These days, very few organizations operate by having everyone in the same place at the same time. They rely on home office workers, road warriors, branch offices, overseas offices, contractors, and outsourcing firms for different fractions of their labor.

There are all sorts of synchronous tools we use to collaborate long-distance: Phones, mobile phones, web conferencing, and video conferencing all play a part. Social collaboration is a good asynchronous counterpart, able to work across time zones or generally deliver a message later to someone who is not available now. Compared with e-mail (otherwise, the default), social collaboration provides better context and a wider variety of modes of interaction.

Many social collaboration platforms also include synchronous communication tools such as chat or instant messaging, or the option of integrating with unified communications platforms for Internet video and phone calls.

The most successful users of social collaboration tend to have the need to support a geographically distributed organization, which provides the motivation for embracing the tools and learning to use them effectively. They succeed because they make mastering social collaboration a business priority.

Fight Fragmentation

Social collaboration is often most successful as a unifying force in organizations that are otherwise fragmented.

At SuperValu, that was one of the reasons Yammer was initially adopted on an ad hoc basis as a freemium product and later endorsed by the CEO and IT. Having grown through acquisitions, the grocery chain operated on hodgepodge of systems and management hierarchies that were separated by brands (such as Shaw's in the Northeast and Albertson's in the West). The enterprise social network proved to be a unifying force, bringing together store managers from across the country and across brands to discuss issues they had in common. For example, store managers across all brands who operate in college towns or seashore communities now collaborate on marketing programs to serve those audiences, something they never had a good way of doing before.

A social software project leader at an industrial firm tells a similar story about factory managers from different divisions and different parts of the world making connections they never would have otherwise and solving problems faster as a result. For example, when employees at one location began conferring online about the problems they were encountering with a new fabrication process, their Jive installation was smart enough to give them a "if you like this conversation, you'll probably also like this conversation over here" prompt. As a result, they connected with workers in a factory on the other side of the world who had encountered the same problem.

Maintaining Order

Social collaboration software is designed to help online communities be self-organizing as much as possible, allowing people to connect, share, form groups, and develop content on their own initiative. However, the most successful social collaboration strategists understand that communities don't truly manage themselves, not entirely.

As social collaboration networks mature, they can also accumulate obsolete documents, inactive collaboration groups, outdated answers to questions and other content that could do more harm than good if users stumble across it in a search. Effective community managers try to minimize the accumulation of such cruft in the first place and eliminate it in periodic house cleanings.

Even more importantly, they highlight the best and most useful content and the most active and helpful communities, making those as easy to find as possible.

Showcase Success

Social collaboration can be a powerful force for making people feel better about where they work and the work they do. Encourage the use of the network for peer recognition on an ongoing basis (all those *Great job!* and *Congratulations on winning the sale!* posts) as well as more official recognition for exceptional work.

Consider the use of social recognition apps such as Salesforce.com's Work.com, which encourage employees to award each other badges for desirable behaviors. In addition to serving as visual tokens of recognition, these symbols serve a classification function, allowing managers to go back and see how much peer recognition each person has earned as part of a performance review.

As a selfish interest, community managers and collaboration strategists will also want to showcase the role of the network in promoting success. However, for best results, emphasize the contributions of the *people* on the network rather than the software that drives it.

Chapter 21

Ten Obstacles to Social Collaboration Success

• •

1 like telling social collaboration success stories, and I tell a lot of them, partly because it's easier to get people to talk about their successes than their failures. The success stories really are out there, but the failures are, too. Fortunately, social collaboration failures don't tend to be big, embarrassing, expensive doom-the-company–style failures. Still, a social collaboration system that doesn't accomplish anything is a waste of time.

Some of the material that follows is adapted from a column I wrote for *Information Week*'s social business section. I've also benefitted from reading (and in some cases, editing) the columns on this topic by Dion Hinchcliffe, executive vice president of strategy at Dachis Group and co-author of *Social Business by Design*. The obstacles arise "not because social intranets aren't useful, but coordinating (and sometimes fighting) the IT department, corporate communications, HR, and often competing vendor camps inside the company means that many firms aren't as far along as they should be," he says.

The notion of an Enterprise 2.0 revolution in business around social software goes back to at least 2006 and Andrew McAfee's definition of how Web 2.0 technologies would change business. I admit I tend to take the truth of this as self-evident. Here are ten reasons why it ain't necessarily so.

Overcoming a Commanding-and-Controlling Culture

Who says every organization wants to be transparent and flexible and invite participation from every quarter? What if the CEO sees corporate social media as giving employees the tools they can use to plot against him? Why foster the illusion of democratic organization if that's not the way you want to run the company?

I'm painting an extreme picture, but it doesn't take a Dilbert-style Pointy-Haired Boss. Lots of moderately conservative organizations will think twice — and maybe rightly so — about whether an internal social network makes sense for their corporate culture.

In an organization like this, you might try working with the most forward-thinking divisional leader you can find on a pilot project, which ideally will produce results showing the value of opening up the lines of communication and the possibilities for collaboration.

Ultimately, if senior leaders can't be persuaded to loosen the corporate necktie one notch, your organization may not be ready for social collaboration.

Fending Off Negative Connotations

The phrase "Facebook inside our company" works magic in some quarters. When SAS Institute implemented Socialcast, that was exactly the phrase the corporate communication folks promoting the project used. They heard *Facebook* and thought, *This collaboration system will spread virally through our company — and isn't that wonderful?*

Facebook has other connotations, however. If management hears *Facebook* but thinks *frivolous, time-wasting medium people will use to share jokes and baby photos,* then appealing to a comparison with Facebook or even using the world "social" will only make it more difficult to sell the concept internally.

You might instead try making a comparison to LinkedIn given that social network is all business. Better yet, transition as quickly as possible to showing social collaboration in the context of work. You will probably find yourself falling back on occasional comparisons to how a particular feature like tagging or sharing works on Facebook or Twitter, but make sure you explain how it is used productively for business.

If you think alternate terminology will help, try "networked business" as an alternative to social business, emphasizing the importance of networks between people as well as digital networks. Some consultants talk about "emergent collaboration," where "emergent" means the collaboration emerges naturally from a network of people who share a common goal rather than being imposed by a top-down structure. Instead of saying that you're trying to make the organization more social, you can talk about making it more agile and adaptable — which are indeed goals of social collaboration.

You probably will not be able to edit "social" out of your vocabulary all together, but you can try to put the focus on the power of the network to bind an organization together and make it more effective.

Avoiding Fragmentation

The explosion of social software tools is a source of great innovation, but creates a lot of confusion. Organizations can easily wind up with several enterprise social networks used by different teams or departments, or for different purposes, along with social applications for purposes (such as project management or employee recognition), each coming with their own user profiles and activity streams and notions of how connections are formed.

A *fragmented* social environment — that is, one that promises a global view of people and activity, but in fact doesn't — might be worse than none at all.

Employees and teams may have legitimate reasons for wanting to use a variety of tools for different purposes, but you should try to help them choose wisely and seek opportunities for integration.

Lacking Resources for Integration

In enterprise IT, integration is the universal goal that is never quite perfectly achieved. For every application, there is a threshold of "good enough" integration to make the system usable. One of the hurdles that successful enterprise social networks must clear is having enough integration with relevant systems (such as corporate directories and content management systems) that they deliver on their promise as next-generation, people-centric portals.

The vendors can deliver all the application programming interfaces imaginable, but achieving the necessary integrations still requires IT time and effort. If an enterprise social network launches with significant integration gaps, employees come away unimpressed. For example, if the social collaboration network's search function fails to present search results from other content repositories — and that is where most of the important corporate documents actually reside — it will be much less useful than if it boasted an integrated search capability.

Generating Buzz

Nothing succeeds like success. Users will find a collaboration network compelling if their friends and co-workers are active on it, contributing content and answering each other's questions. More often, early users of the collaboration network find it a ghost town: no citizens and no content.

Community managers refer to a low-traffic community as the *empty bar* problem. No one wants to hang out where there's nothing going on. Somehow, you have to get the party started.

And this is one reason why it's often a bad idea to deploy an enterprise social network company-wide across a large organization, when adoption is unlikely to occur everywhere at the same rate. Instead, start with a smaller group of people — perhaps divided by geography but united around some corporate function or professional interest — and let them prove the value of social collaboration. After you have a good story to tell, it will be easy to get the party started elsewhere in the company.

Competing with Free Public Social Networks

Employees will inevitably compare their experience on an enterprise social network with the experience that they enjoy on consumer sites, such as Facebook. That can be a problem if the enterprise experience suffers by comparison by being awkward to navigate, frustrating to use, or missing important features.

Also, if there is too much bureaucracy and administrative overhead associated with the corporate social environment, some project teams might find it easier to collaborate through a Facebook group or a freemium product (such as Yammer or Teambox).

Is that a bad thing? It certainly can be if sensitive information is being shared through a tool that doesn't meet corporate security and compliance requirements. For example, a Facebook Group could be a fine solution for organizing a holiday party but not a merger.

In the case of a freemium solution (such as Yammer), the open-minded organization might at least consider the solution of "paving the cow paths" by officially sanctioning something that's already working and establishing corporate control over it. Now that Yammer is owned by Microsoft and will be offering increased integration with SharePoint, the cloud service is gaining credibility in the enterprise. However, most organizations would prefer to make a deliberate choice of a collaboration network rather than blessing the work of renegades.

Complying with Industry Regulations

Regulated industries (such as financial services and healthcare) must pay particular attention to whether an enterprise social network meets compliance requirements, such as data archiving for financial advisor communications and protection of patient information under the data security and privacy provisions of HIPAA (the Health Insurance Portability and Accountability Act). Moreover, they might tend to see more risk than benefit in a technology that makes it easy to share information widely when they have a responsibility to keep some categories of information under tight control.

These are not insurmountable obstacles, but they can slow things down. Regulatory strictures may dictate the choice of an on-premises solution over a cloud service, for example. Internal data governance groups may have to review and sign off on implementation plans and may limit the potential applications of a social collaboration network.

Attracting Participants

With few exceptions, such as the case of the French IT services firm Atos banning e-mail in favor of social collaboration, organizations that adopt internal social software promote its use but do not make it mandatory. Dictating a solution might be easier. At least, it might sound easier.

Voluntary adoption is probably the right approach, though. If social software really is so wonderful, employees ought to gravitate to it naturally, as something that makes their lives easier. If the adoption isn't happening, maybe it's the social network that needs to change to accommodate employee behavior rather than the other way around.

If you're having trouble attracting participants, retrace your steps and look for things you can change about how the software is being used and how online communities are forming. Identify advocates who are using social collaboration effectively and ask them to spread the word about its potential.

Think through anything you can do to remove procedural or technical road-blocks to participation and community formation.

Suffering Groupware, Knowledge Management Hangover

Haven't we heard all these promises before? The vision of enterprise social networking sure can sound a lot like the benefits that were supposed to be delivered by previous generations of enterprise collaboration, workflow, and knowledge-management products. Sure, sure, it's different this time.

For social software to be successful, it has to do a better job of living up to its own hype. As a social collaboration advocate, you need to be serious about setting high standards for the software or cloud services vendor of your choice, while setting equally high standards for your own organization to demonstrate how social collaboration can make a difference.

Falling Back on E-mail

E-mail habits have been established by decades of use in the workplace and will not be easily undone. In principle, any internal message that will go to more than a couple of participants — or even one that would be potentially useful to more than a single recipient — belongs on the social collaboration network, not in e-mail. Yet because e-mail is for many people the tool that is closest to hand, it is the one they are more likely to use. Defaulting to e-mail when the social collaboration network is the more useful tool may be like using a screwdriver to pound in a nail, but it's the way many people work.

In Chapter 19, I discuss the tactic of replying to an e-mail with a link to a blog post or wiki article, so that even a discussion that starts in an e-mail moves to the social collaboration network. There are also technological solutions you can experiment with, such as software for integrating e-mail and social modes of communication. For example, the Jive for Outlook plug-in allows you to convert an e-mail to a social discussion thread conversation starter posted to a Jive collaboration network.

There is no one magic solution, other than highlighting specific business collaboration scenarios — such as cooperative editing of a document with many authors or gathering of information from many sources — where the social collaboration network is clearly superior. If employees accumulate enough positive experiences with social collaboration, they may start to form new habits rather than being in thrall to e-mail forever.

Chapter 22

Ten Ways to Make Social Collaboration Pay Off

· ·

*E*very technology initiative is judged by its payoff. The gold standard is *return on investment* (ROI), which is solid proof of a financial return exceeding the money invested. Showing ROI for social collaboration can be challenging. For one thing, when social collaboration is one element of an organizational change process, should the technology be the factor that gets the credit for any positive financial results instead of the leadership or the people who executed the strategy?

I say give the people the credit but give the technology its due for helping produce a positive result. Have a story to tell about how social collaboration contributed, not only to ROI but by making your workplace a better place in which to work.

Starting with a Purpose

Social collaboration software has sometimes been a victim of its own marketing: the dynamic, intuitive technology that "will break down all internal divisions within a company and make everyone work together better." In those ill-fated cases, the contract is signed, the software is deployed, and nothing very dramatic happens. These examples may be classified as failures although whether they truly failed is hard to tell, given that they never had very specific goals in the first place.

The difference between those examples and the most impressive success stories tends to be focus — or the lack thereof. While writing this book, I had a chance to ask about what made the biggest difference in the success of social collaboration when I moderated a panel discussion at the E2 Conference featuring Matt Tucker, co-founder and CTO of Jive Software; Alistair Rennie, general manager of collaboration solutions at IBM; and Sameer Patel, general manager of social and collaborative software at SAP, a business management software company. Interestingly enough, they didn't deny some failures. Tucker even brought up a statistic from Gartner Inc. analysts that nearly 80 percent of social software implementations fail to reach their objectives (although he did say that he believes the odds are better for Jive customers). In one of his own presentations, Patel had cited a Forrester Research study saying that 77 percent of employees never log on to their enterprise social network, and only 3 percent use it once per day.

What makes the difference for the more successful users of social collaboration?

"It's a really simple formula — it's purposeful," Rennie said. "The disasters are always, 'We thought social would be fun, so we'll throw something out there and see what happens.'" Usually, the success stories start with a specific business process, or a handful of processes, that the business believes would benefit from better collaboration and a work-centered social network. That could be found in the health and safety function, mergers and acquisitions, or customer care. What the purpose is matters less than the fact that there is one, he said.

"It doesn't have to be big capital 'T' transformation," he said. And often it's not, but you should have a specific, measurable goal. When someone owns the business process that social collaboration is being applied to and has an interest in seeing it succeed, the tools get used a lot more seriously, and success is more likely. With success comes the opportunity to pursue the broader, company-wide benefits of social collaboration.

"When you say it like that, it sounds so obvious — you should have a purpose," Tucker agreed. Yet when a Jive implementation team asks a customer organization what problems it wants to solve with social collaboration, sometimes that sparks a great conversation — but other times, it prompts a blank stare, he said. When customers aren't certain at the outset, Jive consultants try to help them identify a "deep-use case" with measurable goals, knowing that makes success much more likely, he said. "It can't just be the intergalactic 'Let's all work together better' as the goal."

Patel differed only to say, "The business context, beyond purpose, is actually more important." His company, SAP, is best known for transactional business software, and its SAP Jam social software is intended as a complementary product. Patel said he would start with the point in a process where users might complain that their business software "limited me to 'submit' or 'cancel' when really what I wanted to do was discuss."

Whether you start with a business problem or by analyzing the gaps in processes managed by transactional software, start with a purpose, and you will be more likely to achieve it. This doesn't necessarily mean focusing on one thing only. The international consulting and systems integration company CSC, an early adopter of Jive for social collaboration, had about 200 use cases prior to launch. Each of those was an outline of a business scenario that CSC believed would be helped by better collaboration and information sharing. Claire Flanagan, who led that project as CSC's director of knowledge management, social collaboration, and community strategy, said that broad focus worked because she had also lined up 100 advocates — people who worked directly with those business functions — who saw the potential of the technology and were willing to help make it work.

Flanagan now works at Jive, providing strategic advice to other firms implementing social collaboration.

Accelerating Sales

One good purpose to consider starting with is accelerating sales. Every company likes revenue. If you can figure out how to make the cash register ring, not only will you score points for your social collaboration strategy, but you will have accomplished something for the company.

But wait. How is an internal use of social technology going to drive sales? Isn't that more the role of social media marketing or social CRM?

Social collaboration brings a different but significant value to the sales process. Maybe you will use other technologies and services to increase awareness and generate leads through social media marketing, or you mine LinkedIn for sales prospects. Those are all legitimate parts of a social business strategy and can complement what you do internally.

Internal social collaboration proves most valuable to complex business-to-business sales processes, where your goal is to provide a better total solution than your competitors.

Many businesses that sell consulting services, financial services, or sophisticated technical products report cutting the time required to produce a proposal, while increasing their deal-win rate. In a business where every proposal is different and must be tailored to the customer's needs, you can get a real advantage from the ability to leverage relevant experts within the company and find people who have contacts within or specific knowledge of the target customer.

In that scenario, collaboration within the sales team is important but so are collaboration and discovery of experts and resources throughout the organization. The cast of characters is different each time because every customer presents a unique set of requirements. Social collaboration provides a better way of assembling a team while eliminating inefficiencies, such as missed e-mail messages and chaotic Reply to All message threads.

For example, CSC estimated that it shaved 20 percent to 30 percent off the time required to produce a proposal with social collaboration. KPMG, the global network of accounting and financial consulting partnerships, has a similar story of introducing social collaboration based on Tibco's tibbr and seeing it translate into revenue. Early in the adoption by KPMG's Australian member firm, the social software got credit for bringing together a lot of the right expertise quickly to win a large consulting arrangement. That got management's attention and eventually led to a commitment to deploy the cloud service version of tibbr internationally, giving KPMG partners access to expertise from around the world.

"Bringing people together in such a large machine is not easy," says Vishal Agnihotri, global leader for the project in KPMG's knowledge management organization. Yet winning the business of a multinational corporation with many and varied needs is not a job for one person or even one team, she says. "It's very rare that one service line can answer all the questions a client has."

You don't have to be running a global consulting firm to see the benefits, but the scenario I'm sketching would not be as applicable to selling a simple product defined purely by price and features. There, the role of collaboration might be more limited to defining sales strategy and sharing tips for how to convince customers your product is the better value even though it might be 2 percent more expensive than the competition. Or maybe what makes the difference is the social network of the salesperson who knows who to call internally to secure the best discount for a customer.

See Chapter 18 for more ideas about putting sales at the center of your social collaboration strategy.

Aligning Marketing and Sales

Marketing and sales are two interdependent business functions that never seem to be aligned quite as well as they could be. In addition to general brand-building activities, marketing generates leads for the sales team. The sales team converts the leads into closed deals. At least, that's how the process is supposed to work — but doesn't always.

Instead, marketing and sales sometimes wind up squabbling over whose fault it is when sales goals fall short. Sales complains that marketing didn't deliver enough leads or delivered the wrong sort of leads, while marketing complains about lack of follow-through on the leads it successfully generated. None of that bickering has a place in a social business, where a great many of the leads ought to be coming in through digital channels that are supremely measurable and trackable. Still, the metrics and the reams of click-stream data are valuable only when there is agreement on strategy and goals.

Getting these two functions in better alignment is another path to topline revenue growth and a clear payoff.

No technology will magically break down cultural and organizational barriers. However, one step toward better coordination could be making the members of each group more aware of each other's activities even though they may sit in different departments and get together only occasionally in person. The social collaboration mechanism of following people and groups is a way for salespeople to keep tabs on — and give earlier feedback on — marketing initiatives, helping tune them to target the right audience. Marketing teams developing new campaigns can get more insight into the successes and frustrations of their sales team counterparts, leading to better targeting of future campaigns. Sure, some of this information gathering and market analysis still needs to come from more formal processes, along with system-generated charts and graphs about sales processes. What social collaboration adds is the human dimension: the connection with the person behind the numbers who can say what he really means.

Backing Up Customer Service

Many customer service and support organizations are fielding their own social communities in which they interact directly with customers. This may be part of a broader social CRM strategy that also includes sales and marketing functions. The broad goal is to produce happier customers — and more of them.

Achieving these external goals also requires internal collaboration. When the call center or contact center gets a question it can't answer, a collaboration network can be the key to locating the answer, whether it exists in a document or only in the head of a subject matter expert. Contact center agents can then log that information in a knowledge base so that it's available to the next agent who gets that question. As the information is refined into an authoritative answer, it can also be published into a self-service knowledge base that customers can access directly.

Social collaboration can also be useful within the service and support team for exchanging tips on how to answer thorny questions or handle difficult situations, as well as pursuing operational efficiency. The bigger benefits require more pervasive use of social collaboration, across departments and functions, meaning that subject matter experts take the time to fill out their profiles and share meaningful information about their work, making their expertise searchable and discoverable.

Creating New Products

Another way of boosting revenue is to create new — preferably new hit — products.

In a social business, innovation is everyone's business, and product creation is part of that. See Chapter 8 for tips on organizing brainstorming on a company-wide scale and prioritizing the most promising ideas. Meanwhile, the people whose jobs are specifically tied to developing products and product ideas also have an intense need to collaborate with each other and with other parts of the organization.

The research and development organization at 3M embraced social collaboration partly to compensate for the globalization of its team. Once centralized in Minnesota's Twin Cities, Research and Development (R&D) now has members around the world partly because management believes that will aid in developing products for a global market. (Two-thirds of its revenues come from outside the United States.) Where once 3M personnel relied on informal networks and the maxim that "you're five phone calls away from finding an expert" on any technical topic, now 3M sees the need for a continually updated digital directory of those experts.

Successful new products are never the work of one person. A hit consumer electronics product may start with one person's inspired design, but to get it built, that person had to convince others of his brilliance. That team then needed to coordinate with manufacturing, supply chain, sales, and top management to bring the product to market at the right time, at the right price.

If social collaboration makes that process work better and faster, the payoff will be clear.

Boosting Productivity

One reason why social business strategists emphasize focusing on specific business processes is to identify specific goals that can be tracked with specific metrics. The more generalized promise of social collaboration to boost productivity across the organization is harder to pin down, but that doesn't mean it's not real.

McKinsey Global Institute, a research arm of the global consulting firm McKinsey & Company, estimates that social technologies could add $900 million to $1.3 trillion in annual value to the world's economy. That's a very big-picture number for social technologies, broadly considered, including the value realized every time a consumer saves a few dollars after redeeming a coupon obtained through Facebook. However, McKinsey projected that two-thirds of that value will come from better communication and collaboration within businesses, as opposed to the sales and marketing aspects of social media.

Within every business, there are "interaction workers" whose jobs consist of finding, creating, and communicating knowledge. McKinsey says they currently spend about 28 percent of their day on e-mail, 19 percent searching for and gathering information, and another 14 percent communicating and collaborating internally. Social collaboration can shave time off all those tasks, leading to a total productivity improvement of 20 percent to 25 percent, according to McKinsey.

Your challenge is to translate that potential into more specific results for your firm. Social collaboration has the potential to save time — but only if it's used consistently. If 90 percent of the members of a team cling to using e-mail, even for collaborative work where the social tools clearly would be better, the payoff won't materialize. If sales embraces social collaboration but marketing doesn't, then coordination between the two will not happen.

Increases in productivity have to be earned.

Stopping Time-Wasting Activities

Because productivity is all about saving time, achieving it means not only starting more efficient habits but also stopping less productive ones.

Andrew Carusone of Lowe's Home Improvement argues that having an "unadoption strategy" is just as important as having an adoption strategy for social collaboration. "The goal of social business is performance, not adoption," says Carusone, the director of Lowe's integrated workforce experience and community governance initiative.

If the goal is to make employees more efficient and effective, you ought to be looking at what work they can stop doing. If the actual result is that you're making employees spend twice as much time on communication and coordination, now that they have twice as many ways to do it, what have you accomplished? For example, if you introduce social collaboration as an alternative to traditional e-mail mailing lists, but you leave the mailing lists in place, teams may wind up wasting more time navigating back and forth between the two modes of communication. The same is true of document sharing, project planning, and many other activities.

First, you must prove that the social collaboration environment you're providing really is more productive. Sometimes it may not be. I know of software development teams that held on to their mailing lists because their e-mail software did a better job of preserving the formatting of code snippets, which the social tools provided for their use tended to garble. In a case like that, it's far better to make a compromise than to force the use of a tool that will get in the way of people getting their jobs done.

On the other hand, where the old way of working clearly is not as productive, push hard to put a stop to it.

Improving Employee Engagement

Business research routinely shows that only 25 percent to 30 percent of employees in the average company are actively engaged in their work — meaning that they care about the organization and their contribution to its success and believe they can make a difference. The rest are either going through the motions or actively disengaged: that is, they've lost all faith in the organization and would gladly leave at the first opportunity.

The Gallup organization routinely provides updates on engagement statistics and their significance:

```
http://www.gallup.com/strategicconsulting/en-us/
          employeeengagement.aspx
```

One recent Gallup report, "Engagement at Work: Its Effect on Performance Continues in Tough Economic Times," showed that organizations with high engagement were 22 percent more profitable, 21 percent more productive, and scored 10 percent better on metrics of customer satisfaction. They also reported 41 percent fewer quality defects and 37 percent less absenteeism.

On the other hand, pervasive disengagement can lead to high turnover, which is wasteful given the cost of hiring replacements. On average, surveys estimate the cost of hiring and training a replacement worker at about one-fifth the cost of salary. The Gallup study showed organizations with engaged workforces had 25 percent lower turnover, even in businesses with traditionally high turnover. In businesses where turnover is normally low, it went even lower — by 65 percent — in organizations with high employee engagement.

Improved engagement is one of the important "soft" benefits of social collaboration because it helps employees see how what they do fits into the greater whole of the organization. Even informal "water cooler" discussion on the social network about sports and kids can build stronger networks, making employees feel more connected with their co-workers, which is why some (albeit not all) employee social networks welcome a certain amount of non–work-related chitchat. The work-related content is even more important because it adds to the total knowledge base of the company, but it also pays off for individuals. Given the opportunity to share details about their work and monitor the activity of others, they build awareness of their successes and frustrations while gaining awareness of what others are thinking and doing, including others outside their immediate circle.

Achieving improved employee engagement is also one of the areas where executive leadership on social collaboration is most significant. When the CEO and other company leaders share posts on strategy, invite feedback, and prove that they actually welcome feedback, employees feel more connected to that strategy and perhaps even able to influence it.

Social collaboration can have a particularly big impact on the engagement of younger workers, who are often frustrated when the software they're given to use for work is less effective than what they use in their personal lives.

By no means does implementing social software guarantee improved employee engagement, but the software can be a tool for achieving that goal. The more important prerequisites include having the right leadership, which truly welcomes employee feedback and independent thinking. A collaborative culture encourages people to speak up, rather than shouting down new ideas and reinforcing rigid hierarchies. Where the former exists, employees know that their thoughts and opinions matter.

Breaking Down Silos

In business, silos are organizational units that are isolated from the rest of the organization. IT silos are information systems that exist in isolation. The most harmful silos are not departmental and functional divisions that exist for good reason, but rather boundaries that exist for other reasons, like a history of acquisitions that creates a loosely aligned bundle of organizations, each with their own hierarchies, databases, and business practices.

Information within silos is shared up and down the organization, perhaps, but not horizontally. People within different silos may be developing similar products or wrestling with similar problems but never know about each other's work. Salespeople separated by silos may be approaching the same customers but in an uncoordinated fashion. Organizational silos are often accompanied by fragmented technology, including different systems for managing customer, product, and personnel information.

Implementing a common social collaboration system that stretches across silos can be one way of breaking down those boundaries. For example, within the SuperValu grocery chain, brands brought in through acquisition didn't even have a common e-mail system, but all employees could be offered an account on the Yammer social collaboration network.

Because integrating major enterprise systems can take years, a collaboration network can be a means of unifying the organization in the meantime. By sharing key enterprise data and adding context around it, social collaboration could even prove more powerful than integrating transactional systems alone.

Acting Like a Social Business

The high-concept notion of social business is about more than just social collaboration. It's more than just social CRM or social media marketing. A social business puts all the pieces together in an intelligent manner to drive business results.

At a tactical level, this notion of coordinated response to all the possibilities of social media and social networks denies some common organizational realities. I know of a few executives, such as TD Bank's Wendy Arnott, who have responsibility over both internal and external social media and social technologies. In most cases, internal collaboration and external marketing, sales, and support through social media are handled by different teams. Often, those teams establish their own silos of social technology, with minimal cross-functional collaboration.

What's needed is leadership from the top that recognizes the importance of smooth handoffs from marketing to sales, to service and new product development. If a social media monitoring team picks up on a trend in social media discussions of your product that suggests a change in strategy or an opportunity to create a new product, you want to make it as easy as possible to share your insight with other employees who are in a position to do something about it.

The case for social business may or may not be a good argument for buying a whole stack of social technologies from one vendor. I often joke that technology players like IBM and Salesforce.com use "social business" as code for, "Buy all my products, and you'll be successful." On the other hand, I would argue for a coordinated approach to all the money you spend on social software and cloud services, thinking about both technical and business process integration as you go.

Outside of Silicon Valley, it's unlikely that many company leaders go into work in the morning thinking, "I want to be a social business." Instead, they want to run a better, more profitable business of whatever sort. The airline CEO doesn't want to be social per se, unless social connections will help book more tickets, keep more flights on time, and lower operating costs in a cut-throat business. The manufacturing CEO doesn't want to be social, unless doing so will head off problems on the shop floor, produce new efficiencies, and lead to new products. The point is corporate performance and not just "social for social's sake." Yet, acting like a social business could help them achieve the performance they seek.

Appendix

Case Studies: Learn from Others

• •

Success in social collaboration is often earned by having a good story to tell, which encourages adoption and gives more employees an opportunity to create their own success stories. In other words, "anecdotal evidence" can still be powerful if it is convincing and success stories tend to snowball. While you're waiting for your own success stories to materialize, take advantage of the ones in this appendix to see what others have done that you might be able to apply to your own organization.

Most of these stories are adapted from my work for *InformationWeek* and from the companies I talked with while judging the E2 Social Business Leaders recognition program (which recognized Red Robin Gourmet Burgers as #1 in 2012 and State Street Corp. as top leader for 2013).

SAS Institute: Connecting Experts Worldwide

By the time SAS Institute fielded its internal social network, known as The Hub, SAS already had plenty of other internal collaboration tools in place, including SharePoint, as well as internal blogs and wikis. Yet Rick Wicklin, one of the firm's experts on statistical software development, says that SAS's introduction of a network based on Socialcast caught his attention in a way none of those other tools had.

"I guess the difference between The Hub and all those others is that I use The Hub, and I didn't really use the others," Wicklin says. The Hub did a better job of connecting him with the serendipitous moment of finding something he hadn't been looking for (but still found useful) from someone he never would have connected with otherwise. Internal social networks are often promoted as a tool for connecting ordinary employees with experts, but at SAS, it's also proved valuable as a way of connecting experts with each other. By putting himself forward as a group discussion leader, Wicklin found himself connecting with more people throughout the organization with similar research interests.

SAS, which makes advanced data analysis software, is one of the world's largest private software companies, with a strong reputation for good management. The company was #1 on Fortune's Best Places to Work list in 2010 and 2011 and consistently places near the top of the list (in 2013, it was #2 behind Google). That's why I point to it as an example of a company making intelligent use of social software in the workplace.

Wicklin's discovery of the unique value in the online social experience was exactly what SAS was hoping for when it selected Socialcast, which has a relatively narrow focus on the comment stream and social network profiles, as opposed to something like the Jive Software platform that includes blogging and other content management functions. SAS actually uses Jive to power its customer support communities, but for internal use, it included a lot of features SAS didn't want or need, explains Becky Graebe, the senior internal communications manager at SAS. The existing blogs and wikis were working fine, so rather than replacing them, SAS wanted to supplement them with the social layer proved by Socialcast.

Social collaboration at SAS began as an initiative of the internal communications group although IT provides support and manages the vendor relationship. Because it's relatively easy for web-based tools to link to content in each other's repositories, Graebe saw no need for all those tools to come from the same vendor. Nor has SAS seen any pressing need for deep integration with business applications or business workflow, she says. The Hub does play a supporting role in project management, and SAS is starting to experiment with the Socialcast Projects module.

Mostly, however, The Hub is offered as a tool for communication. SAS's determination to find the unique value of internal social networking also led to some unusual design decisions. Rather like Twitter, The Hub is biased toward current information rather than serving as a historical repository. Postings expire from the site if there is no new activity on them, such as a comment or a Like. This custom configuration of Socialcast is very different from the design of most other internal social networks, which often play a role in preserving information as an extension of knowledge management or content management for the enterprise.

Originally just 180 days, the expiration period has since been extended to two years. Any new activity, such as a reply to a discussion, restarts the clock. Still, an employee who wants to preserve some bit of insight or information uncovered in a discussion would be wise to copy it into a more permanent repository such as a wiki. Again, the goal of The Hub was to focus on things it could do better than those established tools. "We didn't want The Hub to become a graveyard of outdated information," Graebe says.

About 75 percent of the company's 13,600 employees are active on the internal social network — a statistic that's more impressive if you understand that the company employs its own landscapers and cafeteria workers who don't use a computer to do their jobs. In divisions like Research and Development, use of The Hub is nearly universal. First informally launched in early 2011, The Hub attracted 1,000 users within a month and 8,000 by the end of the first year, continuing to grow steadily since.

The network also hosts more than 1,100 professional interest groups. Their proliferation is a mixed blessing, given that Socialcast doesn't make it easy to sort or filter the list of groups. Still, collaboration groups have a lot of advantages over the e-mail mailing lists traditionally used for group discussions. Graebe says her team isn't necessarily campaigning for the elimination of e-mail groups but is trying to make the collaboration platform such a convenient alternative that there is no reason not to switch.

Nor does Graebe see social communication replacing regular old e-mail. When you know exactly whom you want to communicate with, "It's a much straighter shot to send them either an instant message or an e-mail," she says. "Where The Hub comes into play is when you don't know or are not certain who can address your need. Then, The Hub is the better place to go."

SAS hasn't put as much emphasis on community management as some other firms. The project manager for the initial launch of the software played a community management role during that phase, but the online community has been largely self-sustaining since. Graebe says that her team does some troubleshooting: for example, highlighting instances where two online discussion groups are duplicating each other's work and ought to move. As of mid-2013, Graebe was considering establishing a more formal community manager role, but probably just on a part-time basis — maybe two or three hours per day.

The big change for the internal communications team was taking a role in enabling communication between employees, rather than from the corporation to its people. Rather than "pushing things out to the masses, now it's our goal to connect employees with each other," Graebe says.

SAS already had a culture in which people would try to help each other, but the social network allows them to do so on a global scale.

"It provides a way to collaborate across divisions, across departments, and also across countries or time zones," Wicklin says. He particularly values it because the nature of his job in research and development means he works "with a small number of people in a fairly specialized area" and has limited opportunities to meet other people in the company, other than at events like lunchtime seminars or through the soccer league. "This is another venue to meet people and find out who knows what about what," he says, and has helped him identify others in the organization "who really know their stuff."

Wicklin has worked for the company for 15 years, but even people he has known for a long time often reveal expertise and interests through the online forums that he never suspected before.

In one instance, his involvement on The Hub led to a change in corporate policy — or, at least, the scrapping of a policy that was no longer being enforced. Looking at competitors' websites and social media pages, he had noticed that a range of their employees were involved in answering customer questions. He wondered whether SAS employees should be doing the same even though ever since he came to work at the company, he had been told that all such questions should be routed through SAS technical support rather than being addressed informally. When he broadcast that question, he got a response saying that the old policy was outdated, and he could safely ignore it. Because a member of the corporate communications team was monitoring that conversation, that informal ruling was transformed into an official announcement of a new policy empowering employees to engage more in answering those questions rather than leaving them all to tech support.

"I'd never gotten the official word that this was now okay, but as a result of the discussion on The Hub, that comment turned into a corporate decision, which was then advertised," Wicklin says.

In addition to providing a broad company social network for all employees, The Hub includes interest groups that help him connect with other employees who work in his specialty or related specialties. Trying to e-mail everyone who might know the answer to a question would be impractical and awkward, but in a social environment, employees decide which co-workers and what topics they want to follow. If a competitor is making a claim and Wicklin wants to reality-check it or find out how SAS products stack up in comparison, he can post a question like that to the group and get a knowledgeable answer.

Although Wicklin's focus is technical, SAS's Chris Tunstall uses The Hub to share quotes about leadership, links to web resources, and articles from publications like *Harvard Business Review*. As a member of the SAS leadership development organization, he moderates the Leaders Develop Daily, Not in a Day group, which has attracted hundreds of members.

"One of the things that really stands out on The Hub is that it's a one-stop shop you can go to," Tunstall says. "You're not jumping around to different SharePoint sites, but you can get a constant stream" of items of interest, customized on the basis of the people and groups you follow, he says.

Meanwhile, SAS still has 600 internal blogs, which are hosted independently of The Hub. That's fine as long as they continue to serve a purpose, Graebe says, but the volume of posts to them does seem to have fallen off somewhat. Social collaboration lends itself to "a quick thought, versus a formal blog post, which tends to be something more thought out and structured. Some bloggers have gone to more of this microblog feel, which is a little less formal," she says.

Wicklin says the internal blogs were a fine vehicle for "a select few" within the organization who committed to maintaining them, and wikis could be useful for finding specific information. But by encouraging broader participation, social collaboration does a better job of connecting him with all the people doing good work and thinking big thoughts.

TD Bank: Start Small, Think Big

TD Bank's interest in social collaboration began long before it chose an enterprise social networking software package. Headquartered in Canada, where it was founded as Toronto Dominion Bank, TD Bank also operates in the United States and is the sixth-largest bank in North America.

Today, its Connections internal collaboration platform, based on IBM Connections, provides social networking, blog, wiki, discussion, and other tools to more than 85,000 employees. However, social collaboration had far more modest beginnings. Originally, the team exploring the use of social technologies fielded a simple commenting system that allowed employees to give feedback on newsletter articles on an internal website.

Vice president of social media Wendy Arnott says the question was whether employees would take advantage of the opportunity and whether anything useful would result from it. Actually, yes. An online conversation started by a junior teller led to an idea that is now "expected to represent our biggest single productivity improvement" in 2013, Arnott says.

In response to an article asking about bank workers' biggest frustrations, the teller suggested that a paper-based enrollment process could be handled much more efficiently online. Hundreds of other employees quickly voiced their agreement and added their ideas about how it should be done.

"The idea had come up before, but until social [networking] amplified it, it was not a priority," Arnott says. After management saw how unanimous employee sentiment was in favor of the change, it became a priority. Actually getting the signup form online took a couple of years. Still, the fact that social collaboration led to this product idea was a powerful example, Arnott says. "It got us thinking, there must be hundreds of other things that we could be doing better and that we can fix. We started asking, how can we go big with this?"

TD Bank considered about 20 enterprise social networking products, fairly quickly narrowing the field to four leading contenders. Ultimately, IBM Connections was the only one that met every requirement on the bank's list, according to CIO Glenda Crisp.

The major technical challenge has been identity management, which is critical to a system built around employee profiles. Crisp wanted to deliver a single sign-on across Connections, content management systems, and other corporate applications, meaning that employees would be able to use the same login credentials across all of them rather than needing to remember separate passwords. The integration challenge has been further complicated by the acquisitions of U.S. banks with their own systems, she says.

Social collaboration has become part of a broader social business strategy for TD Bank, which also employs a social customer support team to answer questions submitted through Twitter and Facebook. Besides managing its own pages on those sites, TD Bank listens for mentions of its brand elsewhere on social media and responds, where appropriate.

In addition, the bank created a customer-facing community, TD Helps, which allows consumers to ask questions of TD Bank experts in disciplines including mortgages, credit, and small business banking. TD Helps runs on TemboSocial, the same discussion tool TD Bank used for its early internal social collaboration tests.

"We realized that social was going to be a game changer for the organization, especially after a number of large acquisitions with many employees spanning vast geographies," Arnott says. "We basically totally buy in to the idea of social business. Every part of the business will eventually use social" to do whatever it does better, she says.

One rationale for supporting an internal social network was to give employees practice handling business communications through social media, Arnott says. That way, if regulations eventually allow the broader population of employees to engage more freely in social media on behalf of the bank, they will be better prepared. Today, only a small number of people who work for Arnott or have been trained by her group are authorized to speak on behalf of the bank in public social media.

TD Bank is also large enough in terms of both employee base and geographic spread to need a social network to keep everyone engaged and to allow them to connect with the company's best experts in every discipline. In some of her presentations, Arnott uses the example of Adam, a small business credit specialist in a branch in Western Canada. TD Bank has specialists like this wherever it does business, and before the social network, those in remote offices were likely to feel they were on their own. But when a customer comes to Adam with a question he doesn't know how to answer, he knows he can post it on Connections and quickly get a response from experts at headquarters or elsewhere around the organization.

"He can get that answer, get that deal — but what it really means is he helped that customer," Arnott says. Significantly, he also got the answer in a shared community where others who have the same question can see it. "If the answer had been given in an e-mail or telephone exchange, all that knowledge would have been lost," she says.

DenMat: Social Collaboration for Salespeople and Distributors

DenMat's story of social collaboration on Salesforce.com Chatter is hard to disentangle from a broader strategy of using Salesforce cloud services for sales, service, and custom application development.

Founded in 1974, DenMat makes restorative dental and cosmetic products and provides laboratory services for those that must be custom fit to the individual patient. A couple of its best-known products are Lumineers dental veneers and Snap-On Smile partial dentures. Vice President of IT Jonathan Green embraced Salesforce.com's CRM platform partly to move away from green-screen terminal software running on an old AS/400 midrange computer, which was what DenMat used to run manufacturing and sales. Through custom programming on Salesforce's Force.com platform, and use of the Cast Iron Systems integration appliance, he was able to synchronize data between the legacy system and the cloud.

DenMat participated in the original beta test of Chatter, when Salesforce first introduced it as a "Facebook for the enterprise" product that would make commenting on a customer or a sales opportunity recorded in the customer relationship management system as easy as sharing a link or a photo on Facebook. When I first spoke with Green in 2010, one of the reasons he judged Chatter a success was the way it encouraged faster adoption of the Salesforce CRM application by adding a social dimension that made the tools more fun to work with. "You can't estimate fun," he told me then.

Today, DenMat has gotten more serious about both the Salesforce platform and social collaboration on Chatter. The collaboration network isn't entirely internal, including dentists who act as distributors for DenMat products as well as employees. External sales partners can place orders and check the status of orders through the sales and service applications, and they can also use Chatter to discuss anything that may have gone wrong with the process or suggest improvements.

Figure A-1 shows a snippet of a conversation on Chatter between a work-at-home sales representative and a vice president in DenMat's laboratory business, a sales vice president, and Green.

d-RAC Sales Team — Amy Greb
Thank you Robert Brown for adding Dry Bond to DENMAT.COM ordering website :o) if anyone has an office looking for it - can be found https://denmat.secure.force.com/denmatmain/Product_Restorati ve_Dry_Bond
Comment · Like · Share · May 14, 2013 at 8:13 AM via Chatter Desktop

🖒 Shona Murphy likes this.

Rob Clarke
Just an FYI, I recently learned from Perioptix that the 2.7x Mini loupes (TTL and FU's) are recommended over the 2.35x Microlines for DOCTORS for several reasons: Stronger magnification, waterproof, easier to adjust, and little difference in weight. The 2.35x are good for Hygienists. Also, Frames/lenses requiring an Rx usually have a 3 week turnaround.
Comment · Like · Share · May 14, 2013 at 8:11 AM

Donald Park
Our first SOS shipments left the new Lompoc Studio this afternoon. I heard the SOS techs cheered when the first SOS case was completed this morning.

Three milling machines are now operational and the first of the SOS appliances are being milled as of late this afternoon.

Thanks to all of the dedicated people who helped make this a pretty smooth transition. ... More
Comment · Unlike · Share · May 13, 2013 at 7:53 PM

🖒 You, Rob Clarke and 2 others like this.

Shawn Potter
I want to extend my attitude of gratitude to Scott Meija, Carol Newberry, John Green and the facilities and IT teams! The new DenMat Facility in Lompoc is world class. The sales, events and customer care teams are all happy with our new digs and ready to drive some revenue.
Comment · Like · Share · May 13, 2013 at 4:49 PM

🖒 and 3 others like this.

Jonathan Green
Welcome to LOMPOC!!! looks like we are all in, just the one more week until everyone is here with us!! so how do you like it?

○ Better than expected
○ What I expected
○ Did not meet my expectations

[Vote] 8 votes · View results
Comment · Like · May 13, 2013 at 4:34 PM

🖒 Shawn Potter and Donald Park like this.

Figure A-1:
Chatter collaboration at DenMat.

Conversations from the social stream have led directly to product improvements, Green says. For example, when a dentist suggested that a soft-tissue dental laser used to address conditions like gingivitis would be more useful with the addition of a foot pedal, "we got that right to R&D" and before long the accessory was in manufacturing, he says.

DenMat was acquired in late 2011 by a new investment firm, where management was initially "very skeptical of Salesforce.com in general," Green says.

However, the new leaders couldn't help being impressed by the way Chatter helped them connect with employees across the organization, he says. "Now, they want every customer-facing touch point to be through Salesforce."

Adoption of the new tools is not universal. For all that Green has promoted the use of Salesforce, some internal users continue to fall back on the old terminal-based interface because it's what they are used to — and, honestly, because the shortcut key combinations they have memorized can make it faster for routine tasks than working with a web-based user interface. Similarly, some employees have been slow to adopt Chatter "for fear that it could be used against them," Green says. "But then we would hire new people, and they post everything because they're used to working that way. It takes seeing someone do it and not get in trouble" for others to start to change their minds, he says.

At the same time, Green has noticed that usage of the Microsoft Lync instant messaging application is dropping as users find it easier and more convenient to connect with each other through the Chatter realtime chat feature. One of the managers who was an early, determined skeptic has taken to using Chatter regularly, discovering that it really is the best way to connect with and motivate his team, Green says. "I saw three posts from him just yesterday — and he was one of my biggest holdouts."

One of his next targets is the manufacturing production floor, where he is in the process of replacing desktop computers with Android tablets so that manufacturing employees can do their work without being chained to a desk. Next, he wants to rebuild the user interface of the manufacturing software to include Chatter, with the goal of getting "realtime feedback on production cycles."

Unisys: Expanding from Knowledge Management to Social Collaboration

Unisys is taking full advantage of the social capabilities of its platform but within a wider context. "We want to make sure we don't take such a myopic view of social that we don't see how it touches knowledge management and collaboration," says Gloria Burke, director of knowledge and collaboration strategy and governance.

In other words, even as social networking exposes what otherwise might be *tacit* knowledge (not written down anywhere), part of the goal should be to capture that knowledge in an organized way. Meanwhile, social connections are most valuable when they lead to more intensive collaboration on projects and innovation.

Enterprise social networking adds a dimension beyond what previous knowledge management and collaboration initiatives were able to accomplish at Unisys by providing access to people, not just documents. Previously, "One of the things we struggled with was we weren't able to find subject matter experts easily, and our salespeople can't be experts on everything we sell," Burke says. Now, employees are encouraged to tag their profiles with areas of expertise so they will get an automatic notification when someone posts a query about that topic. That profile tagging is a feature of NewsGator Social Sites, the enterprise social network software that Unisys uses in combination with SharePoint.

"We do have a tradition that goes back 10 years where our employee base has been exposed to the technologies for knowledge management," says Rajiv Prasad, director of knowledge management and CTO for operations at Unisys. Adding social is not just about the technology but about getting people to interact and change their behavior, he said. "The technology is needed infrastructure to make it easy to do what you need to do, but if either the capabilities or the content are not up to expectations, they will get turned off."

Instead, 91 percent of the employees in the targeted global audience for the new social platform adopted it within 18 months.

One more basic key to success is helping employees discover how social tools can help them in their jobs.

"We've put a lot of emphasis on helping employees learn how social tools can add value in their particular role," Burke says. After they have it figured out, she encourages them to share. "Nothing drives the adoption of something new more than a colleague telling you it works for them," she says.

In the search for productive uses of social collaboration, experience has proven to be the best teacher, Burke says. "We spent time on a pilot when in retrospect we should have just deployed," She also wishes she had introduced role-based workshops on the value of social networking earlier because "a focused audience approach was much more effective and really drove the usage."

Unisys actually has two social collaboration platforms in play: Chatter for the sales teams, in addition to the NewsGator/SharePoint combination as a company-wide platform. Unisys hopes to achieve a degree of technical integration between the two platforms' social streams so that employees on each will get the notifications they need to see.

Meanwhile, salespeople have access to both platforms, meaning that they can also hop on the NewsGator-powered network to connect with people or find information not present on Chatter.

One of the things that really matters to the sales team is "market agility," Burke says. The kind of ready access to experts provided by the social communities is paying off now that sales can use a mobile device such as a tablet to get answers to customer questions. In the old days, they'd have to go back to the office, figure out who to ask, and then wait for an answer, she says. "Now they can often find out who the subject matter expert is, pose the question, and get the answer before they even leave the [client's] office. That's impressive to the client."

Unisys is also pushing for truly global social collaboration, investing in making translation technology available to allow its professionals around the world to express themselves in their own language and consume content in their own language. Spanish and Portuguese are the priorities.

"It's really an all-in proposition — you can't be just a little social," Burke says. It makes no sense to be "exchanging content silos for social silos," she says. Each nation's organization will still have its own view of the collaboration system, along with nation-specific news feeds, but the content needs to be managed through a common system, or "you lose that transparency social was supposed to bring to the enterprise," Burke explains.

Ford: Driving Social Business Standards

Ford Motor Co. is a social business success story on many levels, but its social collaboration strategy is still a work in progress.

The potential for an end-to-strategy for social business and social technology is enticing but "really, really hard" to execute in a large enterprise says Scott Monty, global director of social media at Ford. "I don't think anybody's really figured it out completely yet."

Monty is best known for his role in formulating the company's social media marketing programs and as the editor of the Social Media Marketing Blog. Ford was an early user of Google+ (where Ford had a company page before other companies were allowed to establish one) and Google+ Hangouts.

Monty is also user #1 on Ford's Yammer enterprise social network, which has grown to have about 17,000 registered users (about 10 percent are active participants). Ford is using Yammer to prove the business value of internal social networking but has not necessarily made a long-term commitment to it as the technology of choice.

Regardless of what technology is selected, social collaboration absolutely makes sense for Ford because it meshes so well with the One Ford strategy that CEO Alan Mulally established when he became Ford's CEO in 2006.

"What it was designed to do was break down all the silos around the company around the world," Monty says, noting that at the time, some car designs would be introduced in Europe and never make it to the United States, while other functional divisions impeded collaboration for people who ought to be working together. Mulally wasn't thinking in terms of social technologies when he first articulated this vision, but they present "just an amazing opportunity to start bridging these gaps," Monty says.

Since joining Ford in 2008, Monty has been seeking opportunities to use social media to distinguish Ford from the competition. One milestone: When Ford introduced a redesigned edition of the Ford Explorer in 2010, it skipped the usual auto show and auto journalist briefings route in favor of simultaneous announcements in eight cities — and on Facebook. The Facebook campaign, created using tools from Buddy Media (now part of the Salesforce Marketing Cloud) prominently featured videos about the vehicle from the product managers and engineers, as well as CEO Mulally and celebrity spokesman Mike Rowe. The Explorer "reveal" campaign attracted 99 million social media impressions and became the #1 trending topic on Twitter and the #2 search for the day on Google.

"We took that as indicator we could be successful in social at the scale we were used to in traditional media," Monty says.

Meanwhile, one of the benefits of bringing social networking inside the company was it shortcut traditional processes. When Monty was planning what became the Summer of Taurus campaign in 2009 (to unveil the 2010 model of that car), he wrote a rough outline of what he wanted and posted it to Yammer, asking whether it could be accomplished by IT or needed to be contracted out.

"He basically says, I need something to bring this technology together and that technology together, and I don't know where to start," recalled IT architect Ed Krebs, part of an advanced technologies group that oversees the Yammer implementation. Within a week, one of the participants to that discussion — from an IT group that typically didn't work with marketing — was able to show Monty a prototype he had built in his spare time, which evolved into a mashup with Bing Maps. The social conversation cut short what could have been a months-long process of gathering requirements for a traditional IT project, while also avoiding the expense of hiring outside developers, Krebs says.

Ford employees have lots of other collaboration tools available, Krebs says. (One co-worker told him, "If you give me one more productivity tool, I won't be able to do my job.") But social networking within the company is something different. "It's much more cross-organizational as a way of identifying issues and allows people who otherwise might not have been engaged to bring in new solutions," he says.

Although the Yammer network has racked up success stories, Krebs says it remains in a test phase where it is available to employees, but the company is not encouraging them to get accounts.

One hesitation in making it the official, IT-blessed social collaboration platform is Yammer's lack of support for standards like *OpenSocial,* a method of application embedding that's so far been embraced most enthusiastically by Jive Software and IBM, as well as a few smaller software firms like SugarCRM. Krebs team has been running some experiments on Shindig, an open source implementation of the OpenSocial specifications. He is also active in a committee of business technology users affiliated with the World Wide Web Consortium (W3C) pushing for social business technology standards.

Krebs thinks the real success of OpenSocial will come when it is pervasive — for example, with engineers able to carry on social conversations from within the context of a computer-aided design (CAD) tool.

Although it doesn't support OpenSocial, Yammer is promoting an alternate Enterprise Graph approach to social application integration, based on extensions to Facebook's Open Graph. Krebs says he considers that a more proprietary approach, and in any case, decided it was more appropriate to do some initial experiments on Shindig than to "get wrapped up in Yammer's weekly releases."

Because he works in an advanced technology branch of the IT organization, "I always have three or four things running back in the lab," Krebs says. In the end, Yammer "might or might not be a winner, but what we didn't want to do was have 50 people on Yammer, 50 people on Socialcast, maybe 50 people on some other tool. We thought it was more important to get critical mass than it was to do tools selection" at this stage of the game, he says.

So is Ford a leader or a laggard? Maybe a little of both, Krebs says. "We've got a lot of elements that are well thought out, where I think we're ahead of where a lot of other companies are. But just like any other large company, we've got a bigger risk footprint. We may move slower than much smaller companies, or companies in different industries, but that's OK."

Index

• D •

• *Q* •

• *R* •

About the Author

David F. Carr is an Editor-at-Large at *InformationWeek,* where his primary coverage areas include social business, collaboration technologies, educational technology, online education, and technologies for the healthcare industry. He was the original editor for *The BrainYard* (since rebranded *InformationWeek Social Business*) and continues to contribute as a columnist. In early 2013, he became editor of *InformationWeek Education.* David previously served as Technology Editor at *Baseline Magazine* and *Internet World Magazine.* He has also worked as a freelance writer, contributing to *CIO Magazine,* Defense Systems, and Forbes.com. In a side business as a web consultant, he has created several WordPress plug-ins, including Facebook Tab Manager and RSVPMaker.

He lives with his wife and three children in Coral Springs, Florida.

Dedication

To Beth Anne, of course. It had to be you.

Author's Acknowledgments

Thanks to Wiley's Amy Fandrei for giving me this opportunity and to project editor Heidi Unger for helping me get it done. My wife, Beth Anne, who is also a talented editor, helped me prepare the book proposal and sample chapter before we had a contract. She also put up with my spending nights and weekends in my office, trying to make progress on the book outside of regular work hours. *InformationWeek* Editor-in-Chief Rob Preston supported my decision to take on this project, trusting me to put in a fair day's work even while juggling this extra job. *InformationWeek* parent company UBM is an active user of Jive Software's social collaboration platform, and CEO David Levin was nice enough to let me share a screen shot of his social profile as part of the chapter on the role top executives play in the success of these tools. UBM Collaboration Systems Manager Tracy Maurer also gave me valuable input, as well as feedback on several chapters.

UBM's conference group also put me to work as the social business track chair for the E2 Conference, and the Social Business Leaders program we ran in conjunction with that event gave me the opportunity to talk with business and technology leaders who are working to maximize the potential of social collaboration for their organizations.

I found the Jive Community website (http://community.jivesoftware.com) and particularly its Internal Community Managers focus group very helpful as a resource for understanding the concerns of large, enterprise social community managers. Although it exists partly as a customer and technical support community for Jive products, membership is open, and many of the discussions are broader than the use of Jive's products alone.

Jive also provided me with access to a cloud-hosted test instance of its software to explore, which came stocked with a cast of fictional co-workers and mock collaboration activities. Salesforce.com did the same with a demo instance of Chatter. IBM Connections product manager Luis Benitez gave me an extensive walk-through and set me up with an account on Greenhouse, which includes a demonstration instance of Connections. NewsGator let me explore the online community for its customers, which is normally restricted to paying customers, subject to some ground rules about not quoting from conversations there without permission.

This access was important because social software products are difficult to test in isolation because by nature they involve interaction with lots of other people. Also, at the time I started writing, my employer's instance of Jive was a version behind the latest release (a common pattern for large enterprises that like to test software thoroughly before deploying it). Jive offers a 30-day free trial of the cloud version of its product, but I was happy not to have to worry about time running out. There were other cloud-hosted products offering free accounts, such as Yammer and Podio, that I could experiment with more easily by asking friends and family to join my collaboration network or creating my own dummy accounts.

Citrix Podio public relations manager Lilly Hanscom gave me a tour of Podio task management capabilities and pointed me to several other useful resources.

Many of the ideas in this book are not original with me. I have tried to acknowledge the thought leaders I spoke with and whose work I read wherever their ideas are cited. Rachael Happe, co-founder of The Community Roundtable, provided insight from her work with large company community managers as well as introductions and access to reports. Many other people gave me encouragement and guidance along the way.

If this book is any good, it's because of my collaborators. If it's flawed, that would be my fault.

Publisher's Acknowledgments

Acquisitions Editor: Amy Fandrei

Project Editor: Heidi Unger

Sr. Copy Editor: Teresa Artman

Technical Editor: Alison Zarrella

Editorial Assistant: Anne Sullivan

Sr. Editorial Assistant: Cherie Case

Special Help: Mark Enochs

Project Coordinator: Kristie Rees

Cover Image: ©iStockphoto.com/Photomorphic